Death to Fascism

THE WORKING CLASS IN AMERICAN HISTORY

A list of books in the series appears at the end of this book.

Death to Fascism

Louis Adamic's Fight for Democracy

JOHN P. ENYEART

UNIVERSITY OF
ILLINOIS PRESS
Urbana, Chicago, and Springfield

1 2 3 4 5 C P 5 4 3 2 1
∞ This book is printed on acid-free paper.

Library of Congress Cataloging-in-Publication Data
Names: Enyeart, John P. (John Paul), 1970- author.
Title: Death to fascism : Louis Adamic's fight for democracy / John P. Enyeart.
Description: [Urbana, Illinois] : University of Illinois, [2019] | Series: The working class in American history | Includes bibliographical references and index.
Identifiers: LCCN 2019001393| ISBN 9780252042508 (hardcover : alk. paper) | ISBN 9780252084324 (pbk. : alk. paper)
Subjects: LCSH: Adamic, Louis, 1899–1951. | Adamic, Louis, 1899–1951—Political and social views. | Slovenian Americans—Biography. | Historians—United States—Biography. | Social reformers—United States—Biography. | Anti-fascist movements—United States.
Classification: LCC E184.S65 E59 2019 | DDC 818/.5209 [B]—dc23
LC record available at https://lccn.loc.gov/2019001393

E-book ISBN 9780252051357

For Aidan

Contents

Acknowledgments

During the winter of 2007–8, I read Louis Adamic's *Dynamite*, the first popular history of labor violence in the United States, as I awaited readers' reports for my first book on working-class politics. I thought a book that started with the Molly Maguires and ended with the Memorial Day Massacre would help to highlight the central role that authoritarianism, brutality, and murder played in capitalism's growth in the United States. Around the same time, I planned a trip for summer 2008 that included a visit to Ljubljana, Slovenia. I kept reading Louis Adamic's work because he was the most popular Slovenian American writer. The more I read, the more Adamic's frequent references to fascism captured my attention, and I started to think I should write a biography of this antifascist activist.

Coincidently, my friend George Matthews was heading to Ljubljana that summer too and one night before we embarked on our overlapping vacations we went out for drinks. George's friend Boris Čibej, a reporter working for Slovenia's leading newspaper *Delo*, happened to be in town and he came along to the bar. George taught me the toast I had to know when I arrived in Ljubljana: *Smrt fašizmu, svoboda narodu* (Death to fascism, liberty to the people). Adamic had repeated the phrase often during the war. I mentioned the biography idea to them, and Boris recalled watching documentaries about Adamic on Yugoslav television when he was a child. A week later, he emailed to me numerous stories about Adamic that had appeared in *Delo* from the 1970s to the present. I remain grateful to George and Boris for the encouragement they provided that night.

Some of the archivists I consulted proved especially invaluable: at Princeton University's Firestone Library, Gabriel Swift, AnnaLee Pauls, Linda Oliveira, and Chloe Pfendler, and their counterparts at Narodna in Univerzitetna Knjižnica (National and University Library of Slovenia—NUK), Marijan Rupert, Matjaž Lulik, and Samo Kristan. They all helped me to navigate the two largest holdings of Adamic/Adamič materials. David K. Frasier at the Lilly Library at Indiana University, Amy S. Wong and Brandon E. Barton at the Charles E. Young Research Library at the University of California–Los Angeles, Ann Sindelar at the Western Reserve Historical Society in Cleveland, and Daniel Necas at the Immigration History Research Center at the University of Minnesota all went out of their way to assist me in gathering Adamic-related materials in the collections their archives hold. I am also grateful for the aid I received from the staffs at the National Archives in College Park, Maryland; the Chicago History Museum; and the people who processed my Freedom of Information Act requests at the Federal Bureau of Investigation. Thanks also to my family in Ohio, Maryland, and New Jersey, who let me stay at their houses when I did research in Cleveland, College Park, and Princeton.

This project also would not have been possible without funding. Bucknell University's Dean's Fellowship allowed me to take trips to many of the archives listed above, and an award from the Friends of Princeton Library provided me with the resources necessary to spend a month combing through Adamic's papers at the Firestone Library. Last, a Fulbright US Scholar's Award allowed me to make a follow-up visit to NUK. Thank you to George Shields, Ann Tlusty, and Karen Morin from Bucknell, Linda Oliveira and Christine Lutz from Princeton, and all those at Fulbright who made these research trips possible.

I am eternally grateful to Rachel Batch, Mehmet Dosemeci, James Englehardt, Alice Kessler-Harris, David Roediger, Jennifer Thomson, Amanda Wooden, Bob Zecker, and a reviewer who chose to remain anonymous for reading the entire manuscript. Jennifer Thomson and Amanda Wooden deserve special thanks for helping me when my chapters were at their worst. I knew the book was moving along when Mehmet stopped saying "oh, dear God" when referring to my writing. James Englehardt's constant support and willingness to discuss readers' reports and revisions are among the many reasons he is a great editor.

Logan Connors, Julie Greene, Tom Krainz, Khalil Saucier, Rich Schneirov, and Shelton Stromquist read multiple chapters and helped me to think through key concepts. They all made this a better book. Paul Barba, Julian

Bourg, Rachel Ida Buff, Michael Drexler, Marisa Egerstrom, Donna Gabaccia, Dan Geary, Kevin Kenny, John Penniman, Doug Rossinow, Joe Scapellato, Anthony Stewart, Gavin Jones, and Richard White all kindly offered their expertise on specific chapters. Each of them came to my aid at key moments in this project. John Bukowczyk provided excellent suggestions on an article I wrote for the *Journal of American Ethnic History* that served as the foundation for this book. The University of Illinois Press publishes the *Journal of American Ethnic History*, and I want to thank the press for granting me permission to publish parts of my article "Revolutionizing Cultural Pluralism: The Political Odyssey of Louis Adamic, 1932–1951," *Journal of American Ethnic History* 34 (Spring 2015), 58–90, in various chapters of this book.

I also appreciate the comments I received from my colleagues in the History Department at Bucknell University who read chapters of *Death to Fascism* in our department colloquia. The members of the Pennsylvania Labor History Workshop, especially Andy Arnold, Rachel Batch, Dennis Deslippe, Francis Ryan, Sharon McConnell Sidorick, Dan Sidorick, and David Witwer, also provided helpful suggestions. Many of these chapters started as conference papers and I want to express my appreciation to those who offered comments on those presentations: Todd Michney, David Roediger, and Fraser Ottanelli. At the 2012 American Studies Association meeting Rachel Ida Buff asked a great question from the audience that got me thinking about Adamic and whiteness. Also, I appreciate the questions about Adamic and diaspora that the University of Maryland history faculty and graduate students asked during a talk I gave there. Thank you, Julie Greene, for inviting me. Geof Garvey and Tad Ringo played vital roles in pushing this book over the finish line. I have a deep gratitude for both Garvey's skillful copyediting and Ringo's various suggestions as project manager that made *Death to Fascism* much better than it was before they looked at it.

Slovenian scholars have been incredibly generous with their time and suggestions. In 2008, 2014, and 2018, Mladen Dolar offered kindness and encouragement on this project from its beginning. Janja Žitnik Serafin spoke with me on my summer 2014 visit and we exchanged emails over the years, for which I am grateful. On my 2014 trip, Božo Repe helped me to understand Yugoslav history better. During my March 2018 visit to Ljubljana, Aljoša Pelhan helped me with details of Adamic's early life and shared photos with me. Aljoša's knowledge of Adamic is vast and I have benefited immensely from our conversations and email exchanges. Milan Mrdenović shared his copy of Adamic's unpublished chapter, "A Game of Chess in an Earthquake," with me. Milan also pointed me to some on-line sources in Slovenia. I also want to thank Larisa Daugul, Jasmina Illić Draković, Simona Zorko, and Tanja Velagić for reminding me how important Adamic remains in Slovenia. Larisa went to the Louis Adamič primary school in Grosuplje and read all his books. Her insights have particularly helped me to think about his legacy. I am especially grateful to her for arranging a tour for me and my family of Adamic's birthplace at Praproče manor in Grosuplje and introducing me to Andrej Kurent, Adamic's nephew. I want to thank Andrej for giving me a copy of his family tree and a copy of the first article Adamic ever wrote when he was still a boy.

I want to offer special thank yous to Amanda Wooden and Mary Margret Rostan. Amanda's love, friendship, encouragement, and criticisms helped to carry me through this project. She made sure that I made it to archives even at moments when she was not in the best of health, and she explains this book to people better than I ever will. Mary Margret Rostan, my mom, watched Aidan Wooden-Enyeart after the bus dropped him off from school and occasionally on a Saturday or a Sunday, so that I had essential writing time to finish this book.

Last, *Death to Fascism* is dedicated to Aidan. Aidan kindly offered to illustrate this book, but I decided that pictures of Lebron James and dinosaurs would not enhance readers' understanding of Adamic's life. Aidan was born in December 2011. He traveled with me to Princeton, Bloomington, Los Angeles, Cleveland, Washington DC, and Ljubljana. He and this book grew up together. Most important, Aidan made me take breaks from Adamic's life to build Legos, go to Reptileland, and enjoy the various rides at Knobles Amusement Park.

Death to Fascism

Introduction

While on his "Tolerance Is Not Enough" lecture tour in February 1947, Louis Adamic spoke to a capacity crowd in Wilkes-Barre, Pennsylvania, a town heavily populated by ethnically Slavic and Italian coal miners. The local journalist covering the event declared that Adamic is "widely regarded as [the] unofficial spokesman for 50 million immigrants and their descendants who came to the United States in the last 100 years."[1] Although Adamic certainly did not speak for all immigrants and their families for the century prior to this speech, the reporter's words conveyed the popularity and influence that the best-selling author wielded from the late 1920s until his death in 1951. On that day, Adamic had come to Wilkes-Barre to repeat his warning that although the Allies had won World War II, the fascist spirit that threatened the world remained alive. Killing fascism was not about tolerance—whites being nicer to African Americans and immigrants. It meant eradicating the belief that the United States was "an Anglo-Saxon country" because such racial nationalist thinking justified Jim Crow and nativism at home and colonialism abroad.[2] Adamic implored his audiences to define democracy and justice in opposition to white supremacy, xenophobia, and corporate hegemony. Recovering Adamic's legacy is essential for remembering that antifascism shaped our understanding of US democracy for most of the twentieth century and has much to teach us today. Although influenced by Marxist ideas and collectivist experiments in governing, antifascists focused on fostering empathy for one another globally in order to create a new humanism as a response to the battles between capital and labor, imperialism, totalitarian governments, and world wars that accompanied modernity in the twentieth century.

Death to Fascism explores Adamic's journey from seeing himself as a Slovenian peasant in exile to joining, shaping, and often leading the coalition of African American and white intellectuals and journalists, working-class militants, ethnic community activists, novelists, leftist politicians, and radicals who made antifascism the dominant US political culture from the mid-1930s through 1948. Adamic and his fellow antifascists contended that at its root fascism was an ethos uniting disparate strands of conservative and reactionary outlooks into an anti-Enlightenment counterrevolution that sought to destroy democracy by appealing to beliefs in racial superiority and by glorifying violence.[3] Antifascists identified democracy as fascism's antithesis. Democracy, to antifascists, included racial and ethnic equality, workers' rights, and the rights of nations to self-determination. Adamic contributed to the antifascist mood by telling stories about injustices focused on the South Slavs he knew: Croatian peasants turned domestic servants, urban Slovenian youths turned Pennsylvania coal miners, and Dalmatian sailors who became California dockworkers. By the end of his career, he had written thirteen books and more than five hundred articles that appeared in periodicals including the *American Mercury*, *The Nation*, *Negro Digest*, *Harper's Weekly*, and the *Saturday Evening Post*. High school teachers and college professors assigned his works in their classes, he made regular radio appearances on nationally syndicated talk shows, crowds filled venues across the country to hear him speak, and he won major fellowships and book awards. Presidents Franklin Roosevelt and Harry Truman, along with numerous other public officials, conferred with him about the relationship between his Yugoslav homeland and the United States. W. E. B. DuBois, F. Scott Fitzgerald, Sinclair Lewis, H. L. Mencken, Eleanor Roosevelt, and Upton Sinclair lauded his work.

Americans have forgotten him because Cold Warriors smeared him as a communist, which he was not. They made a concerted effort to turn his calls for peace, anticolonialism, racial and ethnic equality, and workers' rights into evidence of subversive behavior and thus obscure his progressive politics in the historical record.[4] During the Cold War, Adamic was a leading voice among the many independent leftists pointing out that anticommunist claims of the need for heightened national security masked a corporate-driven imperialist agenda combined with a desire to maintain white supremacy. This view has emerged as a leading interpretation of the period, but Adamic made the public aware of the threat anticommunists posed to cultural pluralism, industrial democracy, and world peace as early as 1936.

Adamic gained recognition as a writer in the United States in the late 1920s by having his characters negotiate their Americanness, which was a reflection of his own struggles to balance his Slovenian and US identities. Adamic declared himself and his fellow immigrants "peasant exiles" who could not escape exploitation whether carried out by Austrian monarchs or American capitalists. He moved away from his feelings of liminality during a 1932 trip funded by a Guggenheim grant to his native Slovenia, which, at that point, was part of Yugoslavia. Yugoslavia emerged at the end of World War I from the wreckage of the Austro-Hungarian Empire, and although Slovenians and Croatians expected to share power with Serbs, Serbian royals took control and established an ethnocentric authoritarian monarchy. After visiting his homeland, Adamic returned to the United States and declared his disgust with Serbian irredentism and US nativism and racism. Soon after that trip, he became the leading advocate for cultural pluralism in the United States and went on to champion Yugoslavism for his homeland. Proponents of Yugoslavism imagined a federated republic where Slovenes, Serbs, and Croats shared political power and recognized each other as ethnic equals. The details of exactly what this hoped-for Yugoslavia would look like remained contested by the various South Slavic groups who trumpeted this vision.[5]

During the Progressive Era, cultural pluralists challenged the proponents of Americanization who contended that the Pilgrims and Puritans established US culture as Anglo and Protestant before the United States existed as a nation. Americanizers ranged from those who embraced the melting-pot ideal that foreigners could come to the United States and be culturally assimilated by learning English and working hard to xenophobes who opposed immigration altogether. Lacking the political power to pass an immigration ban beyond the Chinese Exclusion Act, the anti-immigration wing of the Americanization movement promoted eugenics and advocated for laws that surveilled and harassed the foreign-born and their children. They also portrayed immigrants as a threat to national security, and their propaganda pieces set the context for the immigration restriction acts of 1921 and 1924. Proponents of Americanization treated race as a fixed category despite the fact that the measures and polices they championed updated and advanced the white racial hierarchy built upon the legacies of African American slavery and Manifest Destiny.[6]

In contrast, proponents of cultural pluralism, especially philosophers Horace Kallen and Randolph Bourne, argued that immigrants and ethnics had to be given the choice to participate in the continual process of collectively synthesizing and reformulating the beliefs and values that defined the nation in order to feel a sense of civic solidarity with the Anglo Protestant majority.

Bourne's work in particular influenced Adamic.[7] In 1916, Bourne argued that when people from different places synthesized their values and beliefs, a new federation of cultures emerged that redefined national identity. For Bourne, transcending the racial nationalism Americanizers attempted to impose on immigrants represented the sublime, the moment when the universal citizen was created. Bourne argued that working through the cultural tensions that occurred between ethnic groups and between African Americans and Euro Americans in daily interactions would foster this inclusive culture, which he called a "beloved community." He also emphasized that identities were always in a constant state of flux and that the interactions that held the potential for the ethereal moments of creating universal citizenship were also instances of individuals and groups forging new histories.[8]

The wave of migrants from eastern and southern Europe that Adamic belonged to, along with African Americans who moved north during the Great Migration, physically and culturally built modern urban America. Adamic, following Bourne, believed that US democracy would be remade as these different groups interacted at ethnic festivals, during church gatherings, at work, in schools, at grocery stores, at movie theaters, and, most especially, in unions as the Congress of Industrial Organizations grew and redefined employer-employee relations.[9]

Adamic helped to revive cultural pluralism during the 1930s and 1940s by contrasting it with expressions of national identity in authoritarian Europe. The air of intimidation Adamic witnessed in Mussolini's Italy sparked his embrace of pluralism. Adamic's 1932 voyage to Yugoslavia included a brief stop in fascist Italy. In a letter to his friend Carey McWilliams, a social justice activist and the future editor of *The Nation*, Adamic wrote that fascism "smacks you in the face wherever you turn." Soldiers intimidated everyone as they inspected passports, directed traffic, and marched through city streets. Seeing "little boys snapping to attention, rendering the Fascist salute" whenever a uniformed soldier passed, and men wearing buttons and stickers plastered all around declaring "Viva il Duce" highlighted this spectacle of frenzied nationalism. Mussolini, Adamic declared, "is one smart son-of-a-bitch" for creating a "Fascist army," separate from "the Royal Army," comprising "recruits from among the unemployed" to "whom he would otherwise have to pay a dole; and now he uses them to terrorize" people "into quiet submission."[10] Adamic viewed Adolph Hitler and Mussolini similarly, calling Hitler a gangster who terrorized his own people into accepting a version of their national identity based on an imagined history of past national greatness.[11] In response to a supporter asking how to stop the spread of fascism, Adamic proclaimed that Hitler's "negative, nihilistic, revengeful, [and] destructive" politics could be defeated by exposing his mendacious rendering of the past with a call for compassion. Adamic wrote that the world needs an idea that is "positive and constructive and so sound from the best human angle and so simple that [it] will swing and whirl all over."[12] He turned to pluralism as that positive vision that promoted a new humanity, an updated version of Bourne's beloved community.

Adamic gathered support for cultural pluralism by engaging in a type of covert literary politics. He wrote articles and gave speeches with titles that satirically deployed racial nationalists' sentiments such as "'America' Is a Magic Name" and "Let's Become Americanized, All of Us." In these works he praised the founders for creating a nation that embodied "the highest, most mature concept of human relations yet devised" and then asserted that the "continuous blood transfusions" from non-Anglos into the body politic made democracy thrive. In "'America' Is a Magic Name," he added that a "psychological civil war" to determine the meaning of US identity pitted those who subscribed to "xenophobia, racism, isolationism, and class distinctions" against advocates of "essential human equality."[13] For the United States to be the world's model democracy, he concluded, the adherents of equality had to win. Many politicians cited his work and espoused pluralist ideals in their speeches, but most of those lawmakers rarely enacted policies that aligned with those words. By the early 1940s, Adamic realized that advancing cultural pluralism by appropriating racialist nationalist themes had encouraged some of his supporters to equate cultural pluralism with tolerance, not a commitment to creating a new vision of humanity. As a corrective, he gave lectures pointing out the limits of tolerance, advocating a revolutionary version of pluralism and attacking whiteness as an impediment to democracy.

In 1942, Adamic adopted a more radical version of pluralism that identified peasants as his model democrats. Unlike the exploited exiles he once wrote about, Adamic's model peasants became the guerrilla fighters in Croatian communist Josip Broz Tito's Partisan army. Composed of an array of leftists dedicated to Yugoslavism, which Adamic now saw as a revolutionary form of pluralism, the partisans battled to free their country from its Axis occupiers and the Serbian monarchists.[14] Tito's revolutionary pluralism so inspired the Slovenian-born US writer that he adopted the rallying cry of Tito's Partisans—*Smrt fašizmu, svoboda narodu* (Death to fascism, liberty to the people)—as the closing salutation for the letters that he wrote and the speeches that he gave during World War II. Adamic argued that in some countries, such as his native Yugoslavia, communist revolutions could ultimately foster democracy because they were carrying out a people's uprisings against authoritarian nationalist governments.

By the end of World War II, Adamic linked Tito's militant pluralism to expressions of black anticolonialism. He asserted that killing the fascist ethos required white ethnics to join with black anticolonialists and fight segregation at home and imperialism abroad. W. E. B. DuBois's notion of whiteness especially influenced Adamic's thinking.[15] DuBois argued that children were taught "that every great soul the world ever saw was a white man's soul; that every great thought the world ever knew was a white man's thought; that every great deed the world ever did was a white man's deed."[16] This faith in whiteness offers "conquest sugared with religion; [and] mutilation and rape masquerading as culture."[17] Later DuBois added that African Americans were "nationals without citizenship" and that "the Negro Problem forces the United States to abdicate its natural leadership of democracy in the world."[18] Adamic took DuBois's formulation of whiteness as a global "religion" and presented fascism as that faith's political form. Democracy would not triumph over fascism until racial and ethnic equality became a universally realized practice.

Tracing Adamic's shifting views on how to define and acquire democracy from the 1920s through the 1950s offers us valuable insights into the spectrum of leftist politics in this period. His life adds an important perspective on how antifascist thought came to dominate US leftist politics during the 1930s and 1940s and allows us to see how various transnational democratic projects, such as Tito's Yugoslavism and black anticolonialism, intersected. The lessons he offers remain underappreciated because his initial writings about pluralism during the 1930s led a number of his contemporaries and subsequent scholars to consider him a white liberal who confined his focus to understanding US identity.

Adamic described himself as a progressive because he concentrated on moving democracy "in a forward direction" globally. Liberals and communists used the term *progressive* during the Popular Front era in the 1930s to highlight their shared belief in the Enlightenment vision of human progress and to express their unity within a coalition of leftists fighting against fascism. Adamic from the 1930s through his death in 1951 was willing to work with liberals and communists, but he always remained on guard against both because, he believed, neither group could be trusted. He described liberals as "wishy washy," too willing to compromise on vital issues, and thus not fully committed to killing fascism. Adamic criticized them, most especially Franklin Roosevelt, for accommodating segregationists and imperialists. He distrusted communists because their primary loyalty lay with Moscow, and they would alter their objectives whenever Stalin changed the party line.[19]

After World War II, Adamic argued that Tito's communist government, although not ideal, was better than the Serbian irredentist monarchy that replaced the Austrian Empire and ruled Yugoslavia from the end of World War I through World War II. He believed that Tito's regime would pave the way for the polyglot democracy leftist South Slavs had desired since they sought independence from Austrian rule in the nineteenth century. Adamic's resolve for an ethnically plural and politically equal Yugoslavia grew even stronger after Tito broke from the Soviet sphere of influence in 1948.

Adamic used his storytelling ability to advance his progressive politics. To him, global democracy would flourish through empathy, and he attempted to accomplish that end through his writing. Historian Michael Denning is one of the few scholars to identify the central role Adamic played in shaping culture and politics in this period. After acknowledging Adamic's pivotal role in fashioning the "antifascist common sense" that defined the Depression Era, Denning credited the popular writer as one of the leading "theorists of race and ethnicity" in the early and mid-twentieth century.[20] Although Denning's observations were apt, Adamic described himself more as a storyteller than a theorist. Carey McWilliams more accurately described his friend as a "fabulist" and noted that Adamic burst onto the US literary scene by offering a "refreshing reluctance to accept conventional ideas and the popular notions of the hour." McWilliams also cautioned readers that Adamic's "sense of the dramatic betrays him at times" in that it "is invariably the dramatic incident, and not the facts, that he is after."[21] As McWilliams recognized, Adamic transformed how his readers thought about democracy by getting his readers to relate to his characters' humanity.

Adamic's multiple versions of his migration story from Slovenia to the United States demonstrate how he used storytelling as a political tactic. In his 1932 semifictional autobiography *Laughing in the Jungle*, Adamic explained that when he was still Alojzij Adamič, a fifteen-year-old student in Ljubljana, he joined an underground political organization dedicated to fighting the Austrian monarchy that controlled his homeland. In November 1913, he claimed, his group allied with like-minded activists and staged a mass demonstration for South Slav independence from Hapsburg rule. During this protest, Austrian soldiers charged Adamic and his fellow dissidents and fired on them indiscriminately. Police arrested Adamic when he attempted to flee the melee. While detained, Adamic watched as troops shot his best friend in the head. Released after four days in jail, he learned that school officials had expelled him for his political activities. His family now expected him to join the priesthood. Unwilling to devote his life to God, he fled to the United States. He wrote that he arrived at Ellis Island in December 1913.[22]

This version of the Ljubljana riot made a great story, but it was mostly false. The protest occurred in 1908, not 1913, when nine-year-old Adamic still lived with his parents in Praproče manor near Grosuplje, Slovenia. Also, by 1913, he was already in the United States; he had left Slovenia in the fall of 1912 and landed at Ellis Island that year, not 1913 as he stated in *Laughing*. More important, Adamic borrowed some of the details for his story from his older cousin Ivan's life. Ivan belonged to a resistance group that demanded South Slav independence from Hapsburg rule, and he died during the 1908 demonstration after royal troops shot him.[23] As this story suggests, recapturing an accurate account of Adamic's life is a precarious endeavor. It is easy to mistake his writings for autobiography. They were something more complicated. The main material for Adamic's storytelling did come from his own life and experiences, or rather his invention and reinvention of those experiences in relation to cultural and political battles he fought at a particular moment to advance his vision of democracy.

Adamic's transition from a South Slavic peasant exile to a champion of cultural pluralism led him to revise his narrative of how his Slovenian past informed his American present. That alteration included a retelling of the 1908 Ljubljana riot. In his 1942 book *What's Your Name*, he emphasized that immigrants constantly negotiated between their homeland and host-land identities. He used the seemingly mundane example of immigrants and their last names to make his point. In his case, a United States army clerk in 1916 filled out his induction papers to the army on a typewriter lacking diacritical marks. He went from being Adamič, pronounced "Ah-dah'mitch, with both *a*'s long and full" and "a sizzling tch-ch-ch at the end as in 'pitch'" to "Ad'amic, with the stress on the first syllable and the middle *a* barely heard." Adamic explained that losing the caron above the *c* in his family name literally marked him as American. But keeping the mostly Slovene spelling allowed him to honor his cousin Ivan, who died protesting for South Slav independence. Ivan had become a "martyr-hero to large sections of the Slovenian nation."[24] Louis now claimed that his last name constantly reminded him of the antiauthoritarian spirit his family bestowed upon him, highlighted by Ivan's death. That legacy motivated him to fight to redefine democracy in pluralist terms.

By the time he published *What's Your Name*, Adamic had grown more militant as he determined that the disconnection between the pluralist rhetoric politicians used and the racist and xenophobic policies they implemented created the conditions for fascism to develop in the United States. During the 1930s and 1940s, the US congress repeatedly failed to pass an antilynching law, the State Department refused to suspend quota restrictions and grant Jews asylum from the Nazis, and Roosevelt ordered the incarceration of all Japanese Americans on the West Coast.[25] Native-born whites controlling the levers of power clearly continued to gravitate toward racial nationalism, and their legislative choices indicated that they viewed African Americans and immigrants as threats to American identity instead of seeing them as the nation's source of vitality and progress.

This shift in Adamic's worldview led to another revision in his telling of the 1908 Ljubljana riot that he articulated in his "Yugoslavia and America" lecture in 1947. In the speech, he used the riot to identify himself with the leftist South Slav diaspora that was dedicated to fighting fascism in both Europe and the United States. When he was a boy, Adamic proclaimed, his mother, "a peasant woman with scarcely any schooling," had instilled within him a desire for "Yugoslav unity and freedom" by regularly reminding him of his cousin Ivan's martyrdom. Louis told his audiences that in secondary school he had "hung out spiritually on the fringes" of the "Yugoslav cause" because "political idealism" had fueled his youthful passions.[26] Ivan had protested the Austrians to create a Yugoslavia of ethnic and political equals. Louis supported Tito because Tito, who became Yugoslavia's communist dictator after World War II, made Ivan's dream a reality.

Reading Adamic's numerous iterations of the Ljubljana riot helps us to map his political shifts, which reflected the rise and transformations of the larger antifascist coalition that shaped how Americans defined democracy from the Great Depression through World War II. They also show how narratives are political weapons. When Adamic died in September 1951, either by murder or suicide, the network of anticommunist professional witnesses, journalists, and politicians claimed that Soviet dictator Joseph Stalin had ordered Adamic's assassination. Anticommunists asserted that by supporting Tito after the Yugoslav dictator refused to bend to Stalin's will in 1948, Adamic had deviated from the party line. Stalin, the anticommunists' scenario went, punished Adamic's betrayal by killing him. By October 1951, the leading daily newspapers presented this conspiracy theory as fact.[27] In line with post–World War II McCarthyism, they then claimed Adamic's antifascism was subterfuge that allowed him to advance the communist agenda while claiming to be a democrat. By debating whether Adamic was a communist, the American public and scholars trapped themselves in a Cold War framing of global politics. That outlook prevented them from understanding his argument that destroying the fascist ethos required everyone, especially the people of countries carrying out imperialist projects, to make equality the defining characteristic of human interactions.[28] Adamic understood that this vision was utopian, but he argued so too were the revolutionary impulses inspiring people to rise up around the world.

Death to Fascism joins a growing list of works by scholars—including Benjamin Balthaser, Rachel Batch, Keisha N. Blain, Mark Bray, Rachel Ida Buff, Joseph Fronczak, Barbara Ransby, Christopher Vials, and Robert Zecker—who are looking beyond communist- and anticommunist-centered narratives and demonstrating that antifascist activism should be at the heart of our understanding of democratic politics in the twentieth century.[29] Recovering Adamic's antifascist legacy helps us remember him as a leading voice in shaping US culture and politics in the twentieth century and as someone who can help us make sense of our current moment. As scholars and journalists ask whether we are seeing a revival of fascism globally, debate the meaning of progressive politics, and discuss the efficacy of transnational activism, we can turn to Adamic's life for insights. The chapters that follow trace Adamic through his states of being: exile, cultural pluralist, agent of diaspora, and dedicated anticolonist. *Death to Fascism* then turns to Adamic's controversial demise. The final chapter examines who may have killed him, and how anticommunists successfully authored a version of his life that resulted in his obscurity. An epilogue ties Adamic's legacy to antifascist and progressive politics today.

1

Modernism and Exile

The Origins of Louis Adamic's Politics, 1898–1932

In his 1930 short story "A Bohunk Woman," Louis Adamic invented Mila Tanasich to represent the South Slav "women in America whose men performed the hard, dirty work in industry, and to whom fate was not so gentle." Early in the story, a fictionalized Adamic learned from a friend about a fifty-year-old Croatian immigrant woman who desperately needed work as a cleaning lady. A freight container had fallen on her dockworker husband and crippled him. Now her family had no income. Serving as the narrator, the imaginary Adamic explained that feelings of pity led him to hire her. Near the end of the story, the normally reticent Tanasich exclaimed that "life is cruel and evil," especially in America, which "is big and terrible." Various illnesses, accidents, and war left only one of her seven children alive and led to the deaths of her first three husbands. This had taught her that "perhaps nothing matters. I don't matter. Only life matters . . . life and America. Life must go on. A terrible process, isn't it? America must become great. . . . We all came over from the Old Country to help America become great and terrible." The story ended with Tanasich dying on her way to the hospital.[1]

Adamic used the paradox of America being "great and terrible"—of immigrants providing the labor to make the United States the wealthiest nation on earth while receiving mostly misery in return—to express his sense of being an exile. Adamic and many of his fellow South Slavs grew up feeling displaced because the Austrian Empire controlled Slovenia and Croatia. Then the xenophobes who dominated US public discourse, policy, and law made it clear to those who migrated to the United States that southern and eastern Europeans were not welcome because they were not quite "white" and thus not quite American. Prior to the 1930s, the idea of ethnic groups remained largely outside public comprehension. In the statutes, rulings, scholarship, and reporting that they wrote, lawmakers, judges, academics, and journalists legitimized racial hierarchies that placed Slavs, Italians, Greeks, and Jews above blacks and Asians but below Anglo-Saxons. A 1926 survey asked Anglo-Americans to rank "races" based on their willingness to associate with them. Of the forty choices, Serbo-Croatians, the category that included Slovenes, finished just ahead of Mexicans, Blacks, Filipinos, and Japanese. Those South Slavs seeking inclusion into white America did have a bit of solace. Champions of assimilation attempted to make race mutable. Although most textbooks described race as biologically determined, eastern and southern European immigrants could transcend their genetics by learning English, going to citizenship classes, following the directives of their employers, rejecting radicalism, and convincing native-born whites that the distance between themselves and those groups "below" them was vast.[2]

Adamic and his fellow South Slavs found themselves in between white and black on America's spectrum of racial hierarchy, trapped in between Slovenian and US cultures. This sense of liminality combined with the feeling of dehumanization that accompanied becoming an industrial laborer motivated Adamic to focus both his fiction and journalism on those who faced the pressure to conform without the opportunity to be accepted. Adamic used the exiles he invented, such as Mila Tanasich, to lay bare the myths of US "promises of wealth" and so-called opportunities for newcomers as well as the assurance that if they adhered to Anglo-American middle-class norms they would achieve social acceptance.

Adamic contended that "America broke and mangled the emigrants' bodies, defiled their souls, deprived them of their spiritual and aesthetic sensibilities, corrupted their charming native dialects and manners, and generally alienated them from the homeland." The Austrian monarchy "drove the good Slovenian peasants to America, and America ruined them" as employers and native-born elites continued to treat them as peasants.[3] According to Adamic, this constant suffering had the positive consequence of imbuing some South Slavs with a "peasant wisdom." Adamic used his father as an example of someone who possessed this sensibility and described him as "a hard realist, a practical man, a fatalist, possessing a natural, almost biological good sense and a half-cynical earth knowledge older than any religion or system."[4] Accepting a permanent peasant existence offered a more authentic life because it allowed one to recognize that promises of future economic upward mobility or expanded political rights were chimeras.

Adamic's journey to the United States and his subsequent travels around the country brought him into contact with an array of people whose stories resembled his. Articulating his and their feelings of exploitation and nonbelonging led him to offer a critique of capitalism and express feelings of exile that extended beyond immigrant communities and resonated with the wider native-born working and middle classes. Although native-born whites in particular did not share the sense of liminality that immigrants harbored, they experienced a collective crisis of "being" as the United States industrialized and urbanized at a rapid pace. Recognizing this reality, Adamic promoted empathy between native and foreign-born workers by telling stories about US-born workers losing their Americanness. He did this by borrowing plots from the works of his favorite author, Slovenian modernist poet, essayist, and playwright Ivan Cankar.[5] After gaining some acclaim by questioning the meaning of "American," he turned to writing about South Slavs and received broader recognition as the leading immigrant writer on the immigrant condition. Then, in 1932–33, Adamic added a political dimension to his stories of being and belonging by advocating on behalf of Slovenian culture at a crucial moment in his homeland's history. By questioning employers' right to control workplaces and nativists' influence over defining American identity, Adamic set in motion a cultural shift. His work encouraged immigrants to stop thinking of themselves as exiles and instead fight for a new culture that synthesized their customs with the values of the dominant society to forge a new way of being American and, more important, of being human.[6]

From Slovenia to the United States

On March 23, 1898, Ana and Anton Adamič experienced the arrival of their fourth child, Alojzij (who would become Louis in the United States), at their home in Praproče, roughly fourteen miles southeast of the capital Ljubljana. Louis's father had been born at Spodnje Blato, a village near Praproče, and Louis would usually claim the former as his birthplace to emphasize his peasant origins. *Blato* is Slovenian for mud. Alojzij was Ana and Anton's eldest living child of their ten surviving children; the first three had died of diphtheria. After completing primary school in Praproče, Alojzij attended secondary school in Ljubljana, and his devoutly Catholic mother expected that he would matriculate into the seminary upon graduation. But after his third year, he may have dropped out of school. He later told his mentor and leading US satirist H. L. Mencken that he ran away from school and became a fourteen-year-old hobo. In his semifictional *Laughing in the Jungle* (1932), he offered a different narrative. Adamic claimed to have joined a group of anti-imperialist activists hoping to one day overthrow the Austrian monarchy. He made it clear to readers that he became a student activist out of a search for adventure, not a conversion to radicalism. Later in *Laughing*, he portrayed his decision to go to the United States as stemming from this same yearning for excitement, along with a desire to avoid joining the priesthood. According to a family history, a period of economic distress likely factored into Adamic's decision to migrate. Anton's father Janez had done well enough selling potash that he bought land and, in addition to farming, had a lumber business, making Adamic's family well-off peasants. Anton inherited property at Praproče, which included Janez's manor there. The winter before Adamic left, heavy snows damaged the home's roof and then an earthquake weakened its walls. Expensive repairs, not bad grades, may have prompted Alojzij to quit school and find work in America.[7]

Regardless of his actual reasons for emigrating, Adamic made it to Le Havre, France, in 1913, where he bought a ticket in steerage on the *Niagara* and headed for Ellis Island. He arrived in New York City in late December as a fourteen-year-old who did not speak English.[8] Adamic was one of the 458,580 Croats and Slovenes (the US government did not differentiate) who arrived at Ellis Island between 1898 and 1915. The 1920 census counted 208,552 people who spoke Slovenian as their first language, up from 183,431 in the 1910 census. Although Slovenes settled in eight hundred urban areas in the United States, they concentrated in and around Cleveland, Chicago, and Pittsburgh. In fact, Cleveland became second to Ljubljana in the number of Slovenians in one city. Also, they made significant impacts on the culture and politics of the factory and mining towns of Colorado, Illinois, Indiana, Michigan, Minnesota, Montana, Ohio, Pennsylvania, Wisconsin, and Wyoming. Most men worked in the plants, mills, and mines that formed the burgeoning US industrial landscape, while Slovenian women typically took jobs as waitresses or household servants. More men than women migrated to the United States from Slovenia and Croatia, but exact numbers are hard to find. US officials did not count the number of people leaving the country, and the fact that 47 percent of Slovenian and Croatian migrants journeyed between their homeland, the United States, and back at least once highlighted the problem of acquiring precise data. This pattern of return migration also highlighted the reality that displacement, whether spurred on by economic insecurity or political oppression, fed South Slavs' sense of alienation.[9]

Adamic lived with distant relatives in New York City during his first three years in the country. He took a job as an errand boy for a Slovenian-language newspaper, and by 1916 he had learned English well enough to translate pieces into Slovenian. By seventeen, he had become the assistant editor. Conflicting accounts assert that Adamic was either fired or the paper folded because it did not make a profit. He then took various unskilled jobs, sweeping floors in a Paterson, New Jersey, silk mill being one of them. At night he took English lessons.[10]

Adamic's personal battles with unemployment and possibly his sense of adventure led him to join the army in December 1916. This was the moment when a US army clerk changed his name from Adamič to Adamic because American typewriters had no accent marks. Adamic served two tours. When the United States joined the allies in World War I, federal officials offered immigrant soldiers a fast track to citizenship. He took advantage of this opportunity and became a US citizen in 1917. He spent much of World War I in the Panama Canal Zone rather than Europe, most likely because the US government listed his nationality as Austrian and had a policy of avoiding possible conflicting loyalties in its soldiers. In addition to Panama, the army stationed him in Louisiana, France, and Hawaii. After the war, army officials sent him to Fort MacArthur in the harbor town of San Pedro, California, near Los Angeles, where he continued to live after being discharged in January 1923.

Louis Adamic, US soldier. Courtesy of Public Library of Grosuplje, Grosuplje, Slovenia.

In San Pedro, he started translating pieces by South Slavic authors and taking freelance reporting jobs in hopes of launching a career as a writer. Most notably, he covered a strike by dockworkers affiliated with the Industrial Workers of the World (IWW) in San Pedro. Neither translating nor freelance reporting provided him with steady well-paid employment, and so he went to sea as a cabin boy on five merchant ships and then worked as a construction laborer, a printer, a farmworker, and an autoworker. He continued doing translations and started writing his own short stories when he could find the time.[11]

The Los Angeles literary scene appealed to him and he read voraciously and spent a great deal of time at Stanley Rose's bookstore. There Adamic met established and aspiring writers such as Carey McWilliams, future editor of *The Nation*; Carlos Bulosan, socialist and anticolonialist; and Jim Tully, an originator of the hard-boiled genre of novels that focused on hobos and drug addicts. Hollywood stars such as Charlie Chaplin also frequented Rose's shop, which was rumored to sell bootleg liquor in addition to books. Adamic and McWilliams maintained a close friendship; he and Tully corresponded at least through 1941, and he later joined Chaplin on the boards of many left-wing organizations to raise funds and champion worker, immigrant, and African American rights and oppose fascism.[12]

Needing a steady income, Adamic secured a job as a clerk at the Port of San Pedro in 1925, processing the paperwork of arriving ships. He often had downtime waiting for freighters, and he took those moments to write.[13] Small magazines started publishing his work that year. Between 1927 and 1931, Mencken published eight of Adamic's articles in his *American Mercury*, the country's most popular magazine.[14] Adamic's career blossomed after that.

Also, Adamic's personal life changed dramatically in 1927. At a party in Los Angeles he met Stella Sanders, the daughter of Austro-Hungarian Jewish immigrants. Stella was a student at Hunter College who had come to Los Angeles from her home in New York City to visit her uncles. Adamic and Sanders, twelve years his junior, remained in contact, sporadically meeting during the next two years. By 1929, he and Stella were in love and Adamic believed that he could make a living as a writer. He moved to New York City that year.[15] Louis and Stella married in June 1931 and lived on and off with Stella's mother Minnie Sanders through the summer of 1937.[16] By 1937 he earned enough money to buy a farmhouse in Milford, New Jersey. The couple never had children.

Louis devoted most of his waking hours to his craft, and Stella played an essential role in helping him to succeed. From the late 1920s through at least 1932, Stella heavily edited Louis's work as he fine-tuned his English. She also accompanied him on his 1932 trip to Yugoslavia, which was funded by a Guggenheim Fellowship. Louis won that award to visit his homeland, after being away for nineteen years. In 1934, he published *The Native's Return* about some of the experiences he had on this trip. When he and Stella returned from Yugoslavia, Stella helped Louis promote the book by going on the radio with him.[17] Unfortunately, not much exists about Stella's life in Louis's correspondences. Many of Adamic's letters burned the night he died, September 4, 1951. The two grew estranged after World War II and separated.

The Making of a Modernist

As Adamic started to gain a command of English, he continued to read voraciously, spending much of his free time in public libraries. Upton Sinclair's work appealed to him, especially *The Jungle*. From his experience at various low-wage jobs, Adamic proclaimed that Sinclair had captured the "daily weariness, physical and mental," that one felt after performing the "artless, colorless, [and] toneless" labor that most Americans did for ten to twelve hours per day and "instinctively rebelled" against.[18] But Adamic found Sinclair's protagonist Jurgis Rudkus, who joined the Socialist Party and committed his life to battling capitalist exploitation and nativism, unrealistic because Jurgis eventually found happiness.[19]

Although Adamic's work at moments included romantic and antimodernist accents, he had a greater affinity for the American modernists. Modernists rejected the notion that societies perpetually improved and sought to expose the irrationality of Christianity, capitalism, and the US political system. Adamic specifically noted his attraction to the works of Sinclair Lewis, John Dos Passos, and Theodore Dreiser because they best captured the "dog-eat-dog individualism" of "this machine age" that "terrorized and standardized" the "vainly aspiring masses" and turned their hopes into disenchantment. Adamic appreciated American modernists' attacks on the constellation of Christian fundamentalists, antiunion zealots, nativists, and eugenicists whom he viewed as manipulating the public into equating Anglo-Saxon Protestantism with Americanism and believing that hard work, faith in God, and obeying the law would result in economic security and spiritual fulfillment.[20]

Throughout the 1920s, Adamic found himself drawn to the works of the intellectuals who influenced modernist literature in the United States and Europe, including Sigmund Freud, Fyodor Dostoyevsky, and most especially Friedrich Nietzsche. Collectively, these works encouraged authors and artists to use parody, allegory, and irony to contend that capitalism, democracy, and Christianity destroyed people's humanity and relegated them to spiritual and economic poverty.[21] Adamic found Nietzsche's criticisms of political idealism and Christianity especially compelling. For Nietzsche, idealism grew out of faith, whether in a religion or a political ideology, and therefore it was dangerous because its adherents believed that they understood the truth. Truth "was posited as being, as God, as the highest court of appeal because truth was not *permitted* to be a problem."[22] Nietzsche later asserted that the "*lie* of the ideal has so far been the curse on reality; on account of it mankind itself has become mendacious and false down to its most fundamental instincts—to the point of worshiping the *opposite* values of those which alone would guarantee its health, its future."[23] A "slave morality" had fostered those opposite values.

Nietzsche argued that a slave morality materialized when slaves articulated their resentments but remained trapped in servitude. He called it "protracted revenge" because this set of values, such as forgiveness, humility, and kindness, became the basis of Christianity and eventually the dominant set of values in the western world. The Übermensch, an overman or superman, could overcome this slave morality because he knew that man created the idea of God, and he could demonstrate that universal laws did not exist and create his own morality.[24] By the mid-1920s, American readers found Übermensch references throughout popular periodicals as debates over morality and identity dominated public discourse. Adamic later joined these writers in utilizing the Übermensch concept, and he would repeatedly have his characters transition from reading Sinclair or belonging to a radical organization to recognizing that life was absurd. Reading Nietzsche would typically serve as the catalyst for them to achieve this stage of enlightenment. Adamic proclaimed that he held a Nietzschean point of view in reference to Anglo-Americans' uncritical embrace of materialism and its accompanying inauthentic relationships.[25] In 1928 Adamic wrote his first book (in English) about Nietzsche's ideas. Unfortunately, publishers rejected the manuscript and it is now missing.[26]

Nietzschean ideas, American modernist literature, and a bit of Sinclair's socialist critique of capitalism shaped Adamic's understanding of his *in betweenness* that stemmed from the frustrations of being an immigrant and an itinerant laborer. But his appreciation of Slovenian modernism that he brought with him to the United States, specifically the plots and metaphors he borrowed from Slovenia's greatest writer Ivan Cankar, underpinned his success. Cankar criticized both the Hapsburg monarchy, which ruled Slovenia for much of the eighteenth and nineteenth centuries through 1918, and the landed elites, who controlled the economic system, for dehumanizing Slovene peasants by denying them sovereignty and relegating them to a constant state of economic dependence.[27] Along with a cohort of leftist Slovenian writers including Adamic's eventual friend Oton Župančič, Cankar worked in Vienna at the beginning of the twentieth century studying the works of Dostoyevsky, Immanuel Kant, and Nietzsche. Enthralled by the psychological anguish Dostoyevsky's characters conveyed, Cankar wrote novels and short stories that attacked political and economic injustices. Cankar adopted Dostoyevsky's motif of having innocent people, often peasants, suffer for the aristocracy's transgressions, and he also appropriated the concept that public officials enacted laws to advance their own hedonism.[28] For Cankar, Dostoyevsky's valorization of the purity of Russian peasant wisdom paralleled how he saw Slovenes under Hapsburg rule. Adamic stood out as an influential figure in the 1920s culture wars in the United States because he incorporated Cankar's ideas into his own work.

Adamic's translations revealed his affinity for Slavic modernism. In addition to introducing the English-speaking world to a number of Cankar's short stories, Adamic published Czech poet Josef Svatopluk Machar's story "Superman." Influenced by Nietzsche's focus on alienation and Franz Kafka's expressions of anxiety, Machar, during the 1890s, joined the circle of fin-de-siècle Viennese artists. Machar's superman was a successful commoner who had become the most effective officer in the Austrian army. Yet his superiors removed him from command after he insisted that royals in the army conform to egalitarian rules. Machar's critiques of national identity and the absurdity of politics resonated with Adamic because both men thought that slave morality had become too powerful for the overman to overcome.[29] Five years later, in 1928, Adamic adopted aspects of Machar's "Superman" for his own essay by the same name that depicted an American similarly exiled in his own land.[30] Adamic's writing career took off when he questioned the existence of an American identity.

Challenging American Identity

Adamic's job as a clerk at the Port of San Pedro allowed him time to write.[31] From 1925 to 1928, his articles lampooning Christian evangelicals in Los Angeles appeared regularly in socialist and cultural critic Emanuel Haldeman-Julius's monthly magazine. Through these pieces of journalistic satire, Adamic acquired a following of readers and received encouragement from the most popular writers of his day, including Upton Sinclair, H. L. Mencken, Mary Austin, and Sinclair Lewis.

Adamic made Canadian-born Pentecostal minister Aimee Semple McPherson, Los Angeles's leading evangelist, the primary target of his ridicule. McPherson repeatedly proclaimed that Christians founded America and pointed to the Pilgrims as proof. Then she insisted that the authors of the Constitution and later Abraham Lincoln on the eve of the Civil War received God's guidance to advance US history. But now as schools replaced biblical accounts of life with the theory of evolution and atheists, flappers, and radicals colluded to undermine Christianity and democracy, Satan's influence threatened America's future.[32]

Then on May 18, 1926, McPherson disappeared while swimming at a beach near Venice, California. Editors across the nation assigned more than fifty reporters to the story. The *Los Angeles Times* chartered two airplanes and even hired a parachutist in case they spotted her body in the ocean. Some journalists speculated that she had drowned and others claimed she had been kidnapped. Adamic suggested she had orchestrated a massive publicity stunt. In the midst of the spectacle that saw thousands come to the beach each day waiting to see if McPherson's body washed ashore, investigators realized that the temple's radio engineer, Kenneth G. Ormiston, disappeared at the same time as McPherson. Ormiston's wife had filed papers to divorce him and suspected he was having an affair. On June 23, three days after her congregation assumed that she had died and held a memorial service for her, McPherson reappeared in Agua, a small Mexican town in the Sonoran desert. She claimed that she had been kidnapped and escaped. Detectives believed that she spent at least part of the month with Ormiston in Carmel, California. McPherson denied the allegations, but police found witnesses in Carmel and a grocery list in McPherson's handwriting in the bungalow Ormiston had rented. The Los Angeles district attorney prepared a case against McPherson for faking her kidnapping and offering false testimony. Ultimately, the district attorney determined that he had insufficient evidence to go forward. McPherson's most devout followers remained loyal to her, but the scandal destroyed her reputation and greatly diminished her celebrity.[33] In attempting to restore her reputation, McPherson relied on those who considered themselves 100 percent Americans to come to her aid. She claimed that Satan wanted to destroy fundamentalism and pointed out that those leading the attacks against her belonged to the Catholic Church. As the case went forward, she sought out the Ku Klux Klan's support, and her lawyer called on the "patriots" of Los Angeles to believe in her innocence.[34]

Adamic mockingly framed one piece about her legal troubles as an attack by the devil and ridiculed a radio address where she proclaimed herself innocent. McPherson insisted that she could not possibly be guilty, Adamic noted, because the only man she loved was "Gee-SUS." Adamic also pointed out that she refused to be fingerprinted and to go to Carmel to stand in a lineup.[35] After reiterating the details of the case, he explained that he had "nothing against her alleged relationship with her gentleman friend," but because she became a public character by embracing her role as a religious and political mobmaster, he felt compelled to expose her hypocrisy. He noted that, before her "drowning," the fundamentalist movement appeared likely to win its fight "to place the Bible in the tax-supported schools and bar from them all evolutionary teaching. California seemed to be in danger of becoming a second Tennessee" (referring to the recent Scopes trial). But now "Aimee—bless her soul!—did more to harm religion as a whole in a month than a regiment of debunkers could have done in a lifetime."[36]

Parodying charlatans did not distinguish Adamic from the American authors and journalists he admired. But writing about McPherson served as a stepping-stone for him to find his own voice. As an immigrant criticizing Christian fundamentalism, Adamic understood that he did not possess the same cultural license his Anglo-American middle-class counterparts did. The scandal had made critiquing McPherson a safe way for Adamic to question the realities of American identity without facing too much of a backlash from nativists. It also allowed him to pay homage to Nietzsche's depiction of Christians as herd animals susceptible to slave morality.

In the midst of covering the McPherson story, Adamic made an original contribution to modernist literature with his 1926 piece "The Crusader." He contended that American born workers who challenged their employers became exiles. The story's main character, Lonie Burton, a white native-born patriot turned radical, repeatedly experienced betrayal no matter the politics he practiced. As the story developed, Burton went from supporting the Wilsonian mission of making the world safe for democracy during World War I to advocating syndicalism and joining the IWW. "Lonie's idealism," Adamic declared, was "genuine and poetic," but "seemed to me unsound, romantic, [and] verging on the absurd."[37]

The story takes place over several years, and in the final scenes Burton remained "aflame with desire to improve, uplift the world, to stamp out the countless forms of evil and tragedy," while Adamic portrayed a fictional version of himself as "not unaware of evil and tragedy" but caring "very little" whether "mankind improved or not."[38] Burton's desire for a better world resulted in an employer beating him up during a labor dispute, while his fellow workers watched. The fictional Adamic, seeing Burton shortly after the attack, described Burton as "an old man at twenty-eight, his face battered, his ribs fractured; shabby, bent as though weighed down by a vast burden." In an extended version of the story, Adamic returned to his critique of the dangers of misplaced idealism by adding that Burton "is living proof to me (perhaps soon to be a dead one) that one cannot afford to plunge too far into the economic and social issues of American life. One is too apt to be caught in their ramifications, overwhelmed and crushed, without beneficial result to anyone."[39] Those who acted upon their idealism quickly discovered that American promises of justice were myths. Adamic had Burton lose his American identity to highlight the procapitalist dimension of nativism. The leading voices of coercive assimilation equated radicalism with foreignness, and Adamic, like Sinclair and others, wanted their readers to think about workers' rights to challenge corporate authority. Unlike Sinclair, Adamic was not optimistic about their answer.

Earlier that year, 1926, Ivan Molek, who had arrived in the United States in 1900 and served as Adamic's conduit into the Slovenian American community, criticized Adamic's portrayal of socialism in the person of Burton. Molek, a socialist, edited Chicago's Slovene-language newspaper *Prosveta* ("Enlightenment"), served as an officer in the Slovene National Benefit Society (Slovenska narodna podporna jednota—SNPJ), and played a leading role in championing Yugoslavism, the movement for a democratic federation of South Slavic nations dedicated to political and ethnic equality.[40] His correspondence with Adamic suggested that he read an early draft of "The Crusader." Molek had enjoyed Adamic's pieces on McPherson, and he noted his appreciation of Adamic's attacks on xenophobes and Americanizers and applauded Adamic's criticisms of employers who exploited their workers. But he did raise objections to Burton as a prototypical socialist. Adamic responded to Molek's critique by asserting that championing socialism in the United States "is as futile as spitting into the ocean with the idea of increasing its volume" and added that "equality is a myth."[41]

Adamic not only concluded that radicalism could not affect American social, cultural, and economic relations, he also rejected Molek's belief that Slovenian diasporic activism could change both their homeland and their host land. Leftists such as Molek saw themselves as exiles from Hapsburg-controlled Slovenia who wanted to help make Yugoslavism a reality by engaging in political activism in the United States. Molek helped to start the South Slavic Socialist Federation (SSSF) in 1905, which coordinated with Slovenian and Croatian fraternal organizations to raise money for and lobby on behalf of a Yugoslav confederation. SSSF members affiliated with the Socialist Party of America, but because they were foreign nationals in the United States, they lacked voting rights. As a result, the Socialist Party prevented SSSF activists from formally participating in Socialist Party affairs. SSSF activists did shape the intellectual life of the Socialist Party by publishing newspapers and magazines, holding debates, encouraging workers to join unions, and challenging nativist attitudes. The SSSF had more than 2,600 members at its height in 1916, as they sought to give South Slavic immigrants an alternative to Catholic Church–dominated activities.[42]

Although small, the SSSF did play a role in Slovenian politics. In Slovenia during the late nineteenth century, union leader and journalist Etbin Kristan assisted in the creation of the Yugoslav Social Democratic Party. By 1912, Molek had established firm ties between the SSSF and the Social Democrats. When World War I broke out, Kristan immigrated to the United States and held leadership positions in Slovene fraternal organizations, illustrating the transnational character of Slovene socialism and its focus on workers' rights, political equality, and ethnic justice in Europe and the United States.[43] During the war, the collapse of the Habsburg Empire seemed imminent, which was when the SSSF authored the "Chicago Declaration" that vowed to aid in the creation of Yugoslavia. Unfortunately for Slovenian leftists, the SSSF collapsed soon thereafter as it divided over the Socialist Party's decision to oppose US entry into World War I. The group's Croatian section supported party leaders' contention that the working class killed each other for the expansion of capitalism and therefore all laborers worldwide should oppose sending troops to Europe. Slovenes and the small number of radical Serbs disagreed with their Croatian counterparts because they wanted to hasten the collapse of Austrian rule and called for US involvement in the war.[44] Tensions heightened after the war as some South Slav leftists remained socialists while others embraced communism.

Molek believed that Adamic could help him reignite the Yugoslav movement by joining the SNPJ, publishing some pieces in *Prosveta*, and attending Socialist Party meetings. Adamic declined on all three fronts. Claiming that he wanted to secure the attention of a broader US audience, Adamic refused to write for *Prosveta*. He also added that his translations of Slovenian, Croatian, and Czech authors into English for US magazines signified nothing more than his need for "the few dollars" he received for his efforts. Adamic insisted that he did not possess "any patriotic pride" as a Slovenian and for good measure proclaimed, "I came here in my boyhood, and have lived for the most part among Americans ever since."[45]

Adamic's declaration made little sense. Living "among Americans" certainly did not mean that he saw himself as culturally American. At this point in his life, he equated American with Babbittry—embracing materialism and eschewing critical thought in order to conform to a shallow ideal of success. He also exaggerated his rejection of a Slovenian identity. Although he did not want to agitate on behalf of Yugoslavism, Adamic did firmly embed himself within the Slovenian modernist tradition led by Cankar. Molek and the other adherents of Yugoslavism shared Adamic's sense that Slovenian poems and stories played a fundamental role in defining who they were, and like Adamic, leftist South Slavs viewed themselves as living in a state of exile in the United States. They agreed on their liminality but differed on how to deal with their state of exclusion and the feeling of not belonging that accompanied their marginalization.

Adamic explored the idea of nonbelonging on a personal level and detached it from establishing a nation-state. He displayed his *slovenstvo* (Sloveneness) in March 1926, four weeks after informing Molek that he had "no deep patriotic feeling as a Slovenian," by translating chapters of Cankar's short story *Yerney's Justice* for *Prosveta*.[46] Like most Slovenes, Adamic considered Cankar "the greatest writer Yugoslavia has yet produced." He particularly appreciated how Cankar depicted the "chaotic forces" of life that prevented most people from finding happiness, and how his "pathetic" characters, such as unheroic farmhands, battled systems, conditions, and institutions they could not comprehend, let alone overcome. Their failures turned them into "shadows" lacking in any real humanity.[47] At Upton Sinclair's urging, Vanguard Press published Adamic's translation as a single edition later in 1926.

In Cankar's novella, Yerney's dehumanization resulted from feudal practices Slovenes experienced under Austria's rule. When the son of Yerney's former master took control of his father's land, he dismissed and evicted Yerney, an aging peasant. Yerney, believing that his master's son had violated God's law, appealed to every authority he could find from the village constable to the king of Austria to no avail.[48] The book ended with Yerney starting a fire in the master's house and then laughing righteously. His fellow peasants displayed their rejection of his conception of justice by beating him and throwing him into the burning house to die.[49] Yerney's fellow peasants accepted their nothingness, whereas he did not. His penalty for acting on his idealism was death.

Adamic, as he explained to Molek, was "inclined toward Nietzsche, more than Marx."[50] Even though notions of working-class militancy appealed to

Adamic, he found the advocates of socialism and Yugoslavism to resemble the 100 percent Americans who believed that going to church, working hard, voting, shopping, and buying a house in the suburbs would result in material reward and political freedom. They all allowed their idealism to distort reality, which led them into a paradox where every effort at happiness only increased feelings of despair. Molek and his fellow socialists, Adamic asserted, needed to realize that "everything is futile; nothing is important."[51] Adamic's reading of Nietzsche fueled his aversion to political activism as he shared the German philosopher's distrust of collective action. Nietzsche, however, had only contempt for the crowd, including exploited peasants. Adamic clearly did not share that part of Nietzsche's perspective.

Like Molek, Upton Sinclair, who also helped mentor Adamic, expressed his disappointment over Adamic's treatment of socialism. Sinclair contended that eventually "the working class" will "accomplish its emancipation, and it will be due to the efforts of such idealists as you portray."[52] Sinclair added that Adamic and the other young skeptics Mencken inspired consistently challenged those in power but repeatedly seemed "ignorant of the revolutionary movement."[53] Adamic took umbrage at Sinclair's allegation that he was simply mimicking Mencken. Referring to socialism, Adamic retorted that "I'm incapable of your faith any longer" and then speculated that "perhaps I'm deficient, damaged, tired I don't know what" and therefore "the psychology of cynicism makes" my perspective "unworthy of your respect." But he wanted Sinclair to appreciate his motivations and that he had found his own voice. "The Crusader" genuinely expressed his understanding of America. If "I do jeer, I jeer at myself more than anybody else. I believe the story is the truth as I saw it."[54]

To Sinclair, Adamic employed a mordant style as a strategy for selling articles. Adamic's personal correspondence suggested that he wanted a better world, but his experiences as a working-class immigrant taught him that capitalist hegemony and political corruption meant that Sinclair's faith in socialism rested upon misplaced optimism. Adamic's characters repeatedly held dear various forms of idealism, from hyperpatriotism to socialism, and they failed each time because being American to Adamic meant existing in a perpetual state of alienation and despair. In Adamic's view, Sinclair may have believed too deeply in the American dream, albeit an alternative one, to recognize the depths of immigrants' misery, capitalism's supremacy, democracy's failure, and the limits of radicalism. Adamic believed that at best "The Crusader" would force native-born readers to think about workers' humanity.

Before leaving Los Angeles for New York in 1929, Adamic finished "Land of Laughs." It focused on his experiences with "Americanizers" when he first lived in New York City from December 1913 through December 1916. Groups such as the American Legion and various patriotic women's organizations taught immigrant workers English, a specific version of US history, and the value of hard work and insisted that their classes could help immigrants emancipate themselves eventually from the cultural superstitions, political oppression, and economic backwardness of their homelands.[55] Finding such claims ludicrous, Adamic's story turned these coercive Americanization courses intended to assimilate immigrants into Anglo-American culture into a foil to question the existence of an American identity. He began by inverting the racialized stereotype of new immigrants, eastern and southern Europeans, as diseased and intellectually inferior to the white migrants who had arrived before 1890. He described his teacher as an "unhealthy-looking, undersized Nordic" who appeared "terribly ill at ease before this assembly of thirty-odd Dagoes, Dutchmen, Jews, Bohunks and Turks." The members of the class were "better educated in their native tongues than he was in English." During the day, this "stirrer of the Melting Pot" taught children their ABCs but transformed into an "Americanizer" at night. Each meeting began with the pledge of allegiance, and then the instructor would deliver "a speech, prepared for him by a patriotic society, on the Constitution or the American form of Government." After numerous embarrassing moments that resulted from his inability to answer basic questions about grammar, history, and culture, the "undersized Nordic" became angry and forced the students to sit in silence copying passages from a third-grade history textbook.[56]

Repeatedly compelled to perform this act of pedantry after a long day's work, Adamic wrote that he skipped class to figure out America by wandering the streets of New York City. His adventures often included stops at the public library. He recalled coming across an old article about striking oil workers by socialist journalist John Reed. It provided his first "flash of understanding" of the United States. From there he read Sinclair's *The Jungle*.[57] Although Reed and Sinclair inspired socialist sympathies within him, Adamic explained that he soon thereafter concluded that radicalism mirrored nationalism and capitalism. Native and foreign-born alike could not comprehend the difficulties they faced because they filtered their experiences through the promises of the American dream or a socialist utopia. He concluded "Land of Laughs" by borrowing directly from Cankar in declaring that it "is best to laugh at" America because it "is futile to try to change or influence it deeply: it is immune to reform, and within it operate tremendous economic and other forces that seem to have got out of human control."[58] Without acknowledgment, Adamic, in "Land of Laughs," appropriated Cankar's cruel peasant cosmos.

During his stay in New York City, Adamic focused on spending time with Stella and writing about working-class struggles to highlight just how out of human control America had become. In October 1930, he published a fictional account of IWW activist "Jack Kipps" in the *American Mercury*. Kipps and other Wobblies printed up flyers demanding the release of political prisoners arrested amid the 1919 Red Scare hysteria sweeping the nation. To accentuate their point, they organized a silent protest of President Woodrow Wilson's visit to Seattle. Adamic wrote that Kipps convinced more than five thousand Wobblies to come to Seattle and line six blocks of the president's parade route. When Wilson's motorcade drove through, the Wobblies all folded their arms and remained mute. The display so disturbed Wilson that he invited a delegation of Wobblies to talk with him the next day. Kipps realized, as he explained to the fictional Adamic, that even if Wilson wanted to, he could not have helped because he was part of the system. At that moment, Kipps recognized that "workers must help themselves; nobody else will or can."[59] Capitalism so dominated American life that even presidents were powerless to challenge it. Adamic indicated that he saw no possibility for working-class liberation in the United States.

Despite claims that Adamic mimicked Mencken's style, his work on labor, and then immigrant life, illustrated that he had developed his own voice. Mencken's depictions of absurdity served comedic ends as he presented the divide between American ideals and realities as a farce. Mencken's 1922 essay "On Being American" proclaimed that in the United States "the general average of intelligence, of knowledge, of competence, of integrity, of self-respect, of honor is so low that any man who knows his trade, does not fear ghosts, has read fifty good books, and practices the common decencies stands out as brilliantly as a wart on a bald head." America was the only nation where "third-rate men" are "in full control of the state, and with it of all the national standards."[60] Unfortunately, from Mencken's point of view, the "immigrants who have come in since those early days have been, if anything, of even lower grade than their forerunners," so the quality of the nation had little chance of improving.[61] A peasant sensibility, stretching from the Puritans to the recent eastern and southern European arrivals, defined American identity and thus explained the inferiority of the populace. Mencken asserted that peasants had "practical cunning" but lacked the ability "to see any further than the next farm." A peasant can figure out how to acquire money and property, "but his cultural development is but little above that of the domestic animals.

He is intensely and cocksurely moral, but his morality and his self-interest are crudely identical. He is emotional and easy to scare, but his imagination cannot grasp an abstraction. He is a violent nationalist and patriot, but he admires rogues in office." Mencken then added, "He is violently jealous of what he conceives to be his rights, but brutally disregardful of the other fellow's. He is religious, but his religion is wholly devoid of beauty and dignity. This man, whether city or country bred, is the normal Americano—the 100 percent. Methodist, Odd Fellow, Ku Kluxer, and Know Nothing."[62] Culturally then, Mencken viewed immigrants and their opponents as equally bizarre because they cherished draconian codes, feared the devil, and held the Christian virtues that they often violated in high regard. Becoming a successful American, Mencken suggested, required simply that one take advantage of the opportunities available.

Adamic viewed the gulf between the nation's professed ideals and its realities as a tragedy. The working class, in his opinion, did not yield to exploitation and embrace the illusion of democracy because of stupidity and cultural backwardness. For them, chaotic uncontrollable economic forces had unleashed a pervasive sense of despair that people could not even begin to

Louis Adamic with his wife Stella Sanders in Rogaška Slatina, 1932. Courtesy of National and University Library of Slovenia, Ljubljana, Slovenia.

comprehend let alone confront. This sense of desolation exuded from *Dynamite*, the first popular history of working-class violence in the United States that he wrote. Adamic had trouble finding a publisher for *Dynamite* and in the meantime wrote stories about immigrants whose efforts to achieve the American dream usually culminated in their deaths.

At the beginning of 1931, Viking Press bought *Dynamite*, which appeared to give Adamic enough confidence that he could survive as a writer. He married Stella in June.[63] Despite experiencing a piece of the American dream amid the Great Depression, Adamic's stories of immigrant tragedy and labor oppression illustrated his sense of exile and its resonance with the larger public.

Adamic's Exiles

Echoes of Yerney reverberated throughout Adamic's stories from the late 1920s and early 1930s. His characters appeared as displaced peasants who found that the empty promises of wealth and equality of their adopted land meant that poverty and injustice followed them across the ocean. *Laughing in the Jungle* (1932) offered revised versions of his most popular short stories from this period woven into a single narrative. *Laughing* was part homage and part critique of Sinclair's 1905 *The Jungle*. Sinclair's Lithuanian-born hero Jurgis Rudkus realized that working harder did not yield the success American boosters promised to immigrants. Rudkus's conversion to socialism put him and his fellow workers on the path to liberation from workplace exploitation and land-fraud schemes aimed at those who spoke little English and knew less about the law. In contrast to Sinclair, Adamic's protagonists could never successfully assimilate, whether they embraced capitalist individualism and Anglo-Saxon values or, like Jurgis, converted to socialism. Any effort to become an "American" resulted in death.[64]

Early in *Laughing*, for instance, we meet Peter Molek, named after Adamic's friend and Slovene immigrant community leader Ivan Molek. The fictional Molek returned to his and Adamic's village of Blato to die after spending most of his adult life in Pennsylvania mining coal. Molek suffered asthmatic spasms from an undefined lung disease. When asked what had happened to him, he declared, "America . . . America." In America, immigrants were "dung," mere "fertilizer feeding the roots" of industrial growth.[65] Molek learned too late that hard work did not equal material gain and spiritual reward.

The character Steve Radin best illustrated the danger of privileging idealism over the logic of peasant fatalism. Upon arriving in the United States, the fictional Adamic discovered that his friend Radin earned his living as a boxer and a thug intimidating people for an Irish American political boss and Brooklyn saloon owner named Joe Riley. Just as Radin appeared committed to a life of crime, he found socialism. Riley sent Radin to attack Robert Twombley, a socialist making antiwar speeches, because Riley did not appreciate it when "stevedores and sailors" listened to Twombley instead of drinking. When Radin struck Twombley, the socialist orator refused to retaliate. Surprised, Radin took one of Twombley's pamphlets and walked away. "It was a revelation to him" that war "was a crime." Radin now realized that Riley "was part of the evil capitalistic system."[66] Adamic's character sought an American identity through the idealistic radicalism of Twombley instead of the materialistic self-interested gangsterism of his assimilated patron Riley. Radin's career as a professional agitator appeared promising when he took a factory job and successfully led a strike for higher wages. After the victory, however, his fellow workers did not share his spirit of solidarity. His employer fired him and Radin's brother unionists refused to return to the picket line to save his job.[67] A disheartened Radin read H. L. Mencken and Nietzsche, renounced his militancy, and returned to a life of crime, this time as a bootlegger. Driving a speedboat loaded with $50,000 worth of liquor during a summer night in 1928, Steve crashed into an oil tanker and died.[68]

In narrating Radin's ideological reversals, Adamic explained that the "American success idea" encouraged both the "native and foreign-born" to seek "great material achievements for the sake of these achievements." Beyond their failure to question the value of mindless consumption, "these success-bent men and women," in Adamic's opinion, were "innately unfit to handle wealth and position." By attempting to adopt the capitalist's gangster mentality, most people, especially immigrants, "were headed, sooner or later, toward some such fate, metaphorically speaking, as had finished Steve Radin—a crash in the dark."[69] Confusion and brutality defined South Slav immigrant working-class lives, and idealists could not change the laws of the jungle.

From 1928 through 1932, Adamic's characters, exemplified by Radin "crashing in the dark" in pursuit of wealth, Molek becoming "dung" to fertilize industrial growth, and Tanasich working herself to death "to help America become great and terrible" stressed his point that new immigrants could never succeed in America because economic practices, the social structure, and the dominant culture depended on their failure. Slavs would remain in a state of perpetual alienation if they continued to try to embrace the dominant narratives about hard work leading to opportunity. They would fare no better, however, if they became radicals and attempted to overthrow capitalism. Estrangement remained their permanent state of being.

The only success story in Adamic's jungle was Lenard Podgornik. In a 1928 piece, Adamic portrayed Podgornik as "a professional lazy man" who successfully blends in by being a "bum and gentleman."[70] Adamic treated Podgornik like Job—success followed by reversals. After suffering an industrial accident, Podgornik reads a pamphlet explaining the exploitation of workers and he decides to rebel against work.[71] Podgornik then spends his days in libraries reading Sinclair and other leftist writers, frequenting pool rooms, and socializing with Wobblies. Eventually, he delivers liquor for bootleggers to earn enough money to feed his family and pay his taxes, but he ends his deliveries by noon so he can enjoy life.[72] Lenard's wife, Agnes, ends up taking over his bootlegging business, finding a lover, and acquiring a nice home. Wanting Agnes to be happy, Lenard fakes his own death and moves to Mexico so she could avoid the legal and cultural consequences of living with another man. In making this decision, Lenard found happiness but became "nothing," not "even a Bohunk any more."[73] Adamic did not elaborate on this thought, but he made it clear that success for immigrants meant recognizing their nothingness and refusing to play a rigged game that relegated them to a marginal existence and then an early death.

Adamic used the peasant past as much as the American present to explain how dehumanization followed South Slavs across the Atlantic. America only altered Slavs' sources of alienation. But if they maintained their peasant sensibilities, then they could at least survive in the United States. And for someone who claimed to have lost his Slovene identity, Adamic declared that the "peasant in me gave me the tendency to distrust intangible things, to rely on common sense and keep on guard against high ideals and fancy ideas."[74] By drawing on his peasant roots, Adamic encouraged his fellow South Slavs and other marginalized individuals and groups to embrace their state of exile. Doing so would allow them to collectively disprove the myths that hard work would make them rich, that believing in democracy would make them free, and that socialism could serve as an alternative American identity. Insisting that nonbelonging was a state of being, as he used Lenard Podgornik to demonstrate, Adamic turned to Slovenian modernism to make Americans question how they understood themselves and their nation. High school and college teachers used *Laughing* for this very purpose in the early 1930s. In fact, it was required reading for all English majors in the University of Iowa's 1934 freshmen class.[75]

Revolutionaries and Supermen

Adamic had simultaneously worked on his peasant stories and *Dynamite*. The 1910 bombing of the *Los Angeles Times* building particularly captivated him, but his publisher pushed him to write a more comprehensive book that would appeal to a larger audience. In the end, *Dynamite* was a wildly inaccurate, emotionally charged history of industrial bloodshed. Adamic claimed that he had written it to "shock non-proletarian readers with the story of proletarian suffering" and to depict the "social consequences of the class war."[76] The terms *proletarian* and *class war* implied that he utilized a Marxian analysis. In reality, Adamic relied on newspaper accounts riddled with errors and overgeneralizations from his source materials, and then, in pursuit of good sales, he revealed a penchant for sensationalism.[77] He asserted that workers lacked "social vision and purpose," in effect denying class consciousness as the reason for labor militancy.[78] To him, acts of sabotage, exchanges of gunfire with company guards, and strikes all illustrated spontaneous displays of frustration born out of the combination of starvation wages, draconian workplace practices, and various types of employer intimidation.

Like Yerney's murderers who acceded to the feudal order, Adamic contended that Americans' tolerance for unbridled capitalism had resulted in a widespread acceptance of violent deaths. He stated that "criminal terrorism which reached its heights in the days of Al Capone" directly resulted from "the chaotic, brutalizing conditions in American industry."[79] "Political bosses" also embraced the spirit of savagery underpinning capitalism by employing gangs "as terrorists" to silence opponents and advance their own agendas. Chaos, not democracy, guided American political and social relations.[80] Most labor leaders, he charged, shared employers' opportunism and therefore put their own interests ahead of the workers they claimed to represent, while socialists were either "rogues or lopsided emotionalists."[81] Adamic clearly refused to credit Gilded Age and Progressive Era municipal socialists and union activists with the passage of laws that created city-run electric companies, garbage collection, eight-hour days, and a host of other reforms, not to mention better working conditions on shop floors and in mines.

Adamic maintained continuity between *Dynamite* and his peasant modernist stories when he noted that "the hundred per cent Americans of that day were perhaps justified in characterizing" working-class radicalism "as a 'foreign phenomenon' in the sense that only—or largely—immigrants were guilty of it; but the conditions which provoked them to riots were quite

American." American industrialists "imported these foreigners and then treated them inhumanly."[82] He pointed to the construction of the Erie Canal as one example. Contractors "found no difficulty in replacing the sick and the dead" because "nearly every ship that arrived from Europe brought in more 'dung.'"[83] By which he meant immigrant laborers to fertilize the jungle.

He continued to rely on Nietzschean constructs to help explain US industrial relations. Adamic portrayed IWW leader William Dudley "Big Bill" Haywood as a radical Übermensch. He described Haywood as "a he-man, a man of elemental force, with the physical strength of an ox, a big head and a tremendous jaw; hard, direct, immensely resistant, impatient of obstacles, careless, violent, ready and fit to deal blow for blow; a boozer; a son of the Rockies, risen, as he put it himself, 'from the bowels of the earth,' to grope his way through years of misery and economic injustice to Socialism, to be touched by its idealism, and become a zealot in its cause."[84] Later in the book, Adamic added that Haywood's violence was "revolutionary, not 'racketeering.' Although the press and the pulpit denounced him, deep down in its heart the country felt instinctively that he was no mere murderer, not an 'undesirable citizen.'"[85] Adamic admired real revolutionaries, but Haywood had no place in an America where people failed to grapple with their slave morality. The public curiously ignored Adamic's Slavic modernist approach and Nietzschean references. Instead, they focused on his numerous factual errors and the blame he cast on capitalists for incidents of industrial violence.

The major daily newspapers and middle-class readers celebrated *Dynamite*. The reception by labor and radical periodicals proved more varied, ranging from tempered approval to abhorrence. Socialists Norman Thomas and James Oneal found it a "just" history and "sound" in its argument, but pointed to numerous flaws in the details.[86] Well-known labor lawyer and one-time California socialist gubernatorial candidate Austin Lewis wrote that, broadly speaking, *Dynamite* "has a correct thesis" but contained many errors and said that Adamic clearly did not understand socialism.[87] Delegates attending the International Ladies' Garment Workers' Union annual convention in 1931 passed a resolution criticizing *Dynamite*'s inaccuracies. Prolabor journalist Robert W. Dunn charged Adamic with writing a sensationalist book to make money from royalties; and communist activist William Z. Foster called it "a bizarre mishmash of confusionism, misrepresentation, and sensationalism." From Folsom Prison, labor activist and political prisoner Warren K. Billings informed Adamic that *Dynamite*, which he considered an antilabor book overall, did not in the least capture what had happened in his case. Luckily for Adamic, Sinclair stood by him and other emerging civil libertarians and champions of the working class, such as Carey McWilliams, Arthur Garfield Hayes, and Mary Austin praised the book. Sinclair Lewis showed his support by writing a blurb for the back cover.[88]

James McCann, a carpenter and self-taught writer, offered a more extensive critique. McCann reviewed the book for a radical journal and then carried on a correspondence of nearly three years with Adamic from his prison cell in San Quentin. McCann operated on the margins of the proletarian literary movement that came of age during the Great Depression. He reviewed books for leftist periodicals and regularly exchanged letters with the most recognizable names in this genre, such as John Dos Passos and Jack Conroy. He and Mike Gold, editor of the procommunist *New Masses*, also wrote each other often, and Gold sent McCann the most recent issues of his magazine.[89] Unlike other left critics, McCann had no problem with Adamic questioning the depths of class consciousness, but he wanted the immigrant writer to do so in a much more nuanced fashion. McCann chastised Adamic for not examining why workers and the children of workers became the soldiers, policemen, and company guards "hired to kill off other working stiffs." As it stood, McCann doubted "the value of this book to the working class" and concluded that if you are not clearly on the workers' side, "it follows you are with their oppressors."[90]

Adamic proclaimed that *Dynamite*'s radicalism lay in its challenge to accepted views of American identity. He added that to end industrial violence, curtail poverty, and foster any type of social equality, writers had to convince the bourgeoisie that their interests aligned more with workers than with bosses. Politicians and pundits had manipulated the mostly white middle-class, by generating fears of communism and socialism, to believe industrial violence threatened to usher in a workers' state that would crush economic opportunity and political freedom. Yet capitalism and political corruption had already done that. Americans, from Adamic's perspective, had to understand that they were undergoing a collective crisis of identity because they accepted employer-directed tropes about class relations. To him, the chief site of alienation was not the workplace, as Marxists such as McCann believed, but a misplaced acceptance of the origin stories that defined Americans as Anglo-Saxon, Protestant, and individuals imbued with democratic freedoms. At first, McCann rejected Adamic's position, but after transitioning from his cell at San Quentin to a highway work camp, he wrote Adamic that he heard "so many good words on it from persons of the middle stratum, I began to see the usefulness of such a work."[91]

Adamic had a similar, although more public and more spirited, debate with other radical critics. In a fierce reply to *Dynamite*'s detractors, he explained that he had hoped that the book would elicit sympathy for workers from the middle class. But because "I am not a drastic, wild-eyed Communist," radicals insisted that "I straddle the fence" between labor and capital. They "are wrong" as "I am much more radical—intelligently radical—than" they are. He had little faith that the working class would ever develop a radical consciousness, exhibited by his insistence that "the toiling masses" would not read *Dynamite* because "the working class doesn't read anything but the tabloids and the funny papers." He then claimed that "Karl Marx would revise his ideas and doctrines" if he had known "the American psychology," where life functions as "a hold-up game."[92] Adamic's commitment to Cankar's fatalism and Nietzsche's rejection of slave morality made recognizing reality and accepting exile as a likely permanent state of being, rather than acquiring class consciousness, the first step in living an authentic life.

Slovenstvo

By 1932, Adamic had published repeatedly in the nation's top literary magazine, the *American Mercury*, he had written the first popular history of American labor violence, and *Laughing in the Jungle* received praise for challenging nativism and popular notions of assimilation. Upton Sinclair, H. L. Mencken, and Sinclair Lewis all helped mentor him. In May of that year the John Simon Guggenheim Foundation awarded him a fellowship, which helped confirm that he was succeeding in making writing his career. The Guggenheim Fellowship allowed Adamic to spend the next year in Yugoslavia in order to write about his homeland, which he had not visited since emigrating from it nearly twenty years earlier. Going back to Slovenia for a writer whose work often challenged notions of belonging and identity raised questions about Adamic's own sense of being.

Adamic had refused to participate in the efforts to advance Yugoslavism because he saw it as doomed to fail, an act of misplaced idealism, and, as he explained to Molek in 1926, he now wrote for Americans. He did so as a Slovenian exile by declaring that his peasant egoism allowed him to resist Americanization, asserting that American culture went against his grain, and telling his stories of in-betweenness by borrowing Cankar's metaphors. A number of leading leftist Slovenian intellectuals in the late 1920s noted these aspects of his work when they insisted that *slovenstvo*, the Slovene spirit, guided Adamic.

Adamic became the centerpiece of a larger debate over the meaning of *slovenstvo* during his visit in 1932–33.[93] Because Slovenia had been controlled by other nations for most of its history, Slovenes had to express their cultural identities beyond the nation-state. Conservatives had insisted that Catholicism should be the defining characteristic of Slovenian identity. From the early Middle Ages the Catholic Church had played a central role in educating Slovenes. After the Reformation, embracing Catholicism signified resistance against Germanization for some. At the same time, however, church leaders proffered deals with the Hapsburgs that allowed them to be loyal to the empire while maintaining their political control over Slovenia.[94] Leftists, from liberals to social democrats, argued that the Catholic hierarchy's willingness to make accommodations with the Austrian monarchy represented a betrayal of *slovenstvo*. They maintained that writers had the responsibility to promulgate Slovenian identity whether they lived inside its borders or beyond them.[95]

Shortly after Adamic arrived in Slovenia in spring 1932, leading poet Oton Župančič intensified this debate by proclaiming that Adamic's work conveyed *slovenstvo* more effectively than the "guardians of Sloveneness" who lived in Slovenia. For Župančič, Slovenian identity had more to do with the indomitable peasant resolve in the face of constant suffering, and he insisted that Adamic captured that spirit.[96] The vast majority of the Slovenian intellectuals rejected Župančič's argument, and his piece divided leftists at a crucial moment. The debate over whether Adamic embodied *slovenstvo* continues into the twenty-first century.[97]

Adamic in no way assisted in clarifying how he viewed his relationship to *slovenstvo*. His March 9, 1934, radio interview echoed *The Native's Return* (1934)—the book he wrote after returning from Yugoslavia that mixed travel writing with political intrigue—when he declared, "I thought in English. I had become an American writer and had married an American girl. All my intellectual and emotional interests were here."[98] Then he claimed to not really know his nine siblings or remember Slovenian that well. His oldest sister Tonchka was thirteen when he left and his youngest brother France was one; now they were thirty-two and twenty. Exaggerating for affect, as he typically did in his books, Adamic then claimed that "I could not begin to tell them about America and myself; how I felt about America, what a wonderful and terrible place it was, how it fascinated and thrilled me." He did not want to worry them, nor did he want to encourage his relatives to come to the United States. He maintained that he had lost all but the ability to "express only the most ordinary things in my native tongue."[99] These statements were absurd. His nephew Tine Kurent, Tonchka's son, later wrote that his uncle and mother wrote each other each week. World War I had halted their exchanges, but when Louis settled in San Pedro, he and Tonchka resumed their correspondence.[100] Also, he had translated a number of Cankar's works, and in numerous articles and in *Laughing* he had declared that he would never feel American. In fact, while in Yugoslavia, he started writing *Grandsons*, in which he equated being American with becoming a shadow. The consumerist values that defined modern society had the result that native and foreign-born alike lost their humanity and thus became "shadow people." He proudly declared that he avoided this fate because his Slovenian "peasant egoism . . . stood in the way of" his thorough Americanization. Something about American culture "went against my grain."[101]

Why would Adamic claim an Americanness he had not subscribed to in 1934 only to disavow that claim one year later? If we view him as writing from a position of in-betweenness, his acknowledgment of assimilation can be viewed as framing device to get more non–South Slavic Americans to care about the repression Slovenes and other Yugoslavs experienced under King Alexander's regime. Alexander's rule started in 1921 and over the next decade he grew more autocratic. In 1929, he changed the country's name from the Kingdom of Serbs, Croats, and Slovenes to Yugoslavia, abolished the constitution, and established a monarchical dictatorship.[102] Adamic likely did not want his audience to consider him a Slovenian asking Americans for help for his native land, but rather he probably surmised that he could convince them to support Slovenians by appealing to their general antipathy to dictatorship. According to his correspondence with McCann, he had employed a similar strategy in *Dynamite* to convince the middle class to support the working class.

Adamic may not have embodied *slovenstvo* as Župančič contended, but it motivated him to identify as a Slovenian exile responsible for perpetuating Slovenian identity at a moment when Alexander threatened the very existence of his homeland's culture. The advocates of a secular democratic Yugoslavia were dealt a significant blow at the end of 1918 when South Slav political elites hastily created the Kingdom of Serbs, Croats, and Slovenes. Slovenes quickly discovered that the Serbian officials wielded the most power in this constitutional monarchy and did not view them as equals. For instance, in July 1922, the editor of the popular Zagreb magazine *Nova Evropa*, Milan Ćurčin, dedicated the entire issue to negating the existence of a Slovenian identity. Ćurčin asserted that no biological differences existed between Slovenes, Serbs, and Croatians. Therefore, since Slovenes comprised only 8.5 percent of the Yugoslav population, they should integrate.[103] By the time Adamic arrived in Ljubljana, Alexander demonstrated his affinity for Ćurčin's idea by announcing a Yugoslav unification policy. It included the elimination of Slovene culture, starting with a ban on the teaching of Slovenian in schools.[104] Furthermore, one-third of Slovenians lived outside the kingdom's boundaries in minority communities in Italy, Austria, and Hungary, and those governments actively attempted to assimilate them. Slovenes' sense of exile grew as a result.[105]

Once Alexander eliminated parliament in 1929, he started imprisoning his political opponents, especially communists. Witnessing this repression convinced Adamic, while in Ljubljana in the fall of 1932, to hold a secret meeting with Edvard Kardelj. Kardelj would later become the leading theorist of Yugoslav communism under Josip Broz Tito. Adamic agreed to translate *Struggle*, Kardelj's story of imprisonment and torture under Alexander's "elaborate terror system." Now the English-speaking world would know how the Serbian king treated "political criminals."[106] Then Adamic offered his own account of what he saw in Yugoslavia, *The Native's Return*. He published both books in 1934.

In his introduction to *Struggle* and throughout *The Native's Return*, Adamic emphasized the similarities between Alexander's regime and fascist movements in Italy and Germany. Adamic began with some recent history by noting that after ruling for eight years, Alexander revoked Yugoslavia's constitution and employed a special force of 15,000 secret agents to look and listen for any hint of opposition. In restaurants, one had to suspect that the waiters, the people in the booth next to you, and the men and women "who came to cafes selling flowers, cigarettes, chocolates, or postcards" were spies. Alexander's army of eavesdroppers, like Mussolini's secret police, identified dissidents to the police, who then arrested and tortured them.[107] One day after turning thirty-six, March 24, 1933, Adamic started his journey back to the United States. Safely aboard a ship in the Atlantic, Adamic wrote Molek of what he had witnessed and added that the king's agents were now following him. Molek replied, "They were after me, too, when I visited Jugoslavia in 1930." The "regime over there is practically of the same caliber as Mussolini's barbaric horde" or "Hitler's mad dogs."[108]

The Native's Return became a book-of-the-month-club selection and sold more than seventy thousand copies during its first two weeks in print. Adamic became the loudest voice for Slovenian liberation on both continents. He made Yugoslavia's political dynamics accessible to an American audience through the metaphors he employed. For example, he compared Alexander's secret police force to the Ku Klux Klan by declaring that the groups practiced similar intimidation tactics and shared a fascist attitude.[109] By convincing Americans to care about the authoritarian politics of Yugoslavia and the assault on Slovenian culture, in addition to challenging the dominant white ethnocentric consumerist American culture, Adamic helped keep a version of *slovenstvo* alive.

Conclusion

Adamic saw himself as an exile as a result of his experiences of colonialism in Slovenia and nativism in the United States. Reading Upton Sinclair's critiques of capitalism, American modernists' questioning of progress, and Nietzsche's arguments about slave morality, combined with his abiding devotion to Cankar's peasant existentialism, led Adamic to capture feelings of liminality that pervaded the United States. Leftist Slovenians shared this sense of exile, but unlike Adamic, they saw themselves as part of a diaspora that would eventually help build a new Yugoslavia and with it establish a place for themselves in the world. For Adamic, being trapped between cultures and feeling alienated as a worker led him to become a cultural critic. He attacked the melting pot trope and rejected the vision of a South Slavic federation advanced by leftist Slovenes. As he criticized capitalism, nativism, and the idealism of those who opposed those exploitative ideologies, he gained a public following and laid the foundations of an independent leftist politics in the United States. It turned out that native-born Americans, especially those in the working class, related to his stories because they too felt displaced.

When Adamic witnessed fascism firsthand in Italy and then saw Alexander's terror network, he began to rethink the value of political activism. He may have continued to consider fighting against corrupt politicians, corporate hegemony, and racial nationalism a losing battle, but the consequences of authoritarianism convinced him that the battle had to be fought. The fear of fascism politicized Adamic and led him to stop thinking of exile as permanent state of being. Instead, exile became the starting point for creating a new humanity.

2

Liberating "Shadow" America

Antifascism, Pluralism, and Democracy, 1932–39

By the mid-1930s, Louis Adamic contended that Americans suffered from a collective psychological condition that turned them into "shadows," which made them ripe for fascist exploitation. Jim Crow measures and culture along with immigrant exclusion laws and frequent expressions of nativism purposefully sought to discourage ethnics and African Americans from feeling American. The Anglo majority exhibited their own sense of inferiority, Adamic added, because they constantly questioned whether they were living up to the American dream. Believing that material gain determined one's success led everyone to sacrifice meaningful relationships. Americans, Adamic explained, experienced moments of feeling human by having sex, driving fast, and engaging in illicit activities such as drinking bootleg alcohol and gambling. Yet they remained "hardly alive," for these fleeting instances of humanness provided only momentary releases from the loneliness created by the shared crisis of meaning.[1] Adamic promoted cultural pluralism as a countermeasure to foster the introduction of authenticity into a deracinated American life, as a balm for the existential crisis that bred authoritarian politics.

Adamic's contemporaries recognized him as a popularizer of cultural pluralism, but he did much more than revive the arguments of the losing side in the culture wars of the 1920s. Through his dramatic, often apocryphal, narratives, Adamic played a pivotal role in forging the "antifascist common sense" that characterized the mood of the Depression era.[2]

During the Progressive Era, advocates of cultural pluralism rejected the idea that an "American race," largely defined by its Anglo-Saxon blood and culture, existed. Instead, they claimed that a nation composed of various ethnic and racial groups speaking a multitude of languages and keeping old-world traditions alive made the country stronger. To them, a commitment to the nation's founding principles—a civic nationalism—best defined the US identity. Nativists succeeded in muting the pluralist arguments in 1919 by capitalizing on the fears of "alien" radicalism caused by the Russian Revolution and gained widespread support for the quota laws of 1921 and 1924. Asian exclusion statutes and Jim Crow policies allowed the racial nationalists who equated Anglo to white and white to American to officially define the nation's identity.[3]

Of the leading pluralist thinkers, Adamic had a particular affinity for the Progressive Era philosopher and public intellectual Randolph Bourne (1886–1918). Advocates of pluralism sought to discover how selfhood emerged, especially in the early 1900s, when the ideal for Americans changed from independent farmers and small proprietors to captains of industry. In this new world, the self was subjective and created through social interactions. Bourne contended that the dialectic between the self and the community contained the possibility for developing a new democratic culture if people could emancipate themselves from the urge to try to alleviate anxiety through consumption. Bourne pointed to immigrants and ethnics as the most likely social groups to establish this democratic culture, or what he called a beloved community. Alternatively, corporate leaders and other proponents of the emergent mass culture hoped that most people would embrace their consumer selves.[4]

Adamic contended that by 1934 the mindless consumerism Bourne and other feared had combined with the dominance that nativism and white supremacy asserted over laws and cultural practices. A society where most of the population felt neurotic and empty resulted. Adamic presented "Americanization," the process racial nationalists favored to assimilate immigrants, as deeply flawed and overlapping with fascism by opposing radicalism and promoting white supremacy. A democratic US identity, he asserted, required that the larger public embrace a more accurate version of US history that recognized immigrants, ethnics, and African Americans for making modern urban America through their labor and their cultural practices.[5] Adamic contended that thinking of "American" as a fixed identity subverted the democratic spirit that animated the country.[6] He identified pluralism as the underpinning of democracy and simultaneously linked racial nationalists to the fascist spirt pervading Europe.

In addition to promoting pluralism, Adamic determined that fighting the inchoate fascism he saw emerging in the United States during the 1930s included championing industrial democracy. He covered the rise of the Congress of Industrial Organizations (CIO) for *The Nation* and other left magazines and published his proworker novel *Grandsons* that offered his clearest discussion of the "shadow" condition. Proponents of industrial democracy joined pluralists in the antifascist coalition as they argued that in addition to greater ethnic and racial equality, defeating fascism required the expansion of worker rights. Industrial democracy included laborers possessing some say in determining wages, hours, and workplace relations. The CIO's strength and successes in unionizing the largest manufacturing industries in the 1930s and 1940s stemmed from the fact that many of its union organizers embraced pluralism in order to foster cross-ethnic and cross-racial solidarities.[7]

Although recognized as one of the nation's leading authorities on ethnic issues by 1939, Adamic had grown increasingly frustrated because a number of journalists, politicians, and public intellectuals presented his work as a celebration of America's ethnic character. Adamic feared that if this simplistic understanding of cultural pluralism persisted, antifascism would become an anodyne campaign against bigotry instead of a democratic revolution for a new humanity. Such an attenuated approach to pluralism pushed Adamic to become more vocal about confronting racism. His initial attacks proved tame at best, as they revealed his developing understanding of how pluralism should function. Ultimately he adopted a militant anticolonialist position after World War II.

In addition to criticizing those who tied their identities to the new mass culture, Adamic also attacked the procommunist left in the United States for its blind loyalty to Moscow. Throughout the 1930s, Adamic limited his associations with activists in the Communist Party of the United States of America (CPUSA), as he agreed with Sinclair Lewis's assertion that there "is no excuse for anyone to swallow the Bolshevik claim" that only communists offer a "defense against Fascism."[8] In 1935, Adolf Hitler and the Nazis had frightened the Comintern—the assembly of all communist parties throughout the world charged with promoting global revolution—to the point that Soviet premier Joseph Stalin and party leaders instructed communists to enter into the Popular Front with leftists of all stripes to defeat fascism. The Comintern's policy change established the notion among many historians that communists drove antifascist politics.[9] Adamic and other independent leftists expressed their appreciation of the communists' courage to challenge nativism, racism, imperialism, and unregulated capitalism, but they repeatedly warned their supporters not to ally too closely with party-led efforts because CPUSA members would change direction whenever Moscow instructed them to do so.[10] In August 1939, Stalin agreed to a nonaggression treaty with Hitler and validated Adamic's skepticism of the communists' commitment to antifascism. The Popular Front crumbled.

Adamic's most articulate and strident advocacy for pluralism began a month before the Popular Front collapsed. Since Adamic's contemporaries and some current scholars misidentified him as a communist or a fellow traveler, often on purpose, we must understand his antifascism to grasp his legacy. Adamic recognized that he and his fellow independent leftists shared criticisms of capitalism, white supremacy, and fascism as they jointly shaped 1930s culture and the political mood of the period. But objectives mattered. Communists prioritized serving the party above fighting fascism. Adamic dedicated himself to advancing democracy because, he believed, humanity depended on it. By the end of the 1930s, Adamic battled both communists and racial nationalists. Racial nationalists retaliated against cultural pluralism's advance by uniting under the banner of anticommunism to make their advocacy of white supremacy, nativism, and corporate hegemony palatable to the larger public. Tracing Adamic's journey from a culture critic in exile to a leader in the antifascist vanguard begins with probing his decision to popularize cultural pluralism.

"Thirty Million New Americans"

Adamic's battles with both communists and nativists as well as his alliance with the leading pluralist organization of the 1930s, the Foreign Language Information Service (FLIS), highlighted the contours of the antifascist spectrum that enlivened Depression Era politics. His antifascism at times confused his contemporaries and some subsequent scholars, as he appeared to vacillate between affiliating with organizations led by the Communist Party and denouncing CPUSA members as "hysterical" propagandists beholden to dictates from Moscow and lacking any real understanding of the US working class. In actuality, Adamic distinguished between "Communists," those he considered zealots, and communists, whom he identified as idealists searching for ways to fight against "injustice, want, [and] frustration." Small-c communists kept "the unemployment problem on the front page" and forced Americans to confront racism in relation to cases such as the "Scottsboro Boys" (the nine black teenagers falsely accused of raping two white women on a train traveling through Tennessee). Adamic happily collaborated with idealists who advanced social equality and industrial democracy. Conversely, he had little time for the CPUSA's "largely mediocre, crackpot, [and] exhibitionistic" national leadership that eschewed democracy as demonstrated by its "small inner group" that acted "in compliance with orders from the Comintern" and expected party members to follow unquestioningly.[11] Adamic viewed most US Communist Party members as similar to individuals who "converted to religion" and allowed their fanaticism to guide their thoughts and behavior.[12]

Part of the confusion over Adamic's politics stems from the fact that he helped shape the proletarian aesthetic that characterized the cultural works of Depression Era America. Some of his contemporaries associated his embrace of the proletarian aesthetic with an adherence to the subgenera of proletarian literature that attempted to foment working-class consciousness and revolution. To Communist Party officials in Moscow, proletarian literature meant works produced to advance Communist Party perspectives. In the United States, proletarian literature took on three meanings: works by proletarians, works for proletarians, and works about proletarians. Communist Mike Gold's desire to advance "human brotherhood" through his radical literary magazine *The New Masses*, which he launched in 1926, did the most to propel proletarian literature forward in the United States. Quickly discovering that workers needed help transitioning from mills, mines, and factory floors to typewriters, Gold and others established John Reed Clubs to assist aspiring working-class writers in honing their literary skills. Reed had been a socialist journalist who covered many of the most violent strikes in the United States during the Progressive Era as well as the Mexican and Russian Revolutions. By 1934, more than thirty Reed Clubs had formed with more than 1,200 members. In order to remain solvent while laborers learned the craft of writing, the editors of *The New Masses* published pieces written by middle-class radicals.[13]

When proletarian literature came into vogue in the 1930s, communists such as literary critic Granville Hicks expected Adamic to emerge as the quintessential proletarian writer. Hicks regularly wrote for *The New Masses* and then took over editorship for Gold in 1934. He knew that Adamic had arrived in the United States as a teenager and worked a series of unskilled jobs while learning English. Adamic began his career publishing translations and then succeeded in getting his stories accepted in popular periodicals. During the late 1920s, Adamic's work justified laborers' use of sabotage, supported working-class political prisoners, criticized industrialists, and defended immigrants against the various assertions levied by champions of racial nationalism. Adamic's semifictional 1932 autobiography *Laughing in the Jungle*, however, dismissed US radicals as largely comical figures whose ideological commitments limited their understanding of the realities workers faced.

In a letter to Adamic, Hicks sarcastically apologized for "doing" Adamic "an injustice" by assuming that he was "a revolutionary." Hicks realized that Adamic placed himself "with [H. L.] Mencken, finding no ground for hope in the present situation, believing the workers mere boobs, and taking what pleasure you can in looking on the spectacle."[14] Adamic responded to Hicks's condescension in kind. He expressed his envy of Hicks's "blissful ignorance of the American proletariat and the American labor movement, and your neat faith in the imminent coming of the Revolution and the dictatorship of the proletariat."[15] Hicks now saw Adamic as an unskilled immigrant worker who had assimilated by aping the libertarian modernism of Mencken. In reality, Adamic had never forsaken his peasant roots and therefore he located the source of alienation for the vast majority of Americans in the psychic realm. People, especially dispersed immigrant workers, had to recognize themselves as something other than the "dung" enriching the growth of industrial America.[16] Laborers who refused to relinquish their idealism, whether that meant embracing the American Dream or socialism, would never overcome the absurdities that defined their existence. Becoming something new meant synthesizing the various parts of themselves as well as imagining a different America where they and native workers collectively (re)narrated the nation's identity. Adamic directed most of his cynicism toward elites and had great sympathy for the working class. Mencken considered laborers enablers of Babbittry because of their own stupidity. Hicks and other radicals saw Adamic's work as only half good. It criticized capitalism and induced readers to empathize with proletarian suffering, but it did not direct audiences to see working-class revolution as the future.

Adamic's distinctions between communists and "Communists" also included his favorable view of European underground radicals working to overthrow fascists and other authoritarian regimes. With regard to Yugoslav party activists, he explained in 1934 that he had "no quarrel with the ideal of Communism, which is essentially the ideal of equality."[17] Four years later, he added that he backed revolutions as a "method of progress," but he found the CPUSA's calls to Sovietize the United States absurd.[18]

Adamic's support for the South Slav underground illustrated his position. In the spring of 1932, he boarded a ship to visit his native Slovenia, now

Louis Adamic—a portrait, 1932. Courtesy of National and University Library of Slovenia, Ljubljana, Slovenia.

part of Yugoslavia, for the first time since emigrating nineteen years earlier. There he witnessed the autocratic rule of Serbian irredentist King Alexander, which included spying on subjects as well as jailing and torturing political opponents. Alexander, Adamic proclaimed, belonged "in the same category of strong-arm rulers with Mussolini [and] Hitler" because he "was a cog in the new political system of post-war Europe, helping to hold together a crumbling civilization with gangster methods."[19]

On his voyage back to the United States in 1933, Adamic informed Ivan Molek, his fellow immigrant and editor of Chicago's Slovenian language socialist newspaper *Prosveta* (*Enlightenment*), that he had "hot stuff." Upon receiving Adamic's draft article lauding the communist underground's challenges to Alexander's terror network, Molek proclaimed Adamic's "hot stuff" as nothing new. Molek cantankerously explained that this piece resembled the atrocity stories regularly printed in Pittsburgh's Croatian communist newspaper. Although Molek referred to himself as an "enemy of the Jugoslav dictatorship," he cautioned Adamic that authoring pro-underground articles would allow communists to "exploit your literary name." Molek added that he detested "Communist zealotry."[20] Surprised that Molek did not care about Alexander's secret police torturing communists "in the service of reactionary fascism," Adamic declared that he and Molek must "have somewhat dissimilar views on the subject of terror."[21] When Adamic returned to the United States, he sent a bit of his translation of *Struggle*—Yugoslav communist

Edvard Kardelj's memoir of life as a political prisoner under the Yugoslav monarchy—to *The New Masses*, and Gold published it.

Adamic had a hand in confusing people about his politics. In an April 1934 lecture he referred to communists as "not really radical, merely hysterical."[22] Such statements remained consistent with what he had written and said from the late 1920s to that point. Then in July he wrote on a survey conducted by the Russian-based International Union of Revolutionary Writers "that now I consider myself a Communist." He made it clear in his answers to other questions that he meant communist, small c and without quotation marks. What he had seen in Yugoslavia shaped his current position, as did the stories he heard of militants mobilizing in Cuba and the "Far East" in their struggles for self-determination against imperialism. He acknowledged the "growing radicalization of serious writers and artists everywhere" as the Popular Front spread throughout the world, and he counted himself among them. He also stated that Soviet literature was "technically inferior" to works by noncommunist writers in the United States and other capitalist countries.[23] Adamic immediately backed away from his statement of being a communist and emphasized more clearly that antifascism guided him.

Before filling out the survey, Adamic argued that diversity distinguished the democratic US identity—not claims of Anglo-Saxon superiority. During a March lecture in Pittsburgh, he used his own ethnicity as an example and declared that "Slavs have contributed in every way to the greatness of America" by literally doing the work that constructed modern America. Then he quipped that about "the only thing they did not contribute to was the crash of 1929."[24]

A *Saturday Evening Post* editorial convinced Adamic to elaborate on this point. The piece bemoaned the higher taxes that "100 percent American" citizens had to pay for schools and more police protection. Immigrants, the author argued, procreated at a "terrific rate," which created a greater demand for schools, and their "unassimilable blood strains" fed a growing criminal class. Adamic, in his April 1934 *Common Sense* article "Who Built America?," declared that he originally dismissed the editorial as "un-American" nonsense. After reading it, however, he continually encountered similar expressions of anti-immigrant propaganda. He felt compelled to challenge the "small fascist organizations" producing the flyers, pamphlets, and chain letters emboldening xenophobes and shaping public discourse. Repeatedly these media issued the plea to "save America for real Americans." Adamic opposed the notion that Anglo-Saxons were the "real Americans" by noting that South Slavs sailed with Christopher Columbus and ran some of California's best orchards. Then he pointed out that Serbian immigrant Nikola Tesla made modern electrification and wireless communication possible through his inventions. Adamic's fellow Slavs, along with his all other recent immigrants, mined much of the coal, felled most of the trees, and milled most of the steel that created most of America's cities. Adamic concluded by calling anti-immigrant attacks "Hitlerism" and insisted that by disregarding the Constitution and exploiting immigrants, old-stock Americans undermined democracy and caused the current economic crisis.[25]

In asserting that cultural pluralism underpinned democracy and that a fascist ethic guided 100 percent Americanism, Adamic captured the attention of Read Lewis, who directed the FLIS. The FLIS grew out of the Committee on Public Information, which coordinated propaganda efforts for the Woodrow Wilson Administration during World War I. In the 1920s, it became a private organization promoting the coercive form of Americanization that Adamic opposed. Lewis wanted to take the FLIS in a different direction, to make it a voice for pluralism. He considered Adamic the perfect messenger to promote greater understanding between old-stock and ethnic Americans. Adamic agreed to join the FLIS board and Lewis organized a series of lectures for Adamic.[26]

In November, Adamic published his widely circulated "Thirty Million New Americans" in *Harper's Weekly*. He argued that the version of Americanization dominant during the 1920s sought to force southern and eastern European immigrants to adopt Anglo-Saxon culture and levied a psychic toll on those it targeted for assimilation. Instead of examining how this marginalization fostered an existential crisis in newcomers as he had done in his earlier works, he focused on their children, whom he referred to as "New Americans." Adamic contended that while immigrants negotiated between their own values and those of the mainstream white middle class, their children had a different experience. They saw their parents as "pathetic creature[s] constantly at somebody's mercy and repeatedly stepped upon," therefore "not much according to American standards."[27] He feared that these new Americans would become "perennially oppressed by the feeling that they are outsiders and thus inferior."[28] New Americans already behaved "politically neutral, economically unaggressive," and "culturally nowhere."[29] To reverse this trend, the second generation had to take pride in being "a Finn, a Slovenian, a Serbian, a Croatian, a Slovak, a Czech, a Pole, or a Lithuanian" so that they would have a "some feeling of their being part of America, in which immigrants like themselves played an important role."[30] Adamic no longer instructed immigrants to recognize their nothingness and accept the reality that they would never become Americans. He told their children to reject the definition of American as Anglo-Saxon—thus challenging the notion of the melting pot—and instead refer to themselves as Americans who could detail their ethnic group's contributions to modern America.

This article reignited another round of debate to define American identity that periodically erupted from at least 1782. Adamic's argument that all Americans, as opposed to white Anglo-Saxon Protestants, could and should claim their Americanness held sway with the general public because he couched it in an antifascist vernacular. He proclaimed that the combination of patriotic chauvinism—the idea that the only way to become an American was by adopting Anglo-Saxon traditions—and rampant consumerism moved the United States toward fascism. Teachers, he explained, equated white Protestant culture with Americanism, advocated that ethnic children ignore their heritage, and fostered the idea that first- and second-generation Americans were "outsiders who are more or less tolerated." He noted that educators allowed Anglo students to use slurs such as "dago" and "hunky" and even employed such appellations themselves. Being "chauvinistically patriotic," he argued, encouraged young people to accept the virulent forms of nationalism pervading Europe. This "sort of 'patriotism'" rested upon "shallow materialistic concepts." Children learned to mark their country's greatness by being able to claim that "we have the biggest buildings" or "the best ice cream." Without realizing it, these "New Americans are ready for almost any sort of shallow, ignorant nationalist or fascist movement."[31] A truly democratic society depended on the citizenry rooting national pride in the promises of opportunity and cultural heterogeneity, not consumerism and Anglo-Saxonism.

Living up to the nation's democratic promise meant becoming "real men and women on the pattern of their own natural cultures." Adamic provided examples of this happening. In Cleveland, for instance, the city's three largest newspapers had reporters covering the various immigrant neighborhoods and writing "feature articles about the various foreign groups' contribution to the growth and development of" the city. Also, these papers for three years had run stories about events in Poland, Lithuania, Czechoslovakia, Hungary, Rumania, and Yugoslavia. He noted that public school classes in Cleveland are between 40 and 80 percent foreign-born. School administrators, teachers, and parents viewed the second-generation problem as the central issues they had to address.[32] Groups in Pittsburgh, Detroit, Chicago, and Milwaukee created similar programs, but "no central or national organization interested in" challenging patriotic chauvinism existed. Adamic called for an agency, with the FLIS in mind, focused on giving "these millions of New Americans a knowledge of, and pride in, their own heritage, which to some extent, would operate to counteract their feelings of inferiority" and "create a sympathetic understanding toward them on the part of older Americans."[33] Advocates of civic nationalism reprinted this article as a pamphlet and distributed it to fraternal organizations, high schools, and colleges. Adamic's work inspired educational reformers such as Rachel Davis DuBois. DuBois and Adamic met on a number of occasions and she especially identified with his concerns over the sense of inferiority new Americans felt. She pioneered new pedagogies to build students' self-esteem and became part of the larger FLIS network.[34]

Labor Reporter and Novelist

In addition to his commitments to the FLIS and growing reputation as pluralism's chief advocate, Adamic decided to split his time from the end of 1934 through 1937 between advancing pluralism and reporting on working-class activism. The rise of the CIO enthralled him and *The Nation* hired him to write a series of articles explaining the new labor militancy. Adamic had covered class conflict for magazines and newspapers at the end of the 1920s, and he had written *Dynamite*, the first popular history of American working-class violence. Now he circled back to labor journalism but with a different attitude toward unions than he had previously held. Earlier, he had considered worker resistance as retaliatory to abuses by employers and insisted that like businessmen and political bosses, union leaders were racketeers exploiting laborers' hopes for a better future. He saw CIO unions differently, considering them crucibles of democracy that simultaneously advanced worker rights and fostered a sense of equality among unionists of various ethnic and racial backgrounds. Adamic's reporting also exemplified the proletarian aesthetic and simultaneously disavowed proletarian literature.

In December 1934, he reiterated his opposition to proletarian literature, calling it useless propaganda, and insisted that most workers read westerns and the "funny papers." The few laborers who would read serious books and magazines could not afford novels or subscriptions to radical periodicals. In the few cases when workers did read something from this genre, they reacted "unfavorably to exaggerated descriptions of social evils" and became "unfriendly not only to such writing but to radicalism and revolution." Adamic then asserted that stories with multidimensional characters such as those found in the works of Theodore Dreiser, Sinclair Lewis, and Upton Sinclair did more to advance leftist objectives than tales of revolutionary heroes. The working class, he stated, "has no monopoly in charm, graciousness, generosity, and other virtues in personal life, just as the capitalist and the middle class have no monopoly in meanness, greed and other personal faults and vices." All classes in America have members who subscribe to "spiritual vacuity and corruption or general human sordidness." Adamic suggested that radical writers stop creating individual villains and instead make "the capitalist-democratic system" that "causes endless spiritual and physical waste and ruin" among workers and "the middle and upper class" as their antagonist. Champions of the proletariat should leave readers "filled with shame and indignation" that Americans "have made such a mess of ourselves spiritually and culturally." These emotions, he predicted, will "inevitably find eventual expression in political action."[35] Adamic suggested that immigrants and ethnics could appropriate the notion of "American," redefine democracy, and impede the spread of fascism before it moved beyond its embryonic phase in the United States. Unlike his communist counterparts who called for revolution, Adamic proposed that Americans liberate themselves from mass culture through shared interactions and become more human.

The next year he published *Grandsons*, his example of what a proworker novel should look like. According to Adamic, elites, in portraying wealth accumulation and Anglo-Saxon Protestant heritage as the defining characteristics of American identity, created a culture that turned everyone into shadows. He had borrowed this theme from Slovenian modernist writer Ivan Cankar, and it underpinned his work throughout the 1920s and early 1930s. He wrote much of *Grandsons* while in Slovenia in 1932 and 1933 as he took another step toward a fully articulated antifascist outlook. As the novel's unidentified narrator, Adamic declared that "most people in America were shadow-persons, with nothing substantial and permanent in their lives, nothing to hold on to—that they were hollowed out, partly in consequence of their forebears' . . . often pointless experiences during the recent pioneer era, and partly because of the too great and too long an emphasis on the purely material side in American life." The Anglo-American majority promoted ideals that if achieved advanced alienation. Americans "lived in a spiritually and culturally coreless hollow world, and had no dynamic contact with any permanent or continuous reality."[36]

Adamic articulated multiple forms of this shadowiness by telling the stories of the fictional Gale family. Three grandsons—brothers Peter and Andy and their cousin Jack—had their lives shaped by their Slovenian immigrant grandfather who died in the 1886 Haymarket riot. The novel revealed Adamic's independent leftist politics as Jack, the revolutionary union organizer, was the character closest to escaping from the shadows and becoming real. His wife, Mildred Adams, a New Englander and descendent of early Anglo settlers, had embraced communism. Mildred married Jack because he was a worker and his grandfather died at Haymarket. Being with Jack gave her cultural capital among her fellow radicals. Ultimately, antiunion vigilantes murdered Jack. Adamic explained that real revolutionaries, such as Jack, "were helpless against the hysterical but articulate 'infantile leftists,' bohemians and psychopaths, the self-styled intellectuals," such as Mildred, "who, desperately struggling against being shadows in a coreless, baseless chaos, used them in their reaching for a sense of reality."[37] Adamic charged most radicals with being unaware "of their personal neuroticism" and with being unwilling to offer a vision of "a better civilization organically developed." To Adamic, radicals were no different from preachers, politicians, gangsters, and other "spouters of phrases, screamers and screechers, citizens of the headline world."[38] He suggested that workers could transform cultural, social, and economic relations by struggling through their own alienation, but they had to tell their stories apart from the framings offered by communists.

Through *Grandsons* Adamic demonstrated his desire to develop a leftist but non-Marxist vision for a new America. In depicting Mildred Adams as neurotic, he equated communists with the Babbittlike majority, as people who sacrificed their own authenticity in service to their ideological commitments. Although provocative, this formulation betrayed his own embrace of a masculine ideal by presenting Adams as a caricature of an irrational Anglo-Saxon Protestant woman.

After reading *Grandsons*, Norman Mini, a Trotskyite and activist on behalf of California agricultural workers, wrote Adamic from San Quentin Penitentiary. One of twelve defendants charged with conspiracy to commit criminal syndicalism, Mini received a sentence of three and a half years. An appeals court reversed the lower courts' decision in September 1937.[39] Mini exclaimed it is "funny business" that a "political prisoner" wrote in hopes of "cheering up a novelist." While awaiting sentencing, two of the men convicted with Mini disparaged *Grandsons*. Mini wanted Adamic to know that he "sympathize[d] with" him. Although now "cut off from that smug little world that gives out official evaluations of everything 'proletarian,'" he realized that his fellow prisoners likely captured the "dirty digs" and other forms of criticisms Adamic "must be getting." Mini thought that although "hazily and abstractly," Adamic expressed "the chief problem facing our movement." That "the majority of America, workers and all, were on edge and worried and half psychopathic, and wavering and groping for a solution of their big problem." All the while radicals, who only understood actual laborers through "fifth-rate rehashes of Lenin," seek "to go on undisturbed . . . issuing manifestos." Mini hoped Adamic would keep thinking about how people can find their authentic selves.[40]

Grandsons showed Adamic's embrace of a version of the proletarian aesthetic, but his journalism did far more than his fiction to help advance worker rights and spread his pluralist view of democracy. His pieces covering the emergence of the CIO collectively suggested that workers were finding their shared identities through collective action. In a January 1935 article about Shamokin, Pennsylvania, coal miners, he argued that workers' desire to survive served as the foundation of their militancy. Seeking to feed their families, pay their bills, and heat their homes, these unemployed miners started sneaking onto company land, drilling or dynamiting holes, and bootlegging coal. Local police and politicians understood the necessity of such appropriations. They informally sanctioned the miners' disregard for coal operator's property rights by refusing to arrest perpetrators. Communist Party organizers claimed that these miners organically embraced communism and convinced city officials of the virtue of their struggle. After interviewing miners and local leaders in Shamokin, Adamic derided communists as naive idealists who followed the party line set in Moscow.[41] As he reported on working-class actions over the next three years, Adamic insisted that workers found their humanity through collective action and advanced democracy as a result.

Adamic presented the CIO as the counterexample to both the American Federation of Labor (AFL) and the Communist Party (CPUSA). Although many viewed the AFL and CPUSA as political opposites, Adamic referred to them both as top-down organizations that imposed dictates from leaders onto workers. The CIO, alternatively, grew organically out of workers' collective desires for greater democracy in their workplace and in the nation as a whole. He used rubber workers in Akron, Ohio, who engaged in a 1936 sit-down strike, to illustrate his point. Most "workers distrust—if not consciously, then unconsciously—union officials." With this action there are "no leaders or officials to distrust" because the "initiative, conduct, and control of the sitdown come directly from the men involved." The sit-down strike was "a purely democratic action" as well as "a social affair." By sitting down, workers had time to talk, and these conversations furthered pluralism and strengthened class consciousness. Those coming from West Virginia and the South and Polish immigrants, for instance, recognized their shared grievances and became better connected with each other.[42] He saw workers struggling through their angst, seeing themselves as deserving a greater voice, finding American forms of militancy, and overcoming cultural differences. Interactions such as these, Adamic insisted, resulted in workers forging new democratic identities.

Also, Adamic praised CIO head John L. Lewis for expressing the federation's objectives in the populist language of the haves versus the have-nots instead of speaking in the Marxist vernacular of class struggle. Populist idioms allowed Lewis to dissociate himself from the "infantile leftists" and differentiate his vision of industrial democracy from their proposed workers' state. He believed that Lewis and other CIO leaders had convinced the public that capital "is wild, irresponsible, [and] unsocial."[43] In his conclusion, Adamic did warn readers that Lewis was "a dangerous man" who, if unchecked by the rank-and-file, could "become the leader of a kind of labor fascism."[44]

In a follow-up piece, Adamic credited the CIO with leading the vanguard of a new wave of change. American progress had ebbs and flows. The Revolutionary War signified the first climax in producing the Declaration of Independence and the Constitution. The Civil War represented the second climax in establishing "theoretical equality." Now the "instinctive struggle of labor for democracy in the shop and factory" against "undemocratic, absolutist, or (to use a popular word) fascist institutions, with the employer the sole authority" signified the most recent climax.[45] Adamic noted that working class's advancement "was won not by labor alone" but by "small, aggressive labor movements" working with "a majority of the politically active American people who, consciously or otherwise, were addicted to democracy as a principle and a way of life."[46]

Adamic was building on the words of Lewis's adviser W. Jett Lauck. Lauck, an economist, argued that political democracy emerged in 1776. The lack of regulation during the Industrial Revolution, however, allowed corporate leaders to concentrate their wealth and use their financial power to undermine political democracy. CIO officials insisted that economic democracy had to accompany political democracy to save the republic. Lauck made this argument as early as 1926. CIO members presented their militancy as distinctively American. When they struck, they held American flags to emphasize the point and union officers often mentioned how their actions enlivened the bill of rights, especially the First Amendment. Union activists after the 1936 hearings spearheaded by Senator Robert M. La Follette Jr. proclaimed that the fascist ethic motived their employers. La Follette's investigation revealed that corporations spied on workers, threatened employees who demanded rights, and amassed arsenals in preparation to arm the mercenaries they would hire to put down strikes. By 1938, CIO media linked corporate abuses of workers' rights to Germany's treatment of unions and Jews.[47]

Adamic framed the CIO as an agent of antifascism and pluralism when he proclaimed that it embodied "the laboring masses' urge" for "democracy and equality" against "absolutism or fascism, in the shop and factory and for more democracy, more liberty, less absolutism generally in the life of the American people." He then argued that the public has "only theoretically accepted [the] idea that labor is a human element in the establishment of actual democracy or equality in industry."[48] By achieving industrial democracy, laborers would acquire their humanity. He also celebrated the CIO for having "no Jim Crowism or alien baiting" and proclaimed that "this is a victory for equality that is of paramount importance to all America."[49] Adamic's comments reflected his optimism that the CIO was going to play an essential role in liberating Americans from their shadow condition by fostering a new, collectively constructed, democratic identity. Historians have recognized that CIO leaders, with the support of most white union members, limited their organization's commitment to equality. While African Americans were welcome in local unions and on picket lines, the CIO did not seek to challenge discrimination in the labor market that prevented people of color from obtaining the highest-paying jobs.[50] Adamic believed the CIO would progress toward a broader culture of equality that in turn fomented larger structural changes to the economy.

Adamic's labor journalism helped amplify the proworker mood being broadcast throughout the larger culture. He highlighted how CIO unions could function as incubators for pluralism. But as Nazi aggressions increased and another world war appeared likely, Adamic returned to focusing solely on immigrants, new Americans, and refugees.

Redefining Democracy

At the apex of his work on the labor movement, Adamic also attacked isolationist and xenophobic policies preventing refugees from entering the United States. He urged the Roosevelt administration to provide asylum to refugees and illegal aliens fleeing Hitler's rule. Employing the documentary style so powerful in this period, he presented the stories of Walter Saupe and Joseph Ganghofer. These two German illegal aliens rejected Nazism and sneaked into the United States to evade Hitler's wrath. After serving thirty-seven weeks in a forced-labor camp in East Prussia, Saupe got a job on a German liner that carried passengers between Hamburg and New York. Once in port, he jumped ship, took an alias, and got a job as a busboy in Manhattan. A Nazi sympathizer reported him to immigration agents, who then arrested him and marked him for deportation.[51] The middle-aged one-time Bavarian hotelkeeper Ganghofer had joined the Nazi Party when Hitler came to power, but by 1935 he despised the Third Reich. Arriving on a vacation visa in the United States, he decided to stay illegally. He took a job as a cook and joined the chef's union. Nazi agents hunted him down and turned him over to US officials for deportation. After recounting these stories, Adamic argued that America either had to be a land of asylum or else collaborate with fascists.[52] He then turned his attention to aiding German Jews.

At that moment, immigration officials counted Jews as German immigrants, and the quota system established by the National Origins Act of 1924 limited the number of people who could immigrate from Germany. Worse, anti-Semitism and fears of adding to the Depression's unemployment rolls led State Department officials to take fewer immigrants than the law allowed.[53] Adamic argued that if politicians and the public continued to turn their backs on the victims of Nazism, the country's "idealism will begin to weaken" and "those mental and spiritual traits" that give life to freedom and equality will melt away.[54] Adamic argued that rejecting the asylum tradition would lead to the deaths of thousands of refugees, serve as a tacit endorsement of Nazi terror, and violate the pluralistic spirit that enlivened democracy.

For Adamic, assisting German refugees, especially Jews, represented just one front upon which to attack the larger nativist outlook that prevented cultural pluralism from becoming the defining characteristic of democracy in the United States. During the 1920s, those who insisted that being Anglo and Protestant defined true American identity used war hysteria and the threat of communism to defeat pluralists and enshrine their views in the 1921 and 1924 National Origins Acts. With the rise of Nazism, Adamic and other antifascists reengaged in this cultural battle by portraying their opponents as fascist sympathizers who opposed democracy and thus betrayed American values. Expanding on "Thirty Million New Americans," he published "Aliens and Alien-Baiters" in 1936 that denounced the "professional patriots" who verged on becoming "fascistic fanatics." Nativists' calls for homogeneity induced public officials "to violate America's traditions of fairness, decency, humanity, and tolerance" in regard to immigrants, thereby threatening to inflict upon the entire citizenry "certain characteristics of European fascist states." Specifically, xenophobes who equated the foreign-born with criminals, claimed that immigrants played a fundamental role in causing the Depression, blocked paths to cultural inclusion for ethnic groups, and demanded an increase in deportations of aliens to improve the economy attempted "to make the alien problem a wedge for the opening of the way to fascism." Adamic pointed out that congressmen and senators introduced bills that would require aliens to carry identification cards, submit to fingerprinting, and periodically report to the local police or postmaster. Once such laws appear, Americans will eventually "be in the general predicament of people now living in fascistic countries."[55] Adamic called on his fellow Americans to reject their fears of foreigners and celebrate the instinct—democracy—that promoted cultural pluralism.[56]

Adamic's antifascism was not just a discursive politics that mirrored the tactics of 1920s anticommunists. Having battled in the culture wars of the 1920s and then seeing fascism in the 1930s, Adamic contended that those committed to creating a militaristic white nationalist authoritarian federal government in the United States shared a worldview with the Nazis. They joined fascists in an effort to eliminate the Enlightenment's promise of progress. A better world to Adamic and other antifascists occurred when interethnic and interracial exchanges led individuals to redefine themselves and then with others collectively revise the nation's identity. Fascists wanted the opposite. They sought to restore a past that had never existed because to them greatness was static and dependent on hypermasculinity. They admired military might, rigid moral codes, authority, and racial purity.

In "Aliens and Alien-Baiters," Adamic identified the person most responsible for promoting the fascist ethic in the United States: John Bond Trevor. During World War I, Trevor, a lawyer, accepted an appointment as an army captain on the general staff of the New York City branch of the Military Intelligence (MI) division. Trevor assumed that "inferior races" subscribed to radical beliefs. Protecting American values, according to Trevor, depended on controlling immigration and maintaining surveillance on ethnic Americans and people of color. He subscribed to the anti-Semitic conspiracy theory that Jewish radicals, funded by German Jewish bankers, had plotted an uprising in New York City. He drew maps of city's "racial colonies," highlighting likely radical meeting places, and recommended that the army send troops to these sites to put down imminent attacks. Trevor's MI colleagues had helped shape his outlook and convinced him that Bolshevik revolutionaries had actually been Jews from New York City who went to Russia and helped Vladimir Lenin establish his communist dictatorship. Although army officials did not follow Trevor's advice, his reports influenced politicians and members of the Justice Department's Bureau of Investigation, which became the Federal Bureau of Investigation in 1935.[57]

From 1919 through the early 1920s, Trevor and other proponents of anticommunism convinced much of the US public, through persuasion and fear, that deporting aliens, reinforcing Jim Crow practices, destroying unions, arresting people for their political beliefs, expanding the reach of intelligence agencies, militarizing police departments, and giving corporate leaders greater control over industrial relations were acts of patriotism that celebrated American identity.[58] Trevor established himself as a leading architect of US anticommunism by aiding the New York Joint Legislative Committee Investigating Seditious Activities, more popularly known as the Lusk Committee, named after its chairman, state senator Clayton Lusk. The committee produced a massive report, over four thousand pages, which became the blueprint for anticommunist tactics and findings after World War II. After his work with Lusk, Trevor played a central role in crafting the Johnson-Reed Immigration Act of 1921, also known as the National Origins Act, and its more restrictive 1924 version. The 1924 measure formally established ethnic and racial hierarchies through the quotas it set. The law also created a federal surveillance system to enforce an Anglo Protestant racial nationalist order. Washington congressman Albert Johnson, one of the act's authors, embraced the eugenics movement and met Trevor in eugenic circles. With its dubious statistics, conspiracy theories, and bad science, Trevor's research on immigrant radicals served as the basis for the national origins law.[59] By the 1930s, Trevor had ties to American fascists and the Nazi movement, and he went on to mentor America's most powerful anticommunists of the next generation: Martin Dies Jr. and Joseph McCarthy.[60]

In "Aliens and Alien-Baiters," Adamic declared that Trevor and his associates "spread alien-hatred" in order to impede "the progress toward a desirable homogeneity of our population," and to undermine democracy by threatening "to inflict . . . characteristics of European fascist states" on the United States. Adamic urged the public to reject their conception of US citizenship and realize that American identity was in a constant state of change because the United States was founded on pluralism.[61] Pointing to Trevor as "America's alien-baiter No. 1," Adamic proclaimed that "if a man's love for his country is measurable by his detestation of all who had the bad taste to be born elsewhere, there probably is no greater patriot in America to-day." Trevor, Adamic satirically added, "discovered the alien problem" while in the army and he left the military to "devote himself to it." Trevor and other "patriots" used the fear of immigrants that they generated to create "rackets" and make "fortunes for themselves."[62] Although Adamic could not pinpoint the source of funding for Trevor's organizations, he discovered that whenever immigration issues appeared before Congress, Trevor would be called upon to testify and a flurry of propaganda would appear in numerous places. Adamic explained that Trevor and his compatriots get "hack journalists to write articles" supporting their positions, while creating "fake societies" that clamor for "the deportation and suppression of aliens and the salvation of America."[63]

"Aliens and Alien-Baiters" solidified Adamic as pluralism's leading champion and a central voice among antifascist activists. People now turned to him for advice on a range of issues in hopes of helping to advance his conception of democracy. The American Jewish Committee, for example, asked the FLIS to turn "Aliens and Alien-Baiters" into a pamphlet and then ordered fifty thousand copies. They considered Adamic an essential ally in the fight against anti-Semitism. Jewish Americans shared their experiences with him and expressed their gratitude for his willingness to challenge the injustices they faced. Some of the letters he received proved slightly comical. In April 1939, a rabbi from Pasadena, California, asked Adamic to solve a disagreement that had arisen within their chapter of the Jewish War Veterans. Some members favored marching in the Decoration Day parade as a unit, while others, including a contingent serving on "the B'nai B'rith Anti-defamation Committee," insisted that our organization should not "separate themselves as a distinct unit at such a time."[64] B'nai B'rith also requested that he serve as a judge for their yearly essay contest for high school students in 1942.[65]

Adamic received hate mail for challenging anti-Semitism. One unapologetic nativist instructed Adamic to stop being "a cog" in the "Jew-baiting machine," suggested that he get a history lesson "of your adopted country" in order to understand that Jews do not assimilate, and read the work of the nation's foremost proponent of eugenics, Madison Grant.[66] More powerful supporters of racial nationalism and anticommunism also disputed Adamic's arguments. Kansas House of Representatives member C. H. Palmer advised Adamic that "many red blooded native born Americans" found pluralism "repulsive." Too many immigrants, Palmer contended, "forget the oppression, disadvantages, and hardships of their native land and start agitating" for "changes in the American system." Palmer then recycled tropes about immigrant criminality in order to assert that "hyphenated citizens" are "not conducive to national stability." He wanted newcomers and their children to renounce their homeland and stop entertaining "thoughts of the 'onions, garlic, and cucumbers' of the 'old country.'" Palmer opposed pluralism because he rejected the idea that immigrants had a "rich culture and strong character." If this were true, he reasoned, "there would be no immigration problem" and immigrants and their children would not be susceptible to the "radical" influences that have made the Dies committee necessary. Palmer concluded, "Encouraging immigrants and denizens to retain their native background and propensities is not conducive to the development of true American patriotism."[67]

Ironically, the Dies committee that Palmer referenced, also known as the House Un-American Activities Committee—which often targeted immigrants and ethnic left-wing activists and union leaders—was created by a segment of the antifascist coalition. During the 1930s and 1940s, a version of antifascism existed that subsequent historians have labeled the "brown scare" after Hitler's Brown Shirts. Politicians, policymakers, and journalists expressed concerns that "fifth columnists," members of fascist sleeper cells, had organized and patiently waited for their opportunity to strike and replace democracy with totalitarianism. Franklin D. Roosevelt and J. Edgar Hoover used the anxieties these stories fueled to depict their isolationist opponents as closeted Nazi sympathizers in order to silence them and to advance the government's preparedness campaign that mobilized the nation to enter World War II. Hoover contended that in order for the FBI to capture these spies it needed to expand its surveillance techniques.[68]

In addition to Roosevelt and Hoover, zealous anticommunists in Congress, most especially Dies, also took advantage of the "brown scare." In 1937, New York congressman Samuel Dickstein reacted to the concerns of his mostly Jewish constituents over the fascist menace and proposed a bill that would establish a committee to investigate more than one hundred alleged profascist organizations operating within the United States. As the bill neared a vote, thousands of German Americans throughout the United States hung swastikas from their apartment windows and marched in their city's streets in hopes of persuading Congress to oppose Dickstein's measure. Some of Dickstein's friends pointed out that a committee on "un-American activities" could just as easily subpoena leftist organizations as it could pro-Nazi groups. Ignoring these words of wisdom, Dickstein agreed to allow anti–New Deal southern Democrats led by Dies to add the investigation of communists to the mission of the House Committee on Un-American Activities. Established in 1938, the committee would quickly make red hunting its primary focus and attack many of the individuals and groups in the antifascist coalition.[69]

Adamic recognized that despite the growing popularity of pluralism, the beliefs that Trevor and Palmer expressed defined immigration law and policy at that moment. Also, his allies now provided the coalition of white supremacists and xenophobes at the center of the anticommunist movement with another weapon to use in this battle to define democracy. Adamic assumed that the United States would eventually be pulled into the war unfolding in Europe and he feared that Trevor, Dies, and others would use that moment to destroy the advances antifascists had made in redefining democracy. He worried that, as during the "Great War," anticommunists would scapegoat immigrants, ethnics, and union activists as security risks and limit refugee rights.[70] In 1939, Adamic suggested that, in order to combat Trevor and the anticommunists, he and Lewis volunteer with federal agencies and promote pluralism.[71] Lewis agreed, and he made lobbying congressional representatives on behalf of immigrants and new Americans one of his tasks as antiradical nativists sponsored a range of measures that included identification cards, registries, and finger-printing immigrants. By September 7, 1939, six days after World War II began in Europe, Adamic wrote to Lewis that a spy hunt had already begun "and everybody is asked to turn informer."[72]

From the late 1930s through 1942, with the aid of Lewis and the FLIS—and its successor, the Common Council for American Unity (CCAU)—Adamic convinced federal organizations to trumpet pluralism as an essential feature of democracy. In exchange, he helped sell war bonds and dedicated himself to keeping morale for the war high within ethnic communities. Adamic consulted on or cowrote scripts for radio programs produced by government agencies. The Justice Department, for instance, asked for his assistance on its radio show that celebrated naturalized citizens. Adamic also coordinated with the Federal Theater Project to arrange performances depicting the vital role immigrants played in making modern America and aided the Department of Education in producing programs.[73]

The federal government provided Adamic with a venue for telling a version of US history that moved immigrants and ethnics from the margins to the center. Lewis, the FLIS/CCAU (Common Council for American Unity), and federal agencies helped promote Adamic's Nation of Nations project. Adamic admired Walt Whitman's writings and borrowed Whitman's phrase in a quest to convince Anglo-American Protestants that they were just one part of the American experience, not the embodiment of it. In one sense, he used Nation of Nations to refer to a four-book series that he wrote—*From Many Lands* (1940), *Two-Way Passage* (1941), *What's Your Name* (1942), and *A Nation of Nations* (1945)—but it also formed part of his overall effort to promote pluralism.[74]

Some of Adamic's critics charged that although he challenged racial nationalism, his pluralist approach ultimately made him an advocate of assimilation.[75] Some leftists, especially communists and Slovene American radicals, illustrated this point when they expressed their shared disdain in response to the praise Adamic received for his 1938 *My America* from the book review editors of mainstream newspapers and magazines.

Communist Robert Forsythe, the penname of humorist Kyle Crichton, led the attack in his *New Masses* column. Forsythe recalled the closeness he once felt toward Adamic. Upon returning from Yugoslavia in 1933, Adamic told stories of the brave communists who maintained their opposition to King Alexander's autocracy despite suffering prison and torture. Increasingly, Forsythe contended, Adamic's militancy faded as insecurities over fitting in led him to become "a 128 percent American." Adamic had eschewed radicalism to become the "Voice of America." Addressing Adamic directly, Forsythe wrote, "[you] have done well; nobody can deny it. The best critics admire you; the best people look up to you," and "you are regarded as a symbol of Americanism."[76] Curiously, Forsythe ignored the fact that Adamic had played a fundamental role in changing the notion of what Americanism meant. By the late 1930s, most Americans—including lawmakers, social activists, intellectuals, and pundits—understood pluralism and industrial democracy as central features of American identity.[77]

Slovene American socialists and communists, who usually criticized each other, concurred with Forsythe. Molek, a socialist and virulent anticommunist, echoed a letter he had sent to Adamic ten years earlier in a new attack on his one-time friend for writing about Slovenes and Slovenian Americans without actually knowing them. Adamic, to Molek's disdain, had lived outside of Slovenian enclaves for most of his time in the United States.[78] Ivan Jontez, editor of *Proletarec* ("Proletarian"), Chicago's underground pro-Yugoslav communist Slovenian language newspaper, concurred with Molek. Jontez proclaimed that "everything I've read about" *My America* in commercial newspapers "was praise, praise, and nothing but praise." Adamic "likes to write about Slovenes," but "he never took his time to find out enough about us to enable him to present an accurate picture of us."[79] Jontez used "us" and "him" throughout his piece to emphasize that Adamic stood aloof from the Slovene American community.

Jontez then cited his "friend's" opinion of Adamic to emphasize his point. Beginning with the *Native's Return*, Adamic has been trying to convince everyone "that he really is a very GOOD American." In that book, Adamic claimed to have forgotten Slovenian. The friend then asked, "Why, is it that such an important piece of news when an immigrant falls in love with his adopted country and becomes a good citizen of it? It has happened so with so many millions of them!" Jontez and his fellow Slovenes found Adamic's books and articles valuable as they challenged the "petty reactionaries" who identify American culture as synonymous with Anglo-Saxonism.[80] It is astounding that Jontez refused to acknowledge that because of Adamic, South Slavs living outside their homeland had a better sense of life in Alexander's Yugoslavia. *The Native's Return* turned many Americans against the Serbian monarch. Also, Adamic's translation of *Struggle* earned South Slavic radicals a great deal of sympathy as Popular Front activists started to redefine American culture. Like Molek, Jontez insisted that Adamic was not one of "us."[81] Forsythe, Molek, and Jontez purposefully misinterpreted pluralism and understated Adamic's role in promoting the Yugoslav communist underground so that they could attack him as a conservative assimilationist.

These three critics, although they did not expressly state it, did raise a valid criticism of Adamic's 1930s activism when they admonished him for not spending more time with Slovenian Americans. By refusing to join fraternal organizations and by not living in Slovenian neighborhoods, Adamic had championed pluralism without living it. Detroit resident Fred M. Butzel, sympathetic to Adamic's efforts, did confront Adamic directly on this issue. Butzel proclaimed that Adamic had "ducked the problem of the obligations of immigrant groups and individuals to the causes of their native lands." Butzel wanted to know what role Irish Americans should play in advancing Irish independence, or Czechs to the restoration of their original homeland, or, as a Jew, what was his responsibility to the Zionist movement?[82] Butzel joined Forsythe, Molek, and Jontez in questioning the extent to which Adamic lived the idea that he championed. Ultimately, these critiques pushed Adamic to explore the politics of diaspora. At this point, however, he responded by clarifying his view of democracy as a universal instinct that all humans possessed and that nations should help them express.

Adamic's critics rejected or mischaracterized his assertion that "America is a process." He made it clear that he wanted to appropriate *Americanization* and revise its 1920s meaning—forcing immigrants to assimilate to Anglo-Saxon culture—and redefine it as an identity that was continuously being updated by newcomers.[83] Pluralism was reshaping US culture and animating antifascism, but racial nationalists' views continued to underpin immigration laws and policies.

Antifascism after the Popular Front's Collapse

When the Soviets and Nazis signed their Nonaggression Treaty in August 1939, anticommunists pushed their agenda more aggressively. With the communists now transitioning in the public's mind from the Nazis' fiercest opponents to their most recent appeasers, Dies seized on the opportunity to portray American communists as potential saboteurs acting on behalf of Hitler. In actuality, the House Un-American Activities Committee spent a great deal of effort undermining welfare and prolabor federal agencies created by the New Deal and championing anti-immigrant and antiunion legislation presented as measures aimed to root out communists and fascists.[84]

The 1939 Hatch Act banned federal employees from belonging to organizations seeking to overthrow the US government. Then, in June 1940, Congress enacted the Smith Act or Alien Registration Act. Resident aliens had to submit to registering and fingerprinting, and if they criticized the military in any way they could be deported. Much of the law resembled the Alien and Sedition Acts from World War I that allowed for the arrest of anyone who criticized the US government or joined organizations advocating the overthrow of the US government. The House Un-American Activities Committee and other groups interpreted phrases such as "advocating the overthrow" broadly and applied such laws to most leftist groups. In September, Congress passed the Selective Service Act, which included a provision barring private employers from hiring communists or supporters of the Nazis for positions that opened because of the drafting of men into the army. The Voorhis Act followed. It compelled any organization with ties to a foreign government to register with the Justice Department and make their records available for inspection by federal agents. During this burgeoning of new measures, anticommunists also succeeded in obtaining the Nationality Act, which granted the executive branch the right to denaturalize a citizen who ten years prior to receiving citizenship had been affiliated with any organization supporting the overthrow of the US government. President Roosevelt, for his part, also permitted the FBI to expand its surveillance operations, which included allowing Hoover to hire more than four thousand new agents and more than six thousand new staff members between 1936 and 1945.[85]

Adamic viewed these measures and the expanding surveillance state as a strategy employed by Trevor, Dies, and others he considered motivated by the fascist ethic to advance their antidemocratic nativist agenda under the cover of championing national security.[86] By having distanced himself from the CPUSA, Adamic could publicly compare these racial nationalists to fascists without fear of reprisal. In fact, during this period of Nazi-Soviet communist friendship and red-scare revival in the United States, 1939 through 1942, Adamic reached the height of his popularity. As he grew into his role as one of the nation's leading antifascists, he recognized that his attacks on racial nationalism failed to adequately challenge racism.

In September 1939, Adamic wrote Read Lewis that he agreed with anthropologist Franz Boas's rejection of eugenics and insistence that cultures could not be ranked.[87] For the next four years, in addition to challenging antialienism and discussing the problems new Americans faced, Adamic argued that fighting fascism and advancing democracy had to address the "Negro problem," investigate Mexican and Mexican American concerns, and challenge anti-Japanese sentiments.

Adamic's opposition to racism in this period was visible but less aggressive than the stance he would take after World War II. He believed that he could convince a large segment of white America to adopt his views. In the fall 1939 issue of the *North Georgia Review*, which then widely circulated as an editorial in southern newspapers, Adamic argued that the "Negro problem" was actually "the American problem." He questioned the notion of black inferiority and challenged southern claims that the problem was a regional concern. He asserted that he understood that white southerners "resent it if a non-Southerner" discusses the issue, but he suggested that an outside perspective might help them recognize that their effort to make African Americans inferior was "helping to degrade the whites who have this attitude," which "is shot through with fear . . . fear that goes through generations, [and] has a corrosive" effect. Now in the South white people did not have to "strive to improve" themselves, they did not have to get "involved in a positive, creative, re-creative process." They simply "look in the mirror" and equate white with superior and thus "there is no need for him to excel or improve himself. The effect is evil."[88]

Then between October 1939 and May 1940, Adamic explained his vision of democracy to more than a hundred audiences in his provocative lecture "Plymouth Rock and Ellis Island." He asserted that the United States experienced a constant state of cultural change because waves of immigrants, including the Pilgrims, advocated democratic ideals that resulted from their encounters with "oppression, terrorism, [and] even massacres." He noted that Anglo-Saxons had produced the American dream, which he defined as "faith in the human individual and the concepts of liberty, fraternity and equality," which the Declaration of Independence and the Constitution symbolized. Yet British migrants did not possess some biological imperative that predisposed them to erecting societies underpinned by Enlightenment ideas, as many believed. Their desire grew out of their refugee experiences, such as escaping religious animus and overcoming monarchical rule. The hopes of these newcomers defined America, and, he contended, "Americanism is nobody's monopoly, but a happy concentrate of some of the highest aspirations and tendencies of humanity." "Americanism" represented a "movement away from primitive racism, fear and nationalism, and the herd instincts and mentality; a movement toward freedom, creativeness," and "a universal or pan-human culture." In a world where fascists justified violence and war on claims of racial superiority and fixed national identities, Adamic insisted that Americans had to live up to "our pretensions of democracy."[89]

In the first month of delivering "From Plymouth Rock to Ellis Island," Adamic went to eleven venues and addressed audiences ranging between two hundred and two thousand. Students at St. Olaf College in Minnesota, he explained to Read Lewis, convinced him that "I'm doing something."[90] Adamic not only communicated the pride he felt in shaping public discourse, his letters to Lewis revealed that he was working fourteen to eighteen hours a day. In one missive, he included his itinerary. One October day began with Adamic meeting a vice principal of a San Francisco high school consisting mainly of Japanese, Mexican, Yugoslav, and Greek students. Then Adamic sat down with students from the University of California at Berkeley for two hours to strategize about how they could challenge prejudice on campus. Next, he attended an assembly of five hundred women members of a Jewish group in Oakland. During the next few days, he planned on speaking at the International Institute in San Francisco and arranging other meetings as his lecture tour took him to Los Angeles and Fresno and then to cities in Oregon and Washington.[91]

In the Plymouth Rock and Ellis Island speech, Adamic made his position on democracy clear, it was stateless, "universal," and "pan-human." To be the model democracy and thus the antithesis to fascism, Americans had to eschew nativism and racism. Adamic hoped that Lewis and FLIS would help him articulate this sharper message. For a brief period, this seemed likely.

Lewis and the FLIS board decided to change their organization's name to the Common Council for American Unity.[92] Comprising mostly well-educated, native-born, middle-class whites, the CCAU board considered themselves the liberal challenge to the nativist movement. They embraced Adamic's pluralist message and delighted in the fact that he agreed to edit the revamped organization's journal *Common Ground* in 1940. *Common Ground* promised to emphasize the "fundamental worth and dignity of every human being."[93] Adamic solicited articles from ethnic and African American writers that offered further examples of how immigrants and blacks helped make modern America and emphasize the pluralist slogan of "unity in diversity."

He also convinced Eleanor Roosevelt, Roger Baldwin, Carey McWilliams, Langston Hughes, and other well-known authors to contribute to the journal, which helped make *Common Ground* a modest success.[94]

The same year *Common Ground* appeared, Adamic officially launched his Nation of Nations project with the publication of his first book in the series, *From Many Lands*. It dealt with immigrant life, but this time he included stories about Japanese Americans and focused the penultimate chapter on the interracial marriage of a white American-born woman and a Mexican man. Although Adamic pointed out instances of racism in both examples, the stories stand out for their lack of sensationalism. He emphasized the mundane, that Americans regardless of color and ethnicity shared similar concerns and struggles. The book ended with reprints of his editorial proclaiming the Negro problem as the American problem and his "Plymouth Rock and Ellis Island" speech.

Adamic's growing concern over racism marked a transition in his thinking and tactics. When his view shifted from Slovenian modernism to pluralism, he attempted to promote ethnic justice by undermining racial nationalism in two ways. First, he wanted old-stock Americans to see their version of American history was the story of white Protestant nationalism. Second, he wanted them to recognize that framing their past that way created the potential for a fascist future. By 1939, Adamic asserted that racial nationalist anticommunists actively pushed the nation toward fascism, but he also found that liberal antifascists presented a danger to democracy as well.

Liberal antifascists seemingly embraced Adamic's pluralist message, but in accepting slow progress and half measures, their lack of vigilance could allow Trevor and his followers to build the America anticommunists wanted. Worse, Adamic asserted that some of his supporters misunderstood his version of pluralism. Too often, politicians, pundits, students, and some teachers identified tolerance as the point of pluralism.

Adamic wanted to stress that his vision of pluralism centered on native-born and foreign alike, recognizing that identity formation was never finished and that they collectively were defining and redefining the nation. Americanness was not a privilege granted by native-born Anglo Protestants to immigrants, ethnics, and African Americans, but a collective project to create a beloved community, a new humanity. Adamic emphasized this point by attacking tolerance. In October 1939, he told a group of white teachers in East St. Louis, Illinois, that being tolerant did not upend the Anglo Protestant narrative underpinning the racial nationalist view of American identity. A "new conception of America is necessary" that acknowledges that "more than 50 races and nationalities" have "fused," have "assimilated" to "one another," not some mythical identity established by the Pilgrims. Tolerance "is a veneer for intolerance" and only strengthened the misperception of a nation founded by Anglos with their superior culture.[95] The next December in Rochester, New York, he added that "America needed to become spiritually, racially and nationally a unit in its stand against totalitarianism."[96] In 1942, he wrote the editorial "Tolerance Is Not Enough" for the *New York Times Sunday Magazine*, where he insisted that winning World War II required a total rejection of Hitler's "nihilist revolution" by living as a nation that celebrated "unity within diversity."[97]

Adamic had to juggle his decision to attack racism with a return to fighting antialienism. The end of the Popular Front rejuvenated anticommunist activism with its definition of American identity rooted in racist and nativist beliefs. His popularity soared at this moment because he could continue to attack anticommunists as fascists and they could not smear him as a communist because he had repeatedly distanced himself from the CPUSA. Adamic had become more militant and a threat to the anticommunist racial nationalists' authority. Realizing that many of the teachers whom he counted on to advance his pluralist message taught tolerance instead of explaining that American identity was never fixed, he started pushing his supporters. This tension within the pluralist ranks ultimately led to Adamic's break from the CCAU.

Conclusion

Adamic helped establish pluralism as the defining characteristic of the antifascist political culture that became dominant during the interwar period. By championing industrial democracy, attacking nativism, and challenging racism through his writings and speeches, Adamic offered a leftist perspective of democracy independent of the Communist Party and more militant than that of the liberals who supported tolerance. Adamic returned to the idea of constructing a democratic culture that philosopher and leading advocate of pluralism Randolph Bourne articulated around World War I, which held that individual identities resulted from social interactions. If one broadened his or her circle of relationships in various ways, including attending lectures and participating in sit-down strikes, the republic would be strengthened because people would be having democratic experiences. To learn other people's stories resulted in revising one's understanding of history, which entailed realizing that Anglo-Saxon Protestants did not create American culture, and therefore they had no right to claim to be its guardians.

As support for Adamic's position increased with the spread of intercultural education and the growing influence of the FLIS, racial nationalists pushed back by linking pluralists to communists. Adamic, by repeatedly criticizing the CPUSA, remained an influential voice in the larger debates over the quota system and refugee policy. But the Hitler-Stalin pact not only limited Adamic's ability to influence the law, it provided an opportunity for racial nationalists to expand nativist control. The resurgence of anticommunism pushed Adamic to become more militant and call for an antifascist revolution.

3

Smrt Fašizmu, Svoboda Narodu!

The Life of a Diasporic Leader, 1939–45

Throughout World War II, Louis Adamic's advocacy of cultural pluralism grew more militant. He insisted that the pursuit of ethnic and racial equality lay at the heart of any meaningful antifascist activism. Eradicating fascism, as he explained in a letter to a friend, did not mean only defeating Axis forces, it also included confronting imperialists and ultranationalists in Allied nations who subscribed to the same "super-race nonsense" as the Germans.[1] Adamic now insisted that antifascists had to unite globally to advance pluralism—and with it democracy—and he pointed to Yugoslav leftist guerilla leader Josip Broz Tito's Partisan army as epitomizing this worldwide fight against fascism. Adamic played the central role in convincing the US public to support Tito's fight against the Nazis and Italian fascists, and in the process he defeated his anticommunist rivals in the contest to define American identity.

By the end of 1942, Adamic contended that the struggle for diversity and the spirit that animated communist revolutionaries were intimately interrelated. Tito convinced Slovenes, Croats, and Serbs to join the Partisans, officially known as the People's Liberation Anti-Fascist Front (LF), by resurrecting the promise of Yugoslavism. Yugoslavism was the nineteenth-century idea that South Slavs should throw off the shackles of Austrian imperialism and create a federation of Balkan peoples that shared political power and embraced ethnic equality. In making Slovenes and Croatians second-class citizens in the first iteration of Yugoslavia, Serbian irredentist King Alexander Karadjordević betrayed this ideal. Tito promised his Serb, Slovene, Croat, Montenegrin, Bosnian Muslim, and Macedonian soldiers that by defeating the Axis forces that overran their nation in April 1941, along with the Chetniks who wanted to reinstall the Serbian monarchy to power, they would make Yugoslavism a reality.[2] Adamic stressed that although Marx and the Russian Revolution inspired Yugoslav radicals, Tito and the LF "were products of the internal conditions in Yugoslavia." By making "cultural diversity" an essential characteristic of a new Yugoslavia, Tito embedded ethnic equality into the "revolutionary process."[3]

Tito's revolutionary pluralism, along with vice president of the United States Henry Wallace's call for a century of the "common man," motivated Adamic to universalize and accentuate the transformative nature of cultural pluralism. Wallace contended that during the prior 150 years, a people's revolution had been occurring with the express goal of giving the common man a better standard of living. To defeat fascism, Wallace asserted, the Allies had to support developing nations' right to self-government, aid them in industrializing, and refuse to perpetuate imperialism. Most controversial of all, Wallace asserted that the American and Russian revolutions had similar aims: to advance equality.[4]

Before the war, Adamic wanted the United States to lead this democratic project. He saw Britain as compromised by its imperialist commitments and he viewed Soviet communism as one stage behind democracy. In January 1941, he felt a surge of confidence that the Roosevelt administration accepted this responsibility when the president called for a globalization of the New Deal's core tenet that governments should protect the general welfare. Roosevelt proclaimed to Congress that he wanted to establish "four essential human freedoms" throughout the world: freedom of speech and of worship and freedom from want and from fear.[5] Later that year, Adamic promoted his Two-Way Passage idea that called for a government-sponsored program to train American ethnics to help reconstruct Europe, and he later added Japan. His Two-Way Passage notion gained popularity after Eleanor Roosevelt endorsed it, and numerous university administrators consulted with Adamic about developing the training programs he envisioned.

The failure of white America to confront segregation, the persistence of nativism and anti-Semitism especially in the application of immigration quota laws, and then witnessing Japanese internment forced Adamic to recognize the limits of the federal government's commitment to democracy. As the war progressed, Adamic criticized the Roosevelt administration's failure to fight for the people battling fascism in "Abyssinia, Spain, [and] Vichy France" and wondered exactly how the government and the people, particularly the white majority, defined "democracy and fascism."[6] Watching the LF battle their Axis occupiers along with observing "open and hidden fascism" in the United States led him to conclude that as a nation we "seem to have lost the creative attitude and energy which wrote the Constitution and built the country." The poll tax and race riots convinced Adamic that a protofascism competed with other worldviews to shape US politics. Adamic also criticized the Soviets for killing, exiling, or denying jobs to "perhaps millions of political dissenters." But, he added, "I wonder how much worse than outright murder or exile is the slower murder of malnutrition in the midst of plenty, or Jim Crow exile. . . . Are the workers who have been killed by company gunmen in our capital-labor 'troubles' during the last 100 years any less dead than the Russian political dissenters?"[7]

Americans, Adamic argued, "must free our mind and spirit and attune them to the insistent revolutionary mood of the contemporary world. We must concretize the Four Freedoms. They have to be made specific, made *operationally visible*, before American idealism and hope and energy can get going again." The "same forces which have exploded in Yugoslavia exist throughout the world. They exist here in America; only here they have not yet been driven into explosion." The "*people* of Yugoslavia" battling for their right for political self-determination "forecasts greater equality and more opportunity for the *peoples* in other countries, including the United States," because all "peoples are now interdependent."[8]

In speeches and the newsletter he edited, Adamic expressed skepticism about the extent to which the United States and other Allied governments would commit themselves to the full eradication of fascism. Specifically, he meant they had to abandon colonialism, which he insisted could revive fascism because of its promotion of national identities through racial hierarchies.[9] This sentiment led him to conclude that helping Tito by reviving the leftist South Slavic diasporic narrative would be the best path he could take to advance the global antifascist movement because of Tito's commitment to ethnic equality. Adamic was certainly not alone in searching for a way to fight fascism by advancing pluralism. African Americans battled for Double V—victory against the Axis and the end of Jim Crow at home—while Jewish, Italian, Japanese, and other ethnic Americans established organizations to fight for pluralism and against fascism in their homelands and host land.[10]

By December 1942, Adamic used *Smrt fašizmu, svoboda narodu* (Death to fascism, liberty to the people)—the Partisans' call to arms—in the titles of book chapters and magazine articles and as his closing salutation in correspondence. At this point, he sought to convince his fellow South Slavs to unite within a diasporic framework and persuade their fellow non-Yugoslav Americans to support the LF. Although Adamic did not use the term *diaspora*, he cited Slovene literary critic and communist underground activist Josip Vidmar's claim that Slovenians "were a little like the Jews. They had tried for a thousand years to cling (with waning success) to their soil," but both groups "did one thing for themselves: they held onto their culture for dear life."[11] Adamic associated the Slovenian and Jewish experiences to help moor his narrative in the imaginations of his fellow South Slavs that they were exiled migrants linked in a larger global network charged with making Yugoslavism a reality. He did not view diasporas as historical conditions but as stories of shared past experiences, migrating to the United States and feeling marginalized, in order to implement an antifascist vision where both Yugoslavia and the United States became more democratic.[12]

Understanding Adamic's reformulation of pluralism as the centerpiece of a global revolt against fascism during World War II begins with his advocacy of Two-Way Passage and opposition to Japanese internment. As he grew incredulous about the US government's willingness to foster actual democracy both at home and abroad, he embraced the South Slavic diasporic narrative he had previously rejected. In presenting Yugoslav Americans as exiles responsible for assisting Tito to make Yugoslavism a reality, Adamic helped establish and lead the Slovene American National Council (Slovensko ameriški narodni svet—SANS) and the United Committee of South-Slavic Americans (UCSSA). These organizations battled Slovenian American Catholics and Serbian Americans who supported the restoration of the monarchy, pressured elected officials and bureaucrats to aid the Partisans, and shaped American public opinion in favor of the LF. This was no simple task, as Adamic's opponents portrayed him and the organizations he led as foreign agents attempting to drive a Soviet agenda dedicated to undermining US values. Advancing the Yugoslav diaspora narrative to advance democratic politics also meant that Adamic worked within a larger network of South Slav LF supporters in Canada and England to provide aid to the Partisan-led government that emerged at the end of 1943.[13] Through his popularity as a writer, connections with friendly politicians and US government officials, and relationships with exiles and ministers in the Yugoslav government and journalists, Adamic played an essential role in making Yugoslavism a reality and advancing the global antifascist revolution.

War Pluralism

Seven weeks before Pearl Harbor, Adamic's *Two-Way Passage* (1941), the second book in his "Nation of Nations" series, appeared on bookstore shelves. In it, he reiterated his view that defeating fascism required the universalization of cultural pluralism, and he proposed the idea that ethnic Americans return to their homelands after World War II to help usher in "an American revolution in Europe." Through this Two-Way Passage plan, the United States would avoid the trappings of European imperialism and instead foster "the *inherent democracy* that exists within the hearts of Europeans."[14]

Adamic gave a copy of the book to Eleanor Roosevelt, who found it "quite exciting" and invited him to dinner at the White House. On January 13, 1942, he and his wife, Stella, ate with the president and Mrs. Roosevelt and Winston Churchill. Disappointed that the president never raised the Two-Way Passage concept, Adamic sent a thirty-two-page memo to the first lady explaining that the current war was an "ideological conflict." Hitler threatened to conquer Europe with an idea, and the United States had to respond in kind. America had to offer Europeans a path toward a "democratic revolution."[15] After his meeting with the Roosevelts through July 1943, Adamic continued to promote his Two-Way Passage idea in a newsletter he started, *In Re: Two-Way Passage*. In it he repeatedly critiqued the State Department for promoting an "appeasement apparatus" and for lacking the vision necessary to truly democratize Europe. Failure to lead meant that only the alternatives of British imperialism and Soviet communism, which he considered better than fascism but inferior to democracy, would define postwar Europe if the Allies won the war.[16] From January 1942 through March 1943, support from various quarters of society appeared to make federal officials consider implementing the passage back proposal. Ethnic fraternal societies passed resolutions championing the idea, talk radio shows discussed it, newspapers editorialized in favor of it, and universities and colleges—including Stanford, Johns Hopkins, Antioch, Columbia, Princeton, Michigan, and Minnesota—created programs to train students for reconstruction missions. As a result, Adamic spent the first two years of the war giving interviews and keynote addresses and consulting with university administrators about the scheme.[17]

The second idea, which he discussed during his January 13 dinner with the Roosevelts and then detailed in a February 1942 memo to the first lady, promoted an "American foreign legion." This organization, led by the US military, would set up "bases in northeastern Africa or/and in the Middle East" and "would consist of small and extremely mobile units of Yugoslav, Greek, anti-fascist Italian, Bulgarian, Albanian, Jewish and other foreign soldiers." Coordinating guerrilla fighting would "serve as a factor in psychological warfare, and prepare for the eventual invasion[s]" to liberate occupied nations. In a February 3 follow-up letter to the president, Adamic stressed that his concern for Yugoslav resistance did not spring from his Yugoslav origin but from his "interest in the eventual total victory of the forces of freedom."[18]

Adamic was struggling to define his place in the United States, his responsibility to Slovenia, and the best way to fight fascism.

During the meal with the Roosevelts and Prime Minister Churchill, Adamic raised a third point that concerned him: the proposed evacuation of Japanese immigrants (Issei) and their American-born children (Nisei). Adamic contended that "chauvinistic groups and newspapers" and white farmers who "desired to eliminate" their Japanese American competitors generated the anti-Japanese hysteria on the Pacific Coast. He recalled being shocked when Mrs. Roosevelt, who frequently praised his pluralist writings in her syndicated weekly newspaper column, proclaimed that federal agencies had captured spies working on behalf of the Japanese government. Adamic could only guess that the first lady had been misled by military leaders or succumbed to the constant attacks of conservative editorialists who continually aimed their vitriol at her. He asserted that the Issei and Nisei were no different from their counterparts among other "enemy aliens," as government officials referred to Germans and Italians.[19]

On February 19, thirty-seven days after Adamic dined at the White House, the president issued Executive Order 9066 that charged Secretary of War Henry Stimson with evacuating almost all Issei and Nisei living in California, Washington, Oregon, and parts of Arizona to prison camps.[20] Adamic went to California in the midst of the evacuation and referred to the orders posted on walls, trees, and telephone poles directing these "enemy aliens" to report for their forced relocation as "one of the most un-American documents ever issued."[21] He came to understand the incarceration experience through his correspondence with Charles Kikuchi, a young writer he had mentored.

In 1939, two of Kikuchi's professors at San Francisco State University, Bertha H. Monroe and Alfred G. Fisk, thought Adamic should interview Kikuchi for his nation of nations project. While in San Francisco in 1940, Adamic met with Kikuchi for the first time. Kikuchi's life story became Adamic's chapter "A Young American with a Japanese Face" in *From Many Lands*. During the war, Kikuchi sent Adamic weekly reports about life in the camps that included inmates' sentiments on being imprisoned and the logistics of daily life. Adamic vowed to help as much as he could and expressed his fear that incarceration could irrevocably alter pluralism's advances to that point.[22]

Between the fall of 1940 and the spring of 1942 he asked six Nisei writers to publish articles in *Common Ground*, the journal he edited, in an attempt to foster opposition to this act of racism. Although Adamic resigned as editor with the publication of the winter 1942 issue, he made sure that the spring edition addressed Japanese imprisonment. Mary "Molly" Oyama's piece about

Los Angeles exclaimed that in this era of "inevitable intensified prejudice, intolerance, and discrimination," we "hope" and "fight" for "a new era wherein we Nisei will be accepted as full-fledged Americans." She reminded readers Nisei men were fighting and dying as US soldiers at that moment "to preserve the ideals of the only country we know."[23]

Adamic and his successor Margaret Anderson wanted to emphasize that Japanese incarceration reflected a larger pattern of US officials and white citizens betraying people of color during wars. In the same issue that carried Oyama's article, Adamic and Anderson printed African American activist Roi Ottley's "A White Folk's War?" Ottley referred to black experiences after World War I when African Americans expected the benefits of democracy after returning from fighting but instead found greater oppression. Now the black community suspected "there is a tacit understanding among the leaders of the white allied nations to limit democracy to white men only," and he warned Roosevelt administration officials that "the black man, like all oppressed peoples, has a long memory."[24] Double-crossing African Americans after World War I and now placing Japanese Americans in what Adamic and other critics referred to as concentration camps certainly made antifascists question liberals' commitment to pluralism, their dedication to democracy, and the extent of their opposition to fascism.

Adamic and Anderson pushed the Common Council for American Unity (CCAU), the organization that sponsored the journal, to be more militant in advancing pluralism and challenging racism. Director Read Lewis kept insisting that doing so would scare off the organization's donors. In fact, in the fall 1942 issue of *Common Ground*, the CCAU board pressured Adamic and Anderson into publishing an article by Robert L. Brown, the public relations director of the Manzanar War Relocation Center.[25] They capitulated, but in the summer 1943, Anderson offered a retort titled "Get the Evacuees Out!" She declared that those claiming to support pluralism could not have exceptions. Embracing a heterogeneous society meant standing up for the rights of black, Jewish, and Japanese Americans because "democracy is no such halfway process. It is a tough belief, and it brooks no emotional withdrawals. We really mean democracy—at home and abroad—or we don't." Supporting civil rights meant challenging claims of national security rooted in xenophobia and racism.[26]

Adamic resigned as editor of *Common Ground* in 1942 and broke off all ties with the CCAU in 1944 because, in his opinion, the board exhibited fascistic tendencies.[27] Tensions between Adamic and the CCAU began in February 1941 when he wrote to Lewis and explained that he did not want to be the face of the organization. Adamic urged the board to directly confront racism, and he became dismayed and angry at their refusal to do so. Years later, Lewis claimed that Adamic grew uninterested in *Common Ground* after realizing that the journal would never achieve a subscriber base large enough to allow it to become a monthly magazine. Adamic, according to Lewis, always wanted to be a part of something bigger.[28] Lewis added that, as the war went on, Adamic wanted to deal with international questions but the CCAU's charge required the organization to concentrate on racial and ethnic tensions as domestic matters.[29] Adamic could be hyperbolic and he enjoyed the public spotlight at times, but he clearly wanted to use the journal to challenge racism and ethnocentrism. In the journal's second and third years, Adamic and Anderson drew fire from critics and then from the CCAU board for printing too many pieces by black authors challenging Jim Crow and then for soliciting articles questioning the legality and morality of Japanese incarceration.[30]

Advancing pluralism to Adamic, Anderson, and all other dedicated antifascists, as Anderson put it, could not occur through "half measures." The limits the CCAU board placed on the messages *Common Ground* could articulate meant that Adamic had to find a new outlet to express his antifascist ideals.

Adamic's Diasporic Turn

Beginning in 1942, Adamic reversed his position from the 1920s and 1930s and adopted the diasporic narrative that leftist South Slavic champions of Yugoslavism brought with them to America. He updated his portrayal of South Slavic peasants, a group he included himself within, as a dispersed people working to remake their homeland. Adamic now advocated Slovene literary critic and communist underground activist Josip Vidmar's assertion that all Slovenes possessed *slovenstvo*, the Slovene spirit, wherever "they were, in Yugoslavia, in Italy or Austria or Hungary, or immigrants in South or North America." *Slovenstvo* would guide Slovenes the world over to join the fight to make Slovenia an equal partner in a new Yugoslavia at the right moment.[31] By employing the leftist Slovene and South Slavic diaspora narrative, Adamic internationalized his pluralist vision and eventually used it to convince the US public to support Yugoslavia's communist guerrillas fighting their Axis occupiers and rival promonarchist Serbian Chetniks. This was no small feat considering that Adamic had to overcome the anticommunist attitudes of federal officials and convince most Americans to rethink their support for the Chetniks.

Adamic's embrace of Yugoslavism began shortly after Adolf Hitler's air force bombed Belgrade on April 6, 1941. German and Italian troops conquered Yugoslavia in eleven days. The Nazis allowed Croatian fascists, the Ustaša, to establish the Independent State of Croatia, which, despite its name, functioned as a puppet regime of the Third Reich. Draža Mihailović—the highest-ranking member of the defeated Royal Yugoslav Army to evade capture—assembled roughly ten thousand soldiers in western Serbia into his Chetnik army and vowed to reestablish the nation's exiled monarchy. Tito gathered the LF at around the same time. Yugoslav government officials fled and eventually reconvened in London as the Yugoslav Government in Exile (YGIE).[32]

From April 1941 through the fall of 1942, Adamic remained well informed about the war in Yugoslavia from the meetings he held with various officials from the YGIE who lived in New York City and Washington, DC. YGIE minister of state Franc Snoj, who at one point requested that Adamic use his celebrity to help save the "Slovene nation," joined Bogdan Raditsa, head of the Press Services at the Yugoslav Embassy in Washington, DC, to provide Adamic with frequent updates on all aspects of occupied Yugoslavia. Adamic also gathered dispatches from journalist Stoyan Pribichevich, who was working in London, and interviewed Slovene and Croatian exiles with ties to the antifascist underground in Europe. In addition, he spoke with his contacts within the Office of War Information, the organization charged with promoting the federal government's official position at home and abroad; the Office of Strategic Services (OSS), the precursor to the Central Intelligence Agency; and the state department. In 1941, like most South Slavic Americans, except those quietly supporting the Croatian fascists, Adamic backed Mihailović and the Chetniks.[33]

Adamic's view about the Chetniks changed after he investigated rumors that the Partisans acted as the true vanguard of antifascism in Yugoslavia and that some of Mihailović's troops had collaborated with the enemy. Although many Slovenian Catholics and Serbian American promonarchical groups dismissed accusations of collaboration as Moscow-directed propaganda, Adamic's network of contacts convinced him the stories were true.[34] Most South Slavic Americans, along with the larger American public, did not know whom they should support. By early 1943, Mihailović had become an antifascist icon in US popular culture. He appeared on the cover of *Time*, 20th Century Fox valorized him in the film *Chetniks! The Fighting Guerrillas*, novelists lionized him, and comic book writers and illustrators presented him as a hero.[35]

Adamic sat at his typewriter in late fall 1942 to sort out the Mihailović versus Tito decision. He filled twenty-six pages with his thoughts on the matter. He noted that Mihailović "did fight Axis troops starting June 1941" and acknowledged that the Chetnik leader wanted to buy time in hopes that US and British forces would eventually invade, defeat the fascists, prevent a Partisan victory, and restore the monarchy. Also, Mihailović defended the Chetnik's lack of engagement with Axis forces by claiming guerrilla actions endangered too many peasants. The Nazis murdered one hundred Yugoslav villagers for every German soldier killed, which they referred to as their depopulation method. Adamic conceded that Mihailović's claim had some merit. Adamic, however, reasoned that the fascists depended on this "appeasement" response in order to rule, and the left-wing press, Yugoslav refugees, and now his sources within the US government verified reports of Chetnik collaboration with fascist units.[36] Adamic asserted that any cooperation with Axis forces was a betrayal of the Yugoslav people and that the LF offered a better future than the Chetniks because they wanted to build a nation of ethnic equals. He reached this conclusion with some trepidation.

Adamic mused that of three ways of life competing against each other—democracy, communism, and fascism—he favored democracy. But in "the face of the horrible present and the even more horrible prospect of a Nazi triumph, anything else" including "a bloody Bolshevik revolution and a Communist system of society, is greatly desirable. If the alternatives are only Hitlerism and Communism, the choice is easy."[37] Adamic publicly declared his support for Tito in a condensed version of his self-reflection piece in the December 19, 1942, issue of the *Saturday Evening Post*. In making this decision, he joined, and then led, the Slovenian and South Slavic left's Yugoslavism project.

In early December 1942, with the promise of a new Yugoslavia looming in the background, Adamic helped arrange a gathering of more than five hundred delegates representing Slovenian benevolent societies, parishes, and political groups gathered in Cleveland to form SANS. Those assembled vowed to provide material and moral support to the Allied war effort in the United States and Yugoslavia. They also elected the founder of Slovenia's Social Democratic Party and political exile, Etbin Kristan, president, and Adamic as honorary president. Adamic had refused the presidency because he worried about overcommitting his time. As it turned out, he worked long hours for SANS and focused most of his writing during this period on the war in Yugoslavia.

During the convention, Adamic took an active role in writing SANS's platform. He hoped to engender support for the Partisans without alienating anticommunist Catholics. The platform emphasized Yugoslavism and used LF rhetoric, but it avoided explicit declarations backing Tito's troops. Fear for Slovenia's future and the fact that Adamic had avoided taking sides in internecine battles between Catholic conservatives and secular leftists prior to this point led Catholic leaders to tentatively accept an alliance with leftists. With Snoj and YGIE ambassador to the United States Konstantin Fotić in attendance to reaffirm the YGIE's acceptance (at least rhetorically) of greater equality in Yugoslavia after the war if the Allies won, the radicals' position appeared less threatening to Catholics.[38] The relationship quickly soured.

By the beginning of 1943, Slovenian Catholics and leftists engaged in fierce confrontations to control SANS, which entailed defining Slovenian American identity and the nature of the South Slav migration narrative. Adamic's faction prevailed, and he emerged as the organization's undisputed leader because of his hard work, the dominance of antifascism in US political culture, his political connections, and his status as one of the nation's leading writers. His framing of the diaspora proved especially effective in shaping how Slovenes and South Slav Americans saw themselves as transnational political actors and how the larger American public understood them. On January 15, Undersecretary of State Sumner Welles and DeWitt Clinton Poole, head of the Foreign Nationalities Branch (FNB) of the OSS, met with a delegation from SANS that included Kristan, Adamic, and Reverend Kazimir Zakrajšek. The FNB monitored war morale in ethnic communities, which included counting on volunteers from those communities to read foreign-language newspapers, listen to radio programs, and then report on instances of dissent and potential subversive activities.[39] Welles and Poole hoped SANS, and Adamic in particular, could help unite Serbs and Croats into a larger Yugoslav bloc dedicated to publicizing Allied war aims. Serbian Americans, however, already despised Adamic because of his criticisms of King Alexander in *The Native's Return*. By the time of this meeting, any notion of Adamic as a peacemaker had vanished in the controversy surrounding his growing insistence that only the LF embodied Yugoslavism, which made him controversial among Croatian liberals and hated by South Slav Catholic anticommunists.

The fragile alliance between leftist and proclerical factions shattered during the meeting. In the presence of Poole and Welles, Kazimir Zakrajšek, SANS's secretary, asserted that "all the evil Communists in Slovenia" necessitated the creation of local armed patrols to protect villages from the Partisans. Adamic wrote to Zakrajšek afterward and asked whether he had thought about how the villagers he spoke of, also known as the Home Guard, had acquired their weapons. Adamic then declared, "the fact that any Slovenian accepted Italian guns with which to shoot any other Slovenian was the most important and an extremely distressing part of your information to us." After chastising Zakrajšek for supporting these fascist collaborators, Adamic sarcastically asked the priest how he felt about Mussolini's troops having destroyed more than one hundred villages in the Julian region, Italian troops forcing "Slovenian girls to serve the[ir] sexual purposes," and the imprisoning of "tens of thousands of Slovenian students and intellectual leaders in their concentration camps." Adamic charged Zakrajšek with allowing his anticommunism to betray his *slovenstvo*.[40]

Adamic's letter had little effect. In February, Vincent Cainkar—head of the leading Slovenian fraternal organization, the Slovene National Benefit Society (*Slovenska narodna podporna jednota* [SNPJ])—informed Adamic that Zakrajšek and other clerics continued to undermine "our cause" when speaking to federal officials.[41] Cainkar feared SANS could not successfully convince the larger US public to support the Partisans as long as Zakrajšek played such a prominent role in the organization. But removing him from office seemed nearly impossible because it "would have an effect like reaching into a hornets' nest among Catholic followers, we would incite trouble and fight among ourselves, and that would mean the end of our Council."[42] While Cainkar and Adamic strategized, a group of Slovene Catholic conservatives from Cleveland, calling themselves the Union of Slovenian Parishes of America, went on the offensive. They informed federal officials that Adamic "does not represent the Slovenian people."[43] Adamic responded by presenting the clerical faction as allied with the Axis forces and proclaiming that the LF embodied transatlantic antifascism.

Ironically, because Adamic had advocated but not lived the pluralism he promoted prior to World War II, he found himself in an ideal position to lead the leftist charge. Cainkar and other Slovene ethnic leaders had to worry about the repercussions from their neighbors and friends if they challenged the Catholic hierarchy. The SNPJ could fall apart if Cainkar publicly denounced Zakrajšek. In contrast, Adamic had the cultural and political influence to make supporting Tito part of a national conversation about democracy and fascism. He could help leftist Slovenes claim to be the true guardians of Slovenian sovereignty and culture. By July, he was repeatedly attacking the Catholic hierarchy as fascist collaborators in speeches and in print. Adamic included Roosevelt in his criticism because the president refused to denounce the church's support of Francisco Franco, Benito Mussolini, and the Slovenian and Croatian bishops and priests working with the Axis occupiers. Roosevelt, Adamic asserted, feared losing the Catholic vote to the point of turning a blind eye to the moral and material support Catholic anticommunists provided to the enemy.[44]

As the battle for control of the diasporic narrative came to a head, Adamic saw a resurgence of his Two-Way Passage idea. When the war began, he had proposed that ethnic Americans return to their homelands after World War II to help usher in "an American revolution in Europe." By having immigrants, instead of military personnel, foster democratic relations, Adamic hoped to avoid making imperialism part of postwar reconstruction. His view of a global antifascist revolution seemed to waver at this moment.[45] On March 28, 1943, papers across the country reported that the Roosevelt administration would appoint New York mayor Fiorello LaGuardia to oversee the reconstruction of Italy once the fascists surrendered. LaGuardia, who had held the rank of major during World War I, would be recalled into the military as a brigadier general and sent to North Africa to await further instructions. Adamic would serve on LaGuardia's staff. Then, on April 7, the major dailies reported that Roosevelt denied the existence of such a plan.[46] Adamic's private correspondence revealed the accuracy of the March 28 version of events.[47] In addition, Adamic had sent LaGuardia a draft of a story he planned to run in the next issue of *In Re: Two-Way Passage*, his newsletter promoting Two-Way Passage. The piece, which never appeared, began with Adamic informing his readers that he had been "sworn to secrecy" since December 1942, when he, LaGuardia, and administration officials started discussing how to implement Two-Way Passage in Italy. LaGuardia, Adamic wrote, would "head a post-Mussolini government or commission which will hold Italy 'in custody' till it can be turned to the status of a normal state."[48]

As newspapers around the country and radio programs analyzed the March 28 story, a rumor circulated that, after serving as LaGuardia's assistant, Adamic would become the head of Yugoslavia's reconstruction project. The editors of the Pittsburgh-based Serbian American promonarchist *American Srbobran* felt it necessary to dismiss the idea and attack Adamic. The piece asserted that "wholesale chaos and destruction" would plague Yugoslavia with Adamic in charge. "The Serbian people hate Adamic" and they "would first embrace a leper." The editor proclaimed if an Adamic-led government came to pass, Adamic would be shot or would have to shoot "hundreds upon hundreds of Serbian Chetniks to force himself upon the Serbian masses." Like Slovene American Catholic leaders, the editor of *American Srbobran* ended by portraying Adamic as a communist propagandist.[49]

As the American public became convinced of Mihailović's collaboration with fascist forces, Adamic's battles with anticommunist Catholics and promonarchical Serbs intensified, as did his commitment to the LF's version of Yugoslavism. He continued to argue that although Tito was a communist, the LF represented a broad-based coalition of antifascists that included liberals, socialists, and some Catholics.[50] To the dismay of the anti-Partisan factions, the US and British governments bolstered Adamic's position by shifting their support from Mihailović to Tito in the summer of 1943. British intelligence officers received consistent reports and intercepted radio communications proving that Chetnik units had made deals with Italian and German forces not to engage each other militarily.[51] Simultaneously, the Partisans kept surviving German offensives. In a May 1943 engagement, for instance, one hundred thousand Axis troops attempted to trap Tito and his twenty thousand men at the base of the Zelengora (Green Mountain) range in Bosnia. Churchill's friend and Special Operations officer Frederick William Deakin witnessed the battle. Deakin saw Chetnik units fighting alongside Axis soldiers. By keeping his army intact, Tito inspired Chetnik defections and convinced the British that the Partisans represented the best hope to liberate Yugoslavia. Also, as Tito assembled a provisional government that November in Jajce, Bosnia, Deakin noticed the absence of Soviet agents. Tito's battlefield victories and independence from Stalin persuaded the British and US governments to supply the Partisans with food and weapons.[52]

Adamic now launched his offensive for the hearts and minds of his fellow Slovenes and South Slavs as well as the larger American public. With SANS splintering, Adamic organized like-minded Slovene, Serbian, and Croatian Americans into the UCSSA. The UCSSA quickly emerged as the point organization presenting Slovenes and leftist South Slavs as a diaspora. In a July 26 letter to Roosevelt, Adamic explained that this group planned to support the war effort by raising funds and morale, to "have a voice in postwar plans and operations," and "to speak in the interest of the South-Slavic peoples who, under the Axis which they are fighting, cannot now speak for themselves." Adamic also hoped the president would support plans to expand Yugoslavia's borders to include lands where South Slavs lived under Italian rule, namely Istria, Trieste, and Gorizia.[53] In August, delegates representing the various South Slav organizations making up the UCSSA held their first official meeting in Cleveland and elected Adamic their president.

The members in attendance from the Serbian National Federation (SNF), which supported the YGIE, walked out of the meeting. They called the UCSSA a communist front and recognized the pro-Tito sympathies of most of the delegates as a threat to their Greater Serbia vision. Advocates of this irredentist ideal wanted to expand Serbia's boundaries by incorporating areas in Croatia, Bosnia and Herzegovina, Montenegro, Kosovo, and Macedonia that had large Serb populations into a single nation. If the Allied governments rejected this plan, the proponents of Greater Serbia at least wanted the restoration of the monarchy as the ruling body in a postwar Yugoslavia. They also intensified their efforts to portray Mihailović as the true hero of Yugoslavia's guerrilla resistance movement.[54] Slovene American anticommunist Catholics voiced arguments to those raised by the SNF, and they too opposed the UCSSA shortly after its inception.[55] Adamic spent the next year battling both groups and lobbying federal officials, shaping American public opinion in favor of Tito, engaging in local political battles in South Slav communities, and coordinating UCSSA efforts with Yugoslav leftists in England and Canada. Examining how he succeeded highlights his influence as a writer and helps us to understand the day-to-day challenges diasporic leaders faced.

"Death in Front of the Church"

Adamic published *My Native Land* in July 1943, a month before being elected UCSSA president. It presented the Partisans as the embodiment of Yugoslavism and revolutionary pluralism and attacked the Catholic Church for betraying Slovenes' desires for political freedom and ethnic equality.[56] Catholic Church officials led the Slovene People's Party (SPP), which ran the day-to-day affairs of Slovenia under both Austrian and Serbian rule. Now the SPP, along with the Vatican, collaborated with fascist governments.[57] Adamic reiterated his criticism that Roosevelt had refused to reproach the Catholic hierarchy's relationship with fascists because the president feared alienating Catholic voters. Anticipating efforts to label him anti-Catholic and determined to convince Slovene Americans to embrace the leftist diaspora's vision of Yugoslavism, Adamic then insisted, "I am not anti-Catholic; I am, as I have said earlier, anti-Clerical; and my anti-Clericalism applies" to "outfits like the Slovenian Clerical party," to "small-time Clerical politicians," and "to the Vatican's international Clerical politics." The "'Catholic issue' is not discussed in the American newspapers and magazines or over the American radio because nearly everybody is afraid to touch it."[58] In a final flourish intended to galvanize ethnic solidarity, he added that in addition to being "fiercely anti-Communist," the "American Catholic hierarchy" is "widely anti-Slavic. It consists largely of bishops of German and Irish ancestry, and some of them consciously or unconsciously discriminate against Polish, Slovak, Czech, Slovenian and Croatian American priests in their parishes." Adamic suggested that to support the "reactionary foreign policy" of church leaders meant appeasing Yugoslavia's fascist occupiers and acquiescing to anti-Slav nativism in the United States.[59]

Two months later, Adamic audaciously defended the LF's program to assassinate those who collaborated with fascists. In his *Harper's* article "Death in Front of the Church," he celebrated the LF's killings of former Slovene governor Marko Natlachen and the University of Ljubljana professor, Catholic priest, and leading political figure Father Lambert Ehrlich. After Ehrlich finished his 7 AM mass on May 26, 1942, two LF members shot him and his bodyguard on the steps of his church.[60] Adamic insisted that Ehrlich deserved his fate because he had repeatedly betrayed Slovenes. During King Alexander's reign, Ehrlich's "spiritual storm troopers," Catholic students loyal to the priest, spied on their leftist classmates and professors. The SPP labeled all their opponents communists no matter what their actual political beliefs. To further stress his point, Adamic recounted an argument he had with YGIE minister of state Franc Snoj. Snoj warned Adamic against straying "too far into pro-Partisanism" and expressed his outrage that the LF killed a priest "right in front of the church!" Adamic retorted that in a "revolutionary situation" a clergyman can do things to "provoke someone to shoot him—even in front of a church." He added that "resistance against the Axis is revolution" and concluded the article by quoting the Partisans' slogan: "Death to Fascism! Liberty to the People!"[61]

Promoting the murder of a priest by a band of communist-led guerrillas would typically have earned Adamic the enmity of most Americans. Instead, "Death in Front of the Church" illustrated Adamic's ability to garner American public support for the LF largely because of his ability to tell compelling stories. Along with his presentations of the drama of the assassination and debate with Snoj over the ethics of revolutionary behavior, Adamic depicted Ehrlich as a Tammany Hall ward boss. For readers in the United States, this framing made the SPP synonymous with the worst form of political corruption Americans could envision.[62]

Adamic's efforts to unite his fellow ethnics and much of the larger American public behind the Partisans got a boost from the British government. "Death in Front of the Church" appeared during the same month that the British government decided to abandon its support for Mihailović altogether. Lee White, one of Adamic's sources in the State Department, informed him that British leaders told Mihailović that they would continue to arm the Chetniks only if the Serbian royalists agreed to take orders from the British general staff in Cairo and work with Tito. Mihailović refused. In addition,

State Department officials had grown "highly critical of the tactics of the government-in-exile," especially of its ambassador Konstantin Fotić's secret propagandistic campaign intended to restore King Peter, the current monarch, to power after the war. White let Adamic know that the US government had "no official policy in regard to Yugoslavia" and none was going to evolve until after liberation.[63]

White leaked information to Adamic because he wanted to do anything he could to help "bring about Serbo-Croatian unity on democratic lines." He clearly saw the LF as Yugoslavia's best option despite being unconvinced that Mihailović "is an evil man, much less a fascist, or that the Partisans are as pure as their supporters in the United States believe." He added that "one thing I learned in the Balkans is that things are never as simple as they seem, and I think that the Yugoslav mess is about as complicated a problem as has yet emerged from the war." Although White requested that Adamic bring more nuance to his pronouncements about the Chetniks, he praised "Death in Front of the Church" as "superb."[64]

Antifascism dominated US political culture, and Adamic's popularity remained high because he had been one of the leading opponents of fascism for roughly a decade. As a result, many government bureaucrats and most of the general public accepted his claims that the LF could advance democratic values, and concomitantly they viewed him as an expert on Balkan politics. A month after "Death in Front of the Church" appeared, Adamic received a letter from Lt. Col. Karl Detzer of the War Department of Army Services. Detzer inquired whether Adamic would write a handbook on Yugoslavia for the army because the entire War Board agreed "that you were the one person capable of turning out the job."[65] Officers, soldiers, and those actively engaged in engineering the war effort shared Detzer's high opinion of Adamic.

Adamic understood that fighting for Yugoslavism as an ethnic leader depended on his making personal connections with his fellow South Slavs. He did so by taking the time to answer letters from supporters and critics. Soldiers of Yugoslav descent fighting overseas wrote to him regularly that they appreciated his work because it highlighted South Slavs' determination to defeat fascism by informing the world about "Marshal 'Tito' and his gallant band of Partisans."[66] Others asked him how they should respond to their priest's criticism that the LF sought to install a totalitarian regime to rule Yugoslavia after the war. Adamic retorted that the Catholic hierarchy was selective in its opposition to dictatorships in that it openly cooperated "with fascist groups and persons: in Spain, Italy, Germany, Poland, [and] South America." He urged this man to inform his priest that he could be nuanced and appreciate the USSR's or Tito's achievements and still be critical of communism.[67] Some Catholic clergy even sent Adamic fan mail to make sure he knew that not all priests followed the dictates of their superiors.[68]

The Slovene Catholic establishment expressed a visceral anger toward Adamic after the publications of *My Native Land* and "Death in Front of the Church." He responded by equating Catholic leaders with southern segregationist politicians and criticizing Roosevelt and the State Department for not challenging these opponents of democracy. Adamic argued that "a vast democratic element" that "favors international cooperation" has always existed but "it has never been organized." Roosevelt and the State Department's willingness "to play along with" the southern bloc and the Catholic hierarchy prevented the United States from embracing a broader notion of democracy. Leaders such as Henry Wallace gained followings by expressing visions of this antifascist sensibility, and examples of individuals and groups going "abroad as ambulance drivers" or "forming little brigades—like the Lincoln Brigade in Spain" illustrated these democratic desires. The future depended "on this vast democratic element" mobilizing. In the postwar world people who understood internationalism as "a natural extension of its domestic democracy" had to become the dominant voices in government to guarantee the destruction of fascism and the natural growth of democracy.[69]

Adamic's Catholic opponents had no counter to his broad framing of the Partisans as part of a larger global revolution to expand democracy through promoting pluralism. They hoped that by repeatedly calling the UCSSA communist they would cause its decline. In early 1944, editors of Cleveland's Catholic Slovene-language newspaper *Ameriška Domovina* highlighted this strategy when they issued a pamphlet proclaiming Adamic a communist agent provocateur who advocated the "Sovietization of the Balkans."[70] Adamic easily defeated this effort by capitalizing on his popularity. Samuel Hazzard Cross, the head of the Slavic Languages and Literature Program at Harvard University and an LF supporter, invited Adamic to respond to these attacks by speaking at the Harvard Club. Adamic accepted the invitation and informed Cross that he would reiterate his argument that priests and bishops who followed the pope's anticommunist position were fascist collaborators. In his speech, Adamic most likely repeated the examples he had used in his newsletter articles and other presentations that he gave noting the SPP's and the Vatican's support of Franco and Mussolini.[71]

Because the Slovene Catholic hierarchy had worked with the Austrian monarchy and Serbian irredentists and then opposed Tito, Adamic successfully presented the SPP as more concerned with maintaining power than advancing Slovenian independence from fascist rule. These attacks forced Slovenian Americans who considered Catholicism as the root of their Sloveneness to separate their religious beliefs from the church's politics. A government study of Slovene Americans conducted after the war suggested that Adamic and his fellow diasporic activists succeeded. It concluded that a majority saw Tito as Slovenia's and Yugoslavia's best option even though they opposed communism. Beyond the Slovene American community, Adamic's fierce opposition to the Catholic hierarchy, which included defending an assassination, did not faze officials in the Department of State or the Department of War, nor did it appear to offend soldiers.

Greater Serbia, Anticommunism, and Antifascism

While defeating his Catholic anticommunist critics for the moment, Adamic faced a fiercer challenge from promonarchist Serbian Americans and their supporters. Despite warmer relations at the beginning of the war between Adamic and ambassador Fotić, a mutual distrust persisted and eventually manifested itself in battles to shape public opinion and influence US government officials.[72] Adamic eventually prevailed.

Fotić promoted the Greater Serbia vision, which meant that by the spring of 1942 he was no longer supporting the YGIE's official position of democratizing Yugoslavia after the war. In addition to battling Adamic and other leftists, Fotić engaged in confrontations with other members of the YGIE and the US government. The heads of Croatian and Serbian sections at the Yugoslav Information Center, Ivan Šubašić and Sava Kosanović, respectively, urged Poole and other FNB officials to confront Fotić. When that failed to produce a result, Assistant Secretary of State Adolf Berle asked Fotić to meet in June. Fotić attempted to win Berle to his side by appealing to the secretary's anticommunist politics. The ambassador insisted that he and the like-minded Serbian Americans belonging to the Serbian National Federation and the Serbian National Defense Council (SNDC), which raised funds for the Chetniks, simply wanted to counter procommunist sentiments expressed by Croatian and Slovenian groups that slandered Mihailović.[73] Fotić had discredited himself in making these claims because officials at the State Department, the Office of War Information, and the Foreign Nationalities Branch knew that the leaders of the SNDC, which had adopted the motto "One People, One State, One King," were on the YGIE's payroll. Shortly after this meeting, the FNB issued a report identifying Fotić as the leader of the Greater Serbia movement in the United States and criticized *Amerikanski Srbobran* for publicizing the Serbian nationalist position at every opportunity.[74]

The FNB's findings appeared shortly before seventeen-year-old King Peter visited the United States in late June 1942. In an effort to promote morale among South Slav Americans, the king and his ministers agreed to allow Oscar Brown of the FNB to help him with his speeches. Brown informed his superiors that Fotić appeared to be the "power behind the throne," and as the tour progressed, the king clearly followed the ambassador's directives. For instance, Peter spoke only of Mihailović's heroic deeds when discussing the resistance after being instructed to make references to a broader Yugoslav guerrilla effort.[75]

After Peter's visit, Adamic's source at the State Department, Lee White, informed him that key individuals have grown "highly critical of the tactics of the government-in-exile" and that they have pointed to Fotić as the leader of the irredentist propaganda effort.[76] Adamic now knew that he could attack Fotić and his network of Mihailović supporters without fear of reprimand from the State Department, the Office of War Information, or the FNB. He hired a newspaper clipping service to send him any article from any paper in the country that printed pieces favoring the Greater Serbian agenda. Once notified of such pieces, Adamic then sent letters to the editors of these periodicals and informed them that they had fallen victim to Fotić's propaganda campaign.[77]

Adamic also confronted the leading American voices supporting the Serbian monarchy. He started with Ruth Mitchell. As a journalist stationed in Belgrade, Mitchell witnessed firsthand the Axis attack on the Yugoslav capital in April 1941. She decided to cover the Chetniks, but her dedication to their cause led her to take up arms and become one of the few women in Mihailović's army. Her tenure as a soldier did not last long; the Gestapo captured her shortly after the Axis occupation of Yugoslavia began. Mitchell spent more than a year in prison and even received a death sentence. A prisoner exchange freed her, and she returned to the United States. Once home, she wrote, spoke, and lobbied on behalf of the Chetniks. After the Allies switched their support to Tito, she persisted in championing Mihailović's cause and joined Fotić's propaganda effort. White informed Adamic that "the State Department is not in sympathy with the ideas expressed by Ruth Mitchell, whom our diplomats regard as a psychopathic case."[78]

In parallel with the Slovenian American Catholic anticommunists, Fotić, Mitchell, Michigan congressman and virulent anticommunist George Dondero, and various journalists allied with the Greater Serbia contingent attempted to smear Adamic and the UCSSA mostly through red-baiting. They also circulated lies. In July 1943, Carleton Kent of the *Chicago Times* printed that Adamic had aligned himself with a Croatian separatist group. Kent implied that Adamic worked on behalf of the fascist Ustaša. Mirko G. Kuhel—a SANS activist in Chicago—not only alerted Adamic to this piece, he discovered that the Serbian National Defense Congress planted the story. Kuhel sent a letter to the *Chicago Times*'s editor to expose this slander and explained that Adamic was the honorary president of SANS and favored a federated Yugoslav built on ethnic equality. The "ultra-pan-Serbian clique" assisted by "anti-Yugoslav stooges in America," Kuhel added, were the actual proponents of ethnocentrism and wanted to preserve irredentism by maintaining "the system of government that brought about the conditions which threaten to annihilate the deceived Yugoslav people."[79]

Before an audience in Detroit, Adamic also fought back. He proclaimed that "reactionary fascist forces within the Yugoslav government-in-exile" have "created a vast propaganda machine in the United States, commanding the services of such curious people as Ruth Mitchell and Congressman Dondero of Michigan, and employing undemocratic, subversive methods to achieve divisive, undemocratic ends in this country, and postwar Yugoslavia."[80] Dondero responded by calling Adamic a communist and demanding a full inquiry into why the army had purchased and shipped fifty thousand copies of *The Native's Return* for soldiers to read. The anticommunist *Detroit News*, part of William Randolph Hearst's media conglomerate, aided Dondero by publicizing the story that the army bought copies of *The Native's Return* for soldiers to read. The article labeled Adamic a "pro-Communist author." Although forty thousand copies were sent to the army and ten thousand to the navy for distribution, the library branch of the US army purchased only thirty copies, as the rest were donated. Dondero claimed that Communist Party agents tricked the armed forces into obtaining these books and attacked Adamic for supporting the Partisans and not the Chetniks.[81] This effort failed as military officials and government agencies continued to ask Adamic to write handbooks about Yugoslavia for troops, brief them on the Partisans, and sell war bonds.

Mobilizing South Slavic Americans around the framework of diaspora included more than battling Catholic and Greater Serbia anticommunists and making appeals to his fellow Yugoslavs to support the Partisans. Adamic understood that SANS and the UCSSA represented only a fraction of his fellow ethnics. His efficacy as a leader stemmed from his ability to shape the attitudes of his fellow South Slavs by influencing the organizations they belonged to, such as the military and most especially their unions. The Congress of Industrial Organizations (CIO) contained hundreds of thousands of people who were of South Slavic descent. Through his labor reporting and advocacy for industrial democracy, Adamic had forged relationships with CIO leaders at the national, state, and local levels, and he encouraged them to promote the Partisan cause. For instance, he wrote New York City CIO council secretary Saul Mills that a "propaganda" campaign "conducted by a clique of corrupt politicians within the so-called Yugoslav government-in-exile" has "obscured" the "truth about the Yugoslav situation" for "two and a half years." He asked Mills to send a resolution for their approval to all New York City CIO affiliates that expressed approval for LF guerillas who "are the fighting vanguard of the new European democracy now being born out of the agony of the war."[82] Adamic then asked CIO leaders in cities all over the country to follow Mills's example and request that their members also declare their local unions' support for the LF. Many unions complied.[83] Adamic understood that some of his fellow Slavs might listen to their priests when it came to dismissing him as a radical but he hoped that those same South Slavs would listen to their union leaders and fellow workers when they contradicted those priests and supported the LF.

Adamic also wrote to South Slav community leaders and asked them to openly back the Partisans. He typically found success with this approach, but a glaring exception occurred in the summer of 1943. Cleveland's mayor Frank Lausche, a friend of Adamic's to that point, rejected Adamic's request. Lausche's refusal was significant because Cleveland was home to the second-largest Slovenian-born population in the world after Ljubljana. Less than a week after Adamic spoke in Detroit, July 22, he invited Lausche, who had become Cleveland's mayor in 1941, to a luncheon hosted by the newly organized UCSSA. Lausche, the son of Slovene immigrants, declined because he believed that the debate over who "ought to be recognized as the official Government" of Yugoslavia "is of a very controversial and explosive character." Lausche then pointed to the race "riots" happening in the United States and proclaimed that he did not want to play a role in escalating tensions between ethnic and racial groups.[84] Between June 20 and 23, race rebellions enveloped Detroit. Fights between white and black young men escalated as white sailors and unemployed white workers accused African Americans of stealing their jobs. White police officers openly sided with white rioters. Police officers shot and killed seventeen blacks and no whites. In total, thirty-four people died, and African Americans accounted for twenty-five of the victims.[85]

Adamic responded to Lausche by arguing that to defeat fascism, all members of the Allied nations had to confront notions of racial superiority, fears of democracy, and greed at home and abroad. And in regard to the race rebellions in the United States, and Detroit in particular, Adamic asserted "the official justice of Detroit" permitted white supremacists to take "a violent crack at the Negroes" while letting "every white rioter go free." Whites who perpetrated violence against blacks, he added, resembled European fascists. Adamic then addressed Lausche's refusal to choose between the Chetniks and the Partisans. He asked whether the mayor understood that Mihailović had collaborated with the enemy and then criticized Lausche for caring more about maintaining his popularity than he did about fighting fascism in Yugoslavia and the United States. Lausche apologized for angering Adamic and he expressed his desire to maintain the "bond of friendship between us." Lausche even offered to come to New York and meet with Adamic so that they could work out their differences.[86] Adamic rejected the mayor's offer.

Adamic's exchange of letters with Lausche clearly revealed that fighting fascism by advancing revolutionary pluralism remained his primary concern. For Adamic, the politics of homeland and host land worked in concert. A number of people who shaped public opinion supported Adamic's position. For example, Estelle M. Sternberger, a reporter and activist on behalf of Jewish women, hosted *Washington Front*, a daily radio show on New York City's WQXR. After Dondero's attempt to red-bait Adamic and prevent troops from getting copies of *The Native's Return*, Sternberger decided to make Adamic the subject of her December 15, 1943, show. She told her audience to reject the efforts of those congressmen currently trying to foment an anticommunist "hysteria" and then called the anticommunists "un-American" for raising "Hitler's cry of Communism to frighten the American public." Adamic's support for Tito, she insisted, "no more stamped him a Communist than Prime Minister Churchill's signing of an alliance with the Soviet Union stamped Churchill as a Communist." Sternberger then asked, "Is a man a Communist because his accurate reporting induces him to express amusement over the startling discovery that in certain countries the Communists seem to be the only ones ready to lead the fight against the anti-democratic forces?"[87] Sternberger joined military leaders, rank-and-file soldiers, academics, Roosevelt administration officials, and CIO union activists in viewing Adamic and his diasporic activism as part of a larger antifascist political culture.[88]

Showdown in Gary

By the time Sternberger's broadcast defending Adamic aired, the British and US governments had shifted their support from Mihailović to Tito. Although the official policy change strengthened Adamic's position, his struggle to advance the diaspora was far from over. The irredentist movement remained vigilant. To claim a complete victory, Adamic and his fellow leftists would need the Allied powers to recognize the Partisans as the official government of Yugoslavia in addition to their acknowledgment of the LF as the army of liberation.

In late 1943, the LF's political arm, the Anti-Fascist Council for the National Liberation of Yugoslavia (Antifašističko vijeće narodnog oslobodjenja Jugoslavije—AVNOJ) declared itself the official government of Yugoslavia. Ivan Ribar presided over AVNOJ's executive board and then became the chairman of the Provisional People's Assembly. Tito served as acting prime minister even though he continued to coordinate military affairs.

Around this same time, Allied leaders met in Tehran, from November 28 to December 1, 1943. In regard to the Balkans, Roosevelt agreed to Churchill's request to aid Tito militarily, but the president refused to recognize AVNOJ as Yugoslavia's ruling body.[89] This was a setback, but Tito and his supporters later had their spirits raised in February. Churchill, while addressing the House of Commons, acknowledged that Mihailović had collaborated with Axis troops and that the Partisans were doing almost all the fighting against the Germans (the Italians had surrendered). Adamic praised Churchill's speech and urged Poole and other US officials to issue similar statements.[90] At this point, the Allies could not support a Mihailović-led government as the irredentists wished, but neither did Churchill and Roosevelt want to name AVNOJ the governing body of Yugoslavia's liberated areas. Churchill proposed a compromise government between Tito and someone acceptable to the monarchy and Croatian liberals. King Peter remained reluctant to consent, but Churchill moved ahead and chose Ivan Šubašić, the former governor of Croatia.

Anticommunists responded by intensifying their opposition to LF supporters, most especially Adamic. Chicago Republican congressman Fred E. Busbey declared on the US House floor that Adamic was "far more dangerous to our American way of life" than Communist Party of the United States of America (CPUSA) head Earl Browder.[91] The Gary, Indiana, branch of the SNF led by former alderman Louis Christopher attempted to capitalize on Busbey's remarks. The Gary branch of the UCSSA had invited Adamic to speak in March on the current state of affairs in Yugoslavia. Citing Busbey and others who identified Adamic as a communist, Christopher temporarily halted Adamic's visit by convincing city leaders that a riot would ensue if they granted the UCSSA permission to hold a rally. Serbian social and religious groups circulated their own petition. They supported the SNF's position that Adamic's "inflammatory, communistic and un-American utterances" could cause disturbances, and they also considered him highly controversial because they feared that he would also speak about "racial and ideological issues."[92] Supporting Tito and racial equality made Adamic a subversive and likely a provocateur in the eyes of anticommunists.

Adamic's supporters challenged the proponents of Greater Serbia by printing flyers, taking out their own ads, and protesting. One UCSSA flyer declared that the SNF and city's Orthodox religious leaders spread their views in the *Srbobran*, which prints "the most vicious race hatred" propaganda. The piece went on claim that by opposing the Partisans, supporters of the monarchy "are opposed to the heroic struggle of the Jugoslav people against the hated Nazi invader." Thus, they must be afraid and make sure that Fotić "and such undemocratic and pro-fascist elements will never again rule Jugoslavia." The flyer then reminded the people of Gary that the Allies now supported Tito and declared that red-baiting "must be treated" as "Fascist propaganda to split the people."[93]

Had this simply been a battle between factions of the South Slavic American community, it likely would have received little attention beyond the immigrant press. But Adamic's celebrity and his ties to the larger web of antifascist activists saw the Indiana CIO state industrial council circulate a petition on his behalf. Indiana's industrial unionists expressed their "shock" at city officials for denying "a group of patriotic American Slavs" the right "to bring to Gary the distinguished Slav writer" to speak. The Slovak National alliance followed suit. As telegrams and letters of support for Adamic mounted, Gary's League of Women Voters and local businessmen demanded that city leaders reissue Adamic a permit to speak. Ultimately, Adamic addressed the people of Gary. Union officials, the mayor, a state senator, and a number of priests and Protestant clergymen sat on stage and listened as Adamic lauded the Partisans, reminded the crowd that the Allied leaders had recognized Tito and the LF as the sole army fighting the Axis occupation of Yugoslavia at that moment, disparaged Mihailović as a Nazi collaborator, and called upon the Roosevelt administration to formally recognize the AVNOJ as the official government of Yugoslavia.[94] Whether they agreed with Adamic or not, local dignitaries sensed that their political futures, the health of their parishes, and the success of their businesses depended on their onstage presence for Adamic's speech.

On April 2, conservative Serbs made one last effort to gain the backing of the larger Gary community by holding an "Americanism" rally featuring

Representative Busbey. Gary's *Post-Telegram* reported that attendance "at the three-hour program was acknowledged by the sponsors as disappointingly small." Ray Brock, a former *New York Times* war correspondent in the Balkans and a Mihailović supporter, tried to bolster the crowd's spirits by promising that American public opinion would shift back in favor of the Serbian general by May.[95]

Various federal agencies, especially the FNB and the FBI, monitored the discord in Gary.[96] Although a devout anticommunist, FNB head Poole had been critical of Serb irredentism. He understood why Croatian and Slovene Americans would support Tito, and he informed his superiors that Adamic was "a first-rate journalist" and a "devoted" American. Yet he deemed the popular writer only "moderately intelligent politically" and thus blind to the dangers of the Sovietization of the Balkans.[97] Poole framed tensions between Serbians and Croatians as resting on ancient hatreds. Adamic disagreed. He did not deny that longstanding hostilities mattered, but he repeatedly published articles in the *Bulletin*, the official magazine of the UCSSA, insisting that the Mihailović-Tito controversy signified a debate about the future. It was an argument over "creating a state system and organization upon the basis of true democracy," not "tribal" grudges. For Adamic, "true democracy" meant equality both for South Slavs in a reconfigured Yugoslavia and for all Americans in the United States.[98]

FBI officials also worried about the consequences of the Mihailović-Tito controversy. J. Edgar Hoover's agents in Gary investigated the role communist propaganda might have played in encouraging South Slavs to support Adamic. Informants reported that Chicago's CPUSA leaders wanted to bring the UCSSA into the party's orbit. During the period when Adamic's speaking permit had been revoked, party officials directed a communist organizer in Gary "to start a propaganda campaign" designed to get the permit reinstated. Although Gary's communists wrote some letters to the local newspapers to "show that most Yugoslavs are behind Adamic and the Partisan movement," FBI agents quickly determined that their effort had little impact. Earl Browder, head of the Communist Party, had come to town recently and the CPUSA failed to round up an audience of any significance. Adamic's visit, as one FBI informant stated, had the feel of "a Crosby-Sinatra affair."[99] The FBI concluded that most of the city's ethnic South Slavs shared Adamic's vision and the agents closed their investigation.[100]

As with the Slovene Catholic press in Cleveland, the advocates of Greater Serbia in Gary saw their efforts to smear Adamic backfire. By denouncing the Partisans and Adamic as agents working on behalf of the Soviet Union instead of antifascists promoting revolutionary pluralism, they allowed Adamic to depict them as both anti-Yugoslav and anti-American. Also like Slovene Catholic anticommunists, supporters of the monarchy failed to recognize that Adamic's celebrity and connections to politicians, government bureaucrats, union leaders, and countless other dedicated antifascists sympathetic to his message would allow him to turn an intraethnic battle into a national event that advanced his position. Seven days before Adamic spoke in Gary, on March 12, New York City mayor Fiorello H. LaGuardia promoted the Partisans during his regular radio broadcast. LaGuardia declared that "I wish our Government would come out and just say, 'Tito, you have done a good job, and Tito, we are for you.' That would help a lot." Adamic sat in the studio during the show and the mayor let his audience know his friend was there.[101]

The Gary controversy bolstered Adamic's popularity within much of the American Yugoslav community and beyond it. Stories about the incident focused on the Gary SNF's efforts to deny Adamic's free-speech rights and thus gave greater credence to Adamic's claims that promonarchist groups harbored fascist aspirations. After the incident, Adamic received numerous requests from various organizations to deliver lectures about the Partisans, conditions in Yugoslavia, US foreign policy, and revolutionary antifascism in general. Between May and October 1944, for example, a Slavic fraternal group from Bridgeport, Connecticut, the Philadelphia chapter of Women's International League for Peace and Freedom, and the chair of the History Department at Monmouth College were among those who invited him to speak.[102] Beyond being popular and influencing the perspectives of those who attended a speech, Adamic's views on Yugoslavia shaped scholarly opinions and military policy. Adamic was in regular contact with Samuel Hazzard Cross, the head of the Slavic Languages and Literature Program at Harvard. Denna Frank Fleming in the Political Science Department at Vanderbilt informed Adamic that he used *The Native's Return* and *My Native Land* to write his lectures, and Kimon A. Doukas, who taught international politics at Indiana University, assigned Adamic's work to help students distinguish between anti-clericalism and anti-Catholicism.[103] Adamic clearly shaped American public opinion in favor of revolutionary pluralism in many ways.

Adamic's tireless attention to detail, popularity as a writer, political connections, and temerity made him an effective leader who demonstrated the efficacy of diasporic politics. In the midst of writing pieces to explain and promote the LF, embarking on lecture tours, doing radio interviews, raising funds for Yugoslav refugees, responding to letters, and meeting with elected officials, Adamic also continued to influence how the military understood the Yugoslav situation. As previously noted, the army asked him to write a handbook on Yugoslavia, the military placed his works in their overseas libraries, and soldiers regularly corresponded with him. In addition, US Army air force private Marion E. Hutton used *Bulletin* articles and *My Native Land* as the basis for the presentation on Yugoslavia that he gave to roughly two hundred service people when explaining the current state of the war in the Balkans. Hutton viewed Adamic's work as vital "in our fight against fascism."[104] Then, in June 1944, Eugene L. R. Lanning, director of the Army Orientation Camp, wrote Adamic that Yugoslavia remained a constant source of interest for the troops and asked him to lecture on the topic.[105]

During the year 1944, Tito and the Partisans received increasingly positive press coverage in the United States. A July 20, 1944, CBS radio broadcast by US army sergeant Walter Bernstein, a correspondent for *Yank Magazine*, reported on the change. Bernstein focused on the central role Partisan women played in fighting the Germans. Most impressive to him was one female guerrilla who "had her grenades" attached "to her belt by the pins" because it saved her time since she just had to pull and throw. Then he spoke of a former Chetnik commander, Kovac Franc, who had defected to the Partisans because, as Franc put it, the Chetniks "weren't fighting for Yugoslavia. We were fighting for the enemy." He went on to explain that in the city of Šibenik, on the Dalmatian coast, he was taking "orders from the German commander-in-chief." Franc added that the Germans paid and fed his unit. Bernstein then reported that he heard stories similar to this one.[106] By the end of the broadcast, Bernstein sounded similar to Adamic. He had interviewed Tito and praised the Partisan commander for his bravery and battlefield successes. Then Bernstein concluded by recounting his visit to "the anti-Fascist Youth Congress," where he encountered wounded children. He realized that even "the kids are fighters." "Those children" wanted "a free and democratic federation of Yugoslav states after the war. . . . And when you fight for a thing, and see your friends die for a thing, you aren't going to be content with any Fascist substitute."[107] Adamic clearly influenced American perceptions of Yugoslavia. By the fall of 1944, Tito was firmly ensconced in US public opinion as the world's leading antifascist guerrilla fighter. *Time* accentuated this point and its editors put the LF leader on the cover of the October 9, 1944, issue.

Despite Adamic's popularity and Americans' growing embrace of the Partisans, Adamic continued to encounter critics determined to expose him as disloyal and thus un-American. During the Gary fight, an editorial in the *Pittsburgh Press* instructed Slavs to act like "Americans." Adamic responded by highlighting his commitment to revolutionary antifascism. He argued that "the same forces which have exploded in Yugoslavia exist throughout the world." By taking up arms to fight the fascists, "the *people* of Yugoslavia" demonstrated the power of collective will, which "forecasts greater equality and more opportunity for the *peoples* in other countries, including the United States." He went on to proclaim that the Tito-Mihailović fight "symbolizes the worldwide rift between progress and reaction." The same reactionary spirit terrorizing Europe underpins "our race riots and anti-Semitism, it underlies our dissensions over the poll and income taxes, it also underlies the vacillating contradictions in our foreign policy." Fascist success in Europe, he continued, "will strengthen reaction in the United States so much that we are apt to go fascist as a country." The Yugoslav situation should concern not only ethnic Slavs but "*all* Americans."[108] For Adamic, the same instinct for democracy that motivated immigrants, ethnics, and African Americans to battle racism and ethnocentrism encouraged the Partisans to fight for a pluralistic Yugoslavia.

The *New York Times* solidified Adamic's image as a successful diasporic leader in June when it credited him with being the primary reason that the fading YGIE recalled Fotić to London. The story proclaimed that the ambassador's dismissal resulted from "his heated disagreement" with the UCSSA "headed by Louis Adamic."[109] Obviously, Fotić had made enemies within the US government, which likely played a bigger role than confrontations with Adamic in his removal from the United States. But by constantly exposing Fotić's propaganda efforts, Adamic certainly shaped the American public's opinion about the ambassador, Mihailović, and the YGIE.

Battling South Slav American Catholics and promonarchist Serbian Americans to shape public opinion, dealing with constant harassment from redbaiters, meeting with government officials, answering letters, writing, speaking, and giving radio interviews for three years without much rest resulted in Adamic suffering a breakdown from overwork. He resigned as UCSSA president in June 1944 and significantly cut back on his duties. Despite his doctor's orders to rest, he did spend the last six months of that year engaged in relief work to aid the Partisans.

Relief and Redbaiting

Performing relief work for Adamic entailed writing letters to potential donors, speaking at fundraisers hosted by pro-Tito benefit societies, negotiating with government agents who oversaw aid distribution, battling conservative South Slav groups in the United States, and coordinating the UCSSA's aid efforts with South Slavic ethnic leaders in other countries. Dealing with government bureaucrats proved particularly onerous for Adamic and Zlatko Baloković, his successor as head of the UCSSA. Adamic and Baloković, a world-renowned concert violinist who emigrated from Croatia, had to navigate federal laws championed by anticommunists in the US Congress that justified nativist polices in the name of national security.[110] The Foreign Agents Registration Act passed in 1938 provided one example. This measure required any group working on behalf of a foreign government—including those raising relief funds—to register with the US government as a foreign agent and disclose its finances.[111]

In conjunction with Foreign Agents Registration Act, UCSSA leaders had to battle the War Relief Control Board, which the Roosevelt administration created in 1942 to streamline the seven-hundred-plus relief agencies that emerged. This board granted each ethnic group one license to distribute aid, and it expressly forbade political organizations from receiving those permits.[112] Adamic and his fellow UCSSA members believed that they could cement the Roosevelt administration's acknowledgment of Tito as Yugoslavia's political leader if they could acquire the control board's license. Adamic also built ties with the United Nations Relief and Rehabilitation Administration. The Relief and Rehabilitation Administration, the precursor to the World Health Organization, was an international organization headquartered in New York City established to coordinate and administer relief especially to politically unstable countries. The US, British, and Canadian governments provided most of the funding during its three years of existence, and its leaders worked with volunteer groups to acquire food, medicine, clothes, tools, and farm equipment. Giving to the Relief and Rehabilitation Administration allowed pro-Tito South Slavic ethnics to feel that were making a contribution to Yugoslavism.[113] The control board surprised both the UCSSA and its Serbian irredentist opponents, who also lobbied for a license, when it granted the Croatian Fraternal Union—representing those Croatian Americans seeking an independent Croatia with a democratic government—a special one-year permit to send aid to the liberated sections of Croatia. This action implied that some federal officials now saw Serbs, Slovenes, and Croats as separate groups. If the Roosevelt administration supported the break-up of Yugoslavia into small republics, Adamic and his followers argued that the chaos that already existed would grow exponentially and hopes for a democratic federation would die.[114]

In addition to the control board's refusal to allot permits to either Serbian irredentist organizations or the UCSSA, Attorney General Robert H. Jackson approved efforts to require these groups to register as agents of foreign governments. After a number of meetings with Justice Department officials, the Serbian American organizations supporting the monarchy escaped registration by agreeing to end their propaganda efforts. In contrast, the UCSSA elected to fight. Adamic insisted that the UCSSA was an "American organization" and reminded investigators that the Treasury Department issued the UCSSA a commendation for the number of war bonds it sold. But federal officials had proof that Adamic had repeatedly contacted and accepted financial support from Boris Furlan, who headed the United Committee of South Slavs in London. Furlan had been a cabinet minister in the YGIE. He and Adamic had coordinated efforts to provide aid to the government Tito established in Partisan-controlled areas of Yugoslavia. US investigators also asserted that the UCSSA acted on the behalf of a foreign power when it granted Yugoslav ministers Sava Kosanović and Ivan Šubašić honorary membership.[115] When Charlotte Slavitt, an attorney from the Justice Department, met with Adamic and Baloković, she acknowledged that the UCSSA rallied South Slavic Americans behind the war effort, but also pointed to the Furlan, Kosanović, and Šubašić examples as evidence of its acting on "behalf of a foreign principal" In a later meeting that spring, Baloković criticized the law and pointed out the absurdity of the situation at hand. The US government was supplying food and weapons to Tito to fight the Nazis. The UCSSA wanted to augment the food, medicine, and clothing that the US government was sending to Yugoslavia in order to engender a double feeling of pride by contributing to their adopted land's assistance to their native land. They wanted to make a clear display of their commitment to a version of cultural pluralism rooted in antifascism. Baloković then declared that the stigma of registering as a foreign agent would so offend the UCSSA membership that they might vote for the Republicans in November.[116]

By summer 1944, the UCSSA's future looked more promising. The Allied powers recognized Tito's Anti-Fascist Council for the National Liberation of Yugoslavia as Yugoslavia's official government, and Laurence A. Knapp became the person in charge of overseeing the registration of foreign agents. After reading that the FBI viewed Adamic as a militant antifascist but not a communist, Knapp ended the effort to force the UCSSA to register as a foreign agent. Joyce Baloković, Zlatko's wife, may have had a degree of influence over Knapp's decision. Joyce Baloković came from a powerful family whose ties to the Democratic Party allowed her to arrange a meeting with Eleanor Roosevelt. Joyce gave the first lady a memo written by Zlatko that asked why a group should register as a foreign agent for supporting "the most active fighters in Europe against the Germans."[117] In addition, the War Relief Control Board in the fall of 1944 granted the UCSSA a temporary license, as it had granted the Croatian Fraternal Union.[118]

With the permit secure, Adamic contacted Baloković with his thoughts for getting the relief campaign off the ground. Adamic stressed that the real significance of this effort rested in its symbolic value because it "will be the first tangible aid which America is sending to Yugoslavia." He recommended that UCSSA officials establish campaign committees in key areas, and include priests, governors, and mayors on those bodies. Union officials, Adamic stressed, were particularly crucial to include because of their organizing skills and the fact they likely had more South Slavs in their locals than did the UCSSA. He also proposed having an event on the ship they would use to carry the clothing, medicine, and food.[119]

In fending off the government's efforts to register the UCSSA as a foreign agent, Adamic and his followers demonstrated that antifascism still trumped anticommunism. The 1944 congressional elections in the state of Washington highlighted the point. Candidates seeking votes to win House and Senate seats knew they had to visit UCSSA-sponsored fundraisers for aid to Yugoslavia in Tacoma if they wanted South Slavic support. After attending one of these events, one UCSSA member asked Adamic whether these candidates really supported Tito or whether they were using "the name Tito just as a medium of getting votes." He assured her that the candidates she asked about backed Tito's government and also urged her to cast her ballot for Congressman Warren Magnuson now running for the Senate. Magnuson regularly spoke in favor of the Partisans and helped to convince his colleagues to vote in favor of providing aid to Tito's forces.[120]

In shaping American public opinion in favor of Tito, winning a permit to send aid to Yugoslavia, and defeating efforts by federal officials to force the UCSSA to register as a foreign agent, Adamic and his fellow leftist South Slavs demonstrated the efficacy of diasporic activism. But as the war drew to a close, an increase in anticommunist mobilization combined with the desire to assimilate expressed by both recent arrivals from Yugoslavia and established South Slavic ethnic Americans undermined Adamic's portrayal of Tito's Yugoslavia as the embodiment of antifascist resistance. A new narrative of Yugoslavia as a nation ravaged by communist debauchery began to compete with the South Slavic leftist narrative. Anti-Tito Slovene émigrés especially embraced anticommunism because it allowed them to justify their collaboration with fascists. (In 1942, Mussolini's troops had organized Slovene peasants into Village Guard units, instructing them to protect their communities from Partisan offensives. Once the Italians surrendered in September 1943, the Nazis reorganized these forces and renamed them the Home Guardsmen. Tito ordered the Home Guards shot without trial on the grounds that they had committed treason.) Like Mihailović, these expatriates claimed that throughout the war they had hoped that the United States and Britain would invade the Balkans and save them from both fascism and communism.[121]

Members of the South Slavic American community in Gary, Indiana, also revealed the diminishing efficacy of Adamic's diasporic narrative. They had embraced intercultural unity before and during the war, but in November 1945 (and then again in 1947) a significant number of Gary's South Slavic ethnics decided to protect the gains they had made rather than advance pluralism, and they played an active role in hate strikes organized to prevent African Americans from integrating the town's high schools and factories.[122]

Beyond Gary, Adamic's diasporic politics started to lose efficacy more broadly in the postwar era. On December 6, 1945, roughly three months after World War II ended, Adamic met with Harry Truman in hopes of convincing the new president to support Tito's government. Adamic claimed to represent 85 to 90 percent "of the Americans who came" from "various South-Slavic countries; perhaps 700,000 to 800,000 people" as a leader of the UCSSA. For most South Slavs in Yugoslavia and the United States, Adamic insisted, "1945 is Yugoslavia's 1776." Adamic wanted the president to recognize the staggering losses Yugoslavs suffered in order to defeat Nazism, avoid a return to the Serbian ethnocentric authoritarian monarchy, and enjoy the right to self-determination. Adamic asserted that roughly 1,685,000 Yugoslavs died since the war started, which would be the equivalent of 15 to 16 million Americans.[123] Unmoved by Adamic's pleas, Truman kept interrupting Adamic to ask his thoughts on Tito's "police government" that shoots dissenters. Adamic countered that some soldiers carried out acts of "personal vengeance" and that Tito ordered the execution of some "war criminals," but the Yugoslav people "are bent on creating a democratic country." Adamic also tried to convince Truman that the United States should help foster democracy in Yugoslavia through diplomatic relations. He added that the Yugoslav people "have to look at . . . what's possible" and "Tito offers to the Yugoslavs [what] seems best to them."[124]

Adamic continued to argue that lacking any type of democratic past, Yugoslavia's communist revolutionaries offered the only possible path toward democracy in the Balkans. Under both Austrian and Serbian rule dissenting parties faced repression and their leaders were exiled or imprisoned. Tito's army and the political party that followed represented the first real effort to forge a truly pan–South Slavic government of ethnic equals sharing power. After the war, Yugoslavism allowed South Slavic groups to carry on their languages and cultural traditions but required nationalists to abandon their commitments to Slovenian, Serbian, or Croatian independence. All Yugoslavs were expected to unite in the "common struggle to build socialism."[125] Eventually, as South Slavs embraced ethnic equality, Adamic speculated, democracy would grow in Yugoslavia.

Conclusion

The persistence of Jim Crow, Japanese internment, and race riots convinced Adamic that the Roosevelt administration and much of white America failed to commit fully to eradicating fascism. As a result, he abandoned his Two-Way Passage idea in favor of a more revolutionary approach. In general, that meant supporting various efforts to expand democracy by fomenting racial and ethnic equality. For him, such support entailed revolutionizing pluralism by adopting the leftist South Slavic diasporic narrative and advocating on behalf of Tito in the United States.

While reporting from the Yugoslav front in February 1944, Stoyan Pribichevich, a regular correspondent for *Fortune*, *Time*, and *Life* magazines, wrote his friend Adamic "that the people in the old country have full confidence in your leading role in America."[126] Later that month, Josip Smodlaka, the former mayor of the Croatian city of Split who joined the Partisan resistance after the Axis occupation began, expressed his appreciation for Adamic's success in convincing the American public to support "our National Liberation Movement." Five months later, Smodlaka let Adamic know that Tito knew all about him and reiterated that all "Jugoslavia is very much indebted to you."[127] Adamic then received a letter from Tito thanking him for his hard work on "behalf of the liberation struggle." Tito congratulated Adamic for exposing the "lie" that the Chetniks had coordinated the guerrilla resistance against the Nazis and Italians, and asked him and the UCSSA to continue assisting Partisan efforts by battling "those exiled politicians whose aim it is to restore the old past."[128] Shortly, after receiving that note, Fotić was recalled, and four months later, the Allies recognized Tito's coalition government as the official ruling body of Yugoslavia. Adamic had served as a transnational political activist championing cultural pluralism through a diasporic framing.

Unfortunately for Adamic, his diasporic narrative that called for alliances with communists to advance antifascism started to falter at war's end. Anticommunists began to succeed in reframing public discourse, as exemplified by Truman's rejection of Adamic's argument that 1945 was Yugoslavia's 1776.

4

"Peace as a World Race Problem"

The Anti-imperialist in an Anticommunist World, 1944–48

In an August 20, 1944, nationally syndicated radio debate titled "Peace as a World Race Problem," Louis Adamic asserted that global hostilities would continue after World War II ended if the United States and Britain did not abandon notions of white supremacy. At various points in the discussion, he argued that "colored" peoples throughout the world "are stirring and heaving toward self-improvement" and that "the chief danger" to their success "actually exists within the white people—within ourselves." Adamic urged the three other panelists and the audience to read "the Negro press in America." In addition to detailing the struggles of African Americans, black newspapers provided insights into black anticolonial activism in the Atlantic world and printed columns "by writers who are Chinese [and] . . . from India." Also, Japanese American newspapers devoted "a great deal of sympathetic discussion to the Negro problem." He wanted white Americans to read pieces by colonized and oppressed peoples in hopes that the white majority would recognize that stereotypes about people of color were created to justify segregation and imperialism. The behavior of the United States government and white Americans in general "toward colored groups," he argued, has "been inexcusable; it is utterly indefensible." Adamic referred to the "ridiculous" treatment of Filipinos—meaning that the United States colonized the Philippines but refused to grant Filipinos citizenship—and the absurdity of segregated training camps for black and white officers in the army as just two examples of the hypocrisy committed by a nation fighting a war against fascism on behalf of democracy.[1]

As World War II neared its end, Adamic joined other leftists in fearing that although the most extreme versions of fascism embodied by Mussolini and Hitler would be defeated, its ethic would live on through British, French, and increasingly US imperialism.[2] Adamic understood fascism as an ethos that rejected the Enlightenment and motivated a counterrevolution against the expansion of democracy. Fascists, according to Adamic, believed in racial and ethnic supremacy as well as corporate hegemony. State-sanctioned violence through both official military actions and unofficially permitting vigilante groups to carry out acts of terrorism, such as lynchings, animated fascism. A true democratic victory meant more than defeating the Axis powers; it included committing to racial and ethnic justice at home and abroad, expanding workers' rights, and establishing the right of nations to self-determination. Adamic and his fellow antifascists, who often referred to themselves as progressives because they focused on the dynamics of advancing democracy over adhering to strict ideological dictates, vowed to continue fighting fascism in the postwar years.[3]

This radio address highlighted Adamic's realization that for democracy to truly defeat fascism, racial equality had to become a reality globally. After World War II, Adamic saw the mostly black writers and activists leading the anticolonial movement as the vanguard in the fight against fascism. He had always understood Yugoslavism as part of a larger international struggle to confront those committed to ethnonational and racial hierarchies. He had persuaded leftist South Slavs, and a majority of Americans, to view Josip Broz Tito as the embodiment of antifascist resistance and to consider a foreign policy based upon nations having the right of self-determination. As he became more explicit in framing Yugoslavism in anticolonialist terms, the Yugoslav American coalition he had mobilized to promote revolutionary pluralism started to collapse under the weight of anticommunist attacks. South Slavs and other ethnics who once gravitated to Adamic's vision started to abandon pluralism for assimilation. That meant that they embraced white supremacist constructions of racial hierarchy and supported the emerging Cold War consensus in exchange for acceptance as Americans from native-born whites who once considered them permanent foreigners.

In a June 1945 interview with the *Chicago Defender*, an African American newspaper, Adamic echoed W. E. B. DuBois when he explained that a "psychological civil war" engulfed the United States in which white ethnics attacked African Americans in a number of riots as "psychological compensation for their own inferior status." By teaching children that the United States was an Anglo-Saxon country, disappearing African Americans altogether from history textbooks, and treating "new" immigrants as invaders threatening "American" culture, Adamic argued, schools set the foundation for this antidemocratic violence. Specifically, Adamic asserted that this national narrative encouraged white ethnics to adopt a *Herrenvolk* sensibility, to link being white to US citizenship, and maintaining this status meant supporting Jim Crow, nativism, and imperialism.[4]

During the 1920s and 1930s, anticolonial activists in the black world held a Leninist view of imperialism. They considered capitalist aggrandizement of wealth as the impetus for the oppression and poverty of colonized nations. The US occupation of Haiti from 1915 through 1934, and Italy's invasion of Ethiopia in 1935—acts that challenged the self-determination of the world's two leading independent black nations—spurred anticolonialists to identify national independence as their primary objective.[5] By the 1940s, anticolonial outlooks shifted as the overlapping movement of Pan-Africanism slightly privileged promoting universal rights above national liberation. Anticolonial activists pressured the newly formed United Nations to foster world peace by devising strategies to end racism while also continuing to advocate for the right of self-determination for smaller nations.[6] By the 1940s, anticolonialism became a synthesis of Marxist ideals and broader assertions for promoting a global democratic culture that grew out of cultural pluralist arguments. Adamic linked the pluralists and the anticolonialists because they shared a similar notion of democracy and a commitment to an antifascist revolution.

Unfortunately for Adamic, postwar antifascism with its focus on spreading democracy by battling racism and establishing a popular front against imperialism became less comprehensible to the American public because political possibilities had narrowed. Cold War liberalism and the anticommunism that underpinned it continuously intensified during this period, and by 1948 a majority of Americans made fear of international and domestic communism and whiteness the defining features of American identity. Advocates of Cold War liberalism eschewed the language of revolutionary change associated with Depression-era politics and instead spoke in terms of preserving democracy by protecting capitalism and defending the noncommunist world from communist aggression.[7] Such safeguarding approaches ranged from forcing non-Communist nations into agreements that undermined their autonomy, to colonialism, to war.

Anticommunists began attacking Adamic's reputation during World War II because they recognized that, in updating antifascism to include imperialism, he posed a very real threat to them. He repeatedly demonstrated that in opposing workers' rights, supporting Jim Crow policies, advocating nativism, and promoting imperialism, anticommunists shared a number of positions with fascists. At first, in 1946, he made light of red-baiters' allegations when he quipped that "one section of the Department of Justice was trying to register me as a foreign agent" devoted to advancing communist interests while the "Immigration and Naturalization service, another section for the Department of Justice, and the Treasury Department" sent "me on tours to persuade people to buy war bonds" and paid him to write "scripts for a morale-building radio show."[8] By the end of the war, anticommunist opposition to his progressive politics had grown more serious.

Anticommunists in the Justice Department, namely D. Milton Ladd—head of domestic intelligence for the Federal Bureau of Investigation (FBI)—found no humor in the contradiction Adamic pointed out. Ladd explained to J. Edgar Hoover that Adamic did not fit the stereotype of a communist apparatchik. Yet Adamic's support for Tito, now Yugoslav's communist dictator, prompted Ladd, a committed Cold Warrior, to declare Adamic a potential threat to national security. Ladd made this choice despite the fact that the United States considered Tito a tenuous ally when Ladd concluded his report in 1951. During the summer of 1948, Stalin had expelled Tito from the Soviet bloc after Tito refused to submit to Stalin's authority. After the Tito-Stalin split, Adamic confounded the bureau because, in addition to denouncing the United States and Britain for keeping fascist ideals alive through their imperialist practices, he also condemned the Russians for their "Red imperialism."[9] For Ladd and other anticommunists, Adamic's position posed a conundrum because they had long insisted that communism was a monolithic international conspiracy directed by Joseph Stalin to destroy democracy and capitalism. Ladd solved his dilemma by creating a new classification of subversive just for Adamic: "A pro-Tito Communist."[10] Ladd purposefully mischaracterized Adamic's postwar politics because the limits of Cold War thinking bounded his analysis.

If Hoover's FBI and other opponents of communism had acknowledged Adamic's framing of postwar politics in the vernacular of anti-imperialism, they would have risked engaging in debates about race, citizenship, and self-determination. Such confrontations would have undermined the hallmarks of Truman's foreign policy: the Truman Doctrine and the Marshall Plan. On March 12, 1947, Truman proposed that the United States replace Britain in funding the Greek monarchy in its civil war against communists in order to prevent an expansion of Soviet influence in the Balkans. The president used the fear of communism to establish the precedent of the United States intervening in another nation's civil war and providing large aid packages to make anticommunist governments dependent on the United States. The Marshall Plan, which began in April 1948, linked Western European nations and the United States economically through US aid packages, including loans, which allowed those countries to rebuild and modernize their industries. To get the money, a country had to agree to lower trade barriers. States associated with the communist bloc were not eligible for US aid even though most of them had helped to usher in the Allied victory that ended World War II.[11] Adamic and other antifascists opposed the Truman administration's policies because the Greek monarchists had fascist ties and they criticized the Marshall Plan for prohibiting nations such as Yugoslavia from receiving aid. Also, the Truman Doctrine and Marshall Plan disregarded the concept of self-determination.

Tracing how Adamic's marginalization as a public intellectual occurred in the postwar years provides insights into how anticommunists established control over US political culture by 1948. Adamic made one last effort to advance antifascism that year by attempting to unite communists and other leftists behind former vice president Henry Wallace's bid for the presidency. Those championing Wallace's Progressive Party never expected to win, but they hoped the campaign would reignite antifascism and offer an alternative to the developing Cold War consensus. As an anticolonialist impulse started to drive the campaign, divisions developed between communists and independent leftists, which the Tito-Stalin split exacerbated. A series of missteps by Wallace and other Progressive Party leaders and the increasing success of anticommunists in shaping public opinion meant that Adamic's gamble failed. Cold War liberalism dominated US politics for the next four decades. In addition to the rise of the Cold War consensus, communists, per Stalin's directive, reverted back to their pre–Popular Front zealotry and labeled anyone who did not adhere to the party line as a "social fascist." To Stalinists' way of thinking, anyone who did not favor the dictatorship of the proletariat sided with fascism.

Although Adamic supported Tito and criticized the Soviets as colonizers by 1948, his red-hunting rivals spent much of that year portraying him as an unassimilated immigrant loyal to a foreign government who possibly spied for Stalin (which he did not). Anticommunists also succeeded in convincing most Americans to equate fascism and communism in that both systems sanctioned totalitarian dictatorships. This discursive struggle refused to acknowledge the characteristics of fascism—organized violence, imperialism, and racism—that Adamic and other antifascists found most threatening to democracy. By successfully painting Adamic as a "red" and continuously sidestepping the Tito-Stalin split, anticommunists distorted Adamic's message. White liberals who otherwise favored his values now abandoned him because they feared anticommunist reprisals. By the late 1940s, only members of the African American press defended Adamic with any regularity.

Adamic's Anti-Imperialist Turn

When pressured to identify his politics, Adamic rejected the terms *liberal* and *leftist*, instead identifying himself as a progressive. Liberals lacked conviction, he argued, and *leftist* had become synonymous with *communist*, an ideology he had long rejected. He defined progressives as those dedicated to advancing democracy and pointed to Vice President Henry Wallace as the epitome of this outlook.[12] In 1942, Wallace proclaimed that for the previous 150 years, a people's revolution had occurred with the express goal of giving the common man a better standard of living. Beginning with the American Revolution, a "millennial and revolutionary march toward manifesting here on earth the dignity that is in every human soul" was happening. The Nazis represented the forces of counterrevolution and the Allies had to win in order for each person the world over to experience the right to self-government and aid in industrializing. Wallace's vision, which he called the "Century of the Common Man," opposed *Life* magazine publisher Henry Luce's call for the "American century," which promoted the dominance of the United States through free enterprise as the basis for remaking the world at the war's end. Luce favored a US economic imperialism. Controversially, Wallace (1944) asserted that the American and Russian revolutions had similar aims. They both wanted to better the lives of everyday people.[13] Adamic had made a similar contention in 1938 when he advocated communist revolutions in places where they fostered greater equality. By 1944, Wallace declared that destroying fascism meant more than defeating the Axis forces. It included the US government enacting greater regulations on monopolies, expanding union membership, putting an end to Jim Crow practices, embracing cultural pluralism, and engaging in a foreign policy that privileged human welfare above economic gain.[14]

Adamic could not have agreed more. In fact, he attended a conference in Havana, Cuba, in 1941 with academics, exiles escaping fascist rule, and writers from the United States, Europe, and Latin America focused on how best to advance democracy globally. W. E. B. DuBois, a featured speaker at the meeting, told a reporter that he left the gathering especially emboldened by those who shared his desire to advance a "fellowship in a new crusade, all men of every race, creed and hue, for a world movement toward . . . a democracy where every man has a voice in government, in art and in work."[15]

Adamic recognized that ushering in the world he desired meant revolutionizing the present by redefining its relationship to the past. That included challenging the idea that US history was Anglo-Saxon history, which he did in his 1945 book *Nation of Nations*. It built on his "Plymouth Rock and Ellis Island" lecture from six years earlier and contended that a misinterpretation of US history created the perception that foreigners and African Americans resided on the periphery of the nation's economic, social, cultural, and political development. Adamic insisted that these groups should be at the center of any narrative explaining the making of modern America because they built it, physically and culturally. Also, he argued that politicians' claims of favoring equality rang hollow until they passed laws to end Jim Crow and nativistic policies.[16] The black press uniformly praised it. A review in the *Chicago Defender* proclaimed that if politicians and educators would read this work, the nation "instead of leaning dangerously toward fascism" might be able to avoid instances when African Americans have to engage in community self-defense against white attackers. The reviewer went on to claim that this book revealed that white ethnics and blacks can be "allies in the struggle to secure more democracy."[17]

In March 1946, the editor of *Negro Digest* asked Adamic to write an article in which he imagined himself as African American. Adamic accepted the offer and extrapolated on his earlier writings. "Diversity," not Anglo-Saxonism, he insisted, "is the American pattern." White Americans had to remember that blacks landed "in Virginia some ten months before the Pilgrims came to Plymouth Rock." If he were a black writer, he would also call attention to moments such as the Gloucester County Conspiracy of 1663, "when Negro slaves and White indentured servants conspired together against their masters." Then he turned to the present day by insisting that this struggle for justice continued in an updated context as part of a "world-wide civil war" over "what has been called 'the march toward freedom of the common man.'" He advised readers to participate in this confrontation by being "actively interested in the race situation the world over, in the politics of Nigeria and Guatemala, Palestine and Yugoslavia, Britain and Russia, India and China."[18] He urged blacks to maintain the transnational perspective that they had adopted over the previous decade. When supporting the Ethiopian resistance to Mussolini's 1935 invasion, black Americans took to the streets of cities across the northeast and confronted profascist Italian Americans. In another instance, African Americans marched in support of Nigerian trade unionists' efforts to challenge British colonialism.[19] Adamic contended that the success of progressive politics depended on African Americans and South Slavs, as well as other ethnics, to appreciate that for democracy to succeed they had to unite in a global project against imperialism.

The next month, Adamic placed fighting imperialism at the center of his activism, joining the African American lawyer turned actor, singer, communist activist, and dedicated anticolonialist Paul Robeson on stage at a "Win-the-Peace" rally. They denounced racism, imperialism, and nuclear weapons.[20] He joined others in also aiding Harold Ickes, Franklin Roosevelt's secretary of the interior, to start the Institute of Ethnic Affairs, an organization dedicated to "achieving solutions to problems within and between white and colored races, cultural minority groups, and dependent peoples at home and abroad."[21]

Adamic's *Dinner at the White House* also appeared that year, 1946, which expressed his view that the fascist ethos underpinned imperialism. Repeating the sentiments expressed by Frederick Douglass, Ida B. Wells, and DuBois, he asserted that a "democratic foreign policy" depended on an infusion of "democracy at home."[22] After championing racial equality, Adamic contended that, by adopting an anticommunist mentality, President Truman led the United States into an "imperialist trap." By accepting the idea that the Soviets had to be contained at any cost, Truman and other US foreign-policy makers rationalized alliances with Spanish fascist Francisco Franco and China's right-wing authoritarian nationalist Chiang Kai-shek. Such associations demonstrated that anticommunists are "*not pro*-democratic. They are chiefly anti-Russian, *not pro*-American." They used the Soviet threat to justify fascist associations and the production of nuclear weapons.[23]

In addition to writing articles, speaking alongside Robeson, helping Ickes start an organization, and writing a book promoting his view of democracy, Adamic also advanced his anti-imperialist message in his newsletter *T&T*. He reprinted articles and editorials from African American newspapers critical of British colonialism in India and South Africa, and he promoted works such as Nigerian nationalist Mbonu Ojike's *My Africa*, which challenged Western notions that African cultures are inferior and attacked colonialism as antithetical to democracy. He also printed his own pieces championing self-determination.[24]

Yugoslavia and American Anticommunism

By the fall of 1946, Adamic worried that by encouraging widespread fears of communism and playing on the citizenry's general ignorance about the Soviet Union, President Truman would unwittingly allow the reactionary forces in the United States to bring a fascist US state to fruition. Adamic explained in *T&T* that the war hawks in Truman's administration easily manipulated the president because Truman did not fully comprehend international relations. Generals, politicians, and journalists misrepresented the aims and behaviors of the Russians and other communists in order to inflate military budgets, play on public fears to expand their influence in Congress, and to sell newspapers.[25] He then pointed out that "using the mask of patriotism" to "inflame the public" created "the atmosphere in which" quasi-fascist organizations such as the Ku Klux Klan are strengthened, reactionary outlooks are presented as mainstream, and those who embodied the promise of antifascism are viewed as subversives.[26] Having a "hack politician" who did not comprehend the "deep-down facts in the Tito-Mikhailovich [Mihailović] matter, the Russian Revolution, the Negro stirrings here, or the upheaval in China" posed a threat to the larger aims antifascists had been fighting for since 1930s.[27]

Truman and other anticommunists demonstrated that Adamic's ability to sway public opinion had clearly declined. Three events in Tito's Yugoslavia—the trial and execution of Draža Mihailović, the imprisonment of Croatian archbishop Aloysius Stepinac, and Yugoslavia's shooting down of two US surveillance planes—demonstrated how anticommunists mobilized support for their position and undermined Adamic's portrayal of Tito as an antifascist hero.

On March 13, 1946, Tito's army captured Chetnik leader Draža Mihailović in a mountain cave and charged him with treason. The Military Council of the Supreme Court of the Federal People's Republic of Yugoslavia set June 10 as the opening day for the Serbian general's trial. Two groups emerged in the United States and shaped public opinion negatively toward Tito's new government. The Committee for a Fair Trial for Draža Mihailović—which included liberals such as John Dewey, Ray Brock (a supporter of the Serbian monarchy and former *New York Times* journalist), and George Creel, the leader of the Wilson administration's propaganda efforts during World War I. They called on Tito to recognize that Mihailović had aided the Allies during the war. A group of US airmen the Chetniks had rescued demanded that they be permitted to go to Belgrade and testify on Mihailović's behalf. Tito consented to include a transcript of their sworn testimony as evidence but refused to allow the airmen to appear in court. Finding Tito's compromise an empty gesture, renowned lawyer and civil libertarian Arthur Garfield Hayes chaired an unofficial commission that held a public hearing in the United States on the Mihailović case. Hayes's commission, after questioning a series of pro-Mihailović witnesses, ruled that no evidence was offered "to show any collaboration between" Mihailović "and the Axis powers." The *Washington*

Post then declared that the mock trial "rendered a real public service" and the next day insisted that Tito give "the Bolivar of the Balkans" a fair trial. In a purposeful act of forgetting, a *Post* reporter then mused that during the war for "reasons never wholly explained, Russia and Britain swung their support" away from Mihailović and to Tito. The story failed to acknowledge that the United States had joined the other Allies in aiding the Partisans. The piece concluded by describing the Chetniks' intrepid struggles against the Nazis in 1941. Other dailies across the country similarly took up Mihailović's plight.[28]

The soberest reporting on the case came from Andre Martin in New York's *Socialist Call*. The left anticommunist reporter pointed out that because Tito is Mihailović's "deadly enemy," the growing cadre of Cold Warriors "has made this general a saint of democracy." Martin then acknowledged that Mihailović's trial resembled a Moscow show trial. Mihailović did rescue US airmen and at one point had fought the Germans. "But," Martin added, those realities do "not exclude the fact that at times he made" deals with "the Nazis against the Partisans," and that he fought Tito's troops "with at least the same cruelty as they used against him." Martin reminded readers that Mihailović was a monarchist, not a champion of democracy.[29] By this point, too many Americans were incapable of distinguishing communists from socialists and too few people were reading the *Call* for Martin's column to challenge the emerging anticommunist consensus.

As the American press attempted to venerate Mihailović, Adamic appeared less engaged with the story than his supporters and critics may have expected. He suffered from exhaustion due to overwork. As a result, he limited his writing and activism. Adamic blamed his successor as head of the United Committee of South Slavic Americans Zlatko Baloković for not raising enough money to maintain relief work and fund the organization's political activities.[30] Referring to Baloković, Adamic wrote a fellow South Slav leftist that "I'm personally through with the bastard, and would like nothing better than to be through with being in the organizations of which he is president."[31] Adamic no longer employed the South Slav diasporic narrative to mobilize antifascist activism, but he continued to use Yugoslavia as an example of democracy's advance globally in the fight against fascism.

As events in Tito's Yugoslavia remained on the front pages of American newspapers, Adamic found fewer Americans willing to consider his point of view. Yugoslav fighter planes forced a reported US cargo transport to land near Ljubljana on August 9 and arrested the crew. Yugoslav officials argued that it was a spy plane. Such encroachments occurred regularly and the Yugoslav government had repeatedly warned US officials to end such flights. The Truman administration criticized the attack and insisted that bad weather had caused the pilot to deviate off course. Ten days later, the American media reported that Yugoslav fighter jets shot down a US military transport plane headed to Vienna. This time the US personnel aboard died. The US State Department demanded the release of the crew from the first plane. Tito complied, but Yugoslav vice premier Edvard Kardelj made it clear to Secretary of State James Byrnes that despite the US "outrage" over these attacks, the Yugoslav government considered the United States fully responsible because of the Truman administration's blatant disregard for Yugoslav sovereignty.[32]

In addition to depicting Mihailović as a democrat and presenting Tito as a despot for shooting down US transport planes, anticommunists turned to the case of Croatian archbishop Aloysius Stepinac in October 1946 to further illustrate the evils of Yugoslav communism. Yugoslav officials arrested Stepinac as a war criminal, charging him with aiding in Croatian fascist dictator Ante Pavelić's mass-murder program intended to create a "pure" Croatia by removing all Serbs, Jews, and gypsies. On April 17, 1941, one day after Yugoslavia's formal surrender to the Axis powers, the Germans allowed Croatian fascists, the Ustaša, to establish the Independent State of Croatia (Nezavisna Država Hrvatska, NDH). Although the Ustaša supported Nazi anti-Semitic laws and practices, such as forced labor, they made Orthodox Serbs their chief target. Of the 1.9 million Serbs living in Croatia in the spring of 1941, Pavelić's government deported one-third of them, converted, or "Croatianized," another third to Catholicism, and murdered the remaining third.[33]

Stepinac did support the NDH at its inception and he clearly embraced its message of Croatian nationalism. By May 1942, however, he opposed the law forcing Jews to wear identity badges, and he requested that Pavelić release imprisoned Orthodox Church members. When his discreet protests went ignored, he criticized Ustaša procedures in his sermons. By October 1943, he condemned the genocidal policies of the NDH. At first glance, Stepinac went from a collaborationist to a reluctant critic to a vocal opponent of the Ustaša. But, as Adamic and subsequent historians pointed out, Stepinac had control over the Catholic Church's official positions throughout Croatia. Catholic newspapers never critiqued Pavelić's government, and clerics supplied most of the Ustaša's propaganda. They considered Catholicism a central characteristic of Croatian nationalism and declared Serbs, Jews, Freemasons, and communists as the principal threats to their nation.[34]

When the communists came to power in 1945, Stepinac assembled a conference of bishops that condemned the communists for killing priests and nuns during the war. The bishops asked for the release of clergy held as war criminals and demanded the return of all confiscated church property. Tito responded by trying to convince the archbishop to sever relations with Rome and create a Yugoslav Catholic Church. When that failed, Tito requested that Vatican officials recall Stepinac to Rome. The pope refused and, seeing no other option, Yugoslav authorities arrested Stepinac for collaboration with the fascists on September 18, 1946. On October 11, the Yugoslav supreme court found him guilty of treason. Tito offered Stepinac one last chance to leave the country, but the archbishop preferred to serve as an instrument of Catholic propaganda. Punishment was never Tito's objective, as evidenced by the fact that Stepinac never had to do hard labor, and he had his own double cell. In 1951, Tito commuted the archbishop's sentence, released him from prison, and required him to remain in his home village.[35]

In the United States, the Catholic hierarchy united with anticommunists to present Stepinac as a victim of godless communism. By late October, the leading dailies rebuked the Yugoslav government. For instance, Cleveland's *Plain Dealer* reprinted Cardinal Francis Spellman's speech declaring that the world had descended into chaos because of the "atheistic Communists" who jailed Stepinac and the "thousands" of other "martyrs of every faith whom corrupt, ruthless dictators daily betray and befoul as they wield poisoned power."[36] No mention of Pavelić or the NDH appeared in the story. By November, Secretary of State Byrnes asserted that the US government would continue to pressure Tito to free Stepinac.[37]

It is interesting that South Slavic American newspapers, except for the staunchly Catholic periodicals, either avoided covering the case or voiced strong opposition to Stepinac because they agreed that he was a war criminal. A researcher for the Common Council for American Unity noted that even the "anti-Tito faction of Serb nationalists is also anti-Croat" because they viewed the Croats as Ustaša "traitors" guilty of massacring "the Serb population of Croatia."[38] Anticommunists had not convinced the South Slav American community to join them, but they did slow activism by mobilizing public opinion through focusing on events in Yugoslavia.

The Eclipse of Antifascism

By early 1947, Adamic dedicated himself to merging antifascists into an anti-imperial consensus by targeting anticommunists as the enemies of progressivism and making references to a global struggle for democracy. He reiterated his 1934 contention that "real" democracy existed only when a citizenry is committed to advancing racial and ethnic equality, and then he challenged tolerance, the watered-down version of pluralism that pundits and many politicians supported after the war. Writers, "preachers, and politicians" have promoted tolerance as "a great virtue," but tolerance, he contended, "is a thin veneer for *in*tolerance." Actual democracy operated when those of different racial and religious backgrounds interacted in schools, factories, and neighborhoods and recognized that they shared the same rights and collective responsibility to solve society's ills. White Americans needed to realize that African Americans and the "colored world" remained intrigued with the Soviet experiment because of the contrast between the Russians' call for an end to prejudice with the perpetuation of "British racism" by "the 'so-called Anglo-Saxon democracies.'"[39] Anticommunists, he asserted, should stop portraying immigrants, ethnics, and African Americans who pointed to the Soviets when making arguments in favor of greater equality as traitors loyal to a foreign government and instead ask why some people living in the United States looked to a dictatorship for lessons on democracy. Adamic presented versions of this message in lectures he gave and in articles appearing in *Negro Digest*, *McCall's Magazine*, and his newsletter *T&T* over the next four years.

Adamic's anticommunist opponents ignored his attacks on various forms of racism and ethnocentrism after the war and concentrated only on his support for the new Yugoslavia. They depicted him as Tito's "stooge" and accused him of seeking to Sovietize the United States. During the first three months of 1947, he went on a lecture tour to "correct" what his audiences had "been reading in the papers and hearing on the radio" about his advocacy of communism. He explained that in the ongoing global "contest between Revolution and Counter-Revolution," between democracy and fascism, anticommunists advanced the fascist ethic because of their commitments to corporate hegemony, segregation, xenophobia, and a foreign policy borrowed from the British that promoted imperialism. Adamic acknowledged that his "special interest in Yugoslavia" resulted from being born in Slovenia, but he added that his homeland represented just one flashpoint on "today's revolutionary" landscape that included "Spain, Indo-China, India, Palestine, Brazil, Bolivia, Greece, Russia, [and] China."[40] Studying Yugoslavia allowed him to recognize how "the larger European process," colonialism, operated, and thus alerted him to the larger "world picture, which I see . . . as a contest between Revolution and Counter-revolution." The forces of counterrevolution proclaimed that communists and democrats were now engaged in a struggle between totalitarianism and freedom. At that moment, Cold Warriors insisted that maintaining freedom meant preventing Greece and China from going communist and stopping Russia and Yugoslavia from spreading their influence.[41]

In this and subsequent speeches, Adamic insisted that Cold War liberals' antidemocratic foreign policy, as designed by the Truman administration, was not only "taking us" into "World War III," but forsaking America's democratic pretense by following "Winston Churchill, the wily chief ideologist of imperialism." Adamic's critics and recent scholars considered such declarations evidence that Adamic allowed his animus toward Churchill and the British to cloud his judgment. Churchill had sued Adamic for libel in 1946 for the disparaging way Adamic characterized him in *Dinner at the White House.* Adamic's and Churchill's lawyers settled the case on January 14, 1947.[42]

Unlike reporters for the leading daily periodicals, P. L. (Percival Leroy) Prattis, Adamic's friend and writer for the African American newspaper *Pittsburgh Courier*, understood that Adamic had not developed Anglophobia. Rather, Prattis noted, *Dinner at the White House* was an attack on colonialism, and he pointed out that Adamic's recollection of events included President Roosevelt's criticism of Churchill: for "every one dollar the British had put in some African colonies, they had taken out ten." Prattis concluded that Adamic had demonstrated that Churchill was "not, nor ever has been, the man to help build a peaceful world." Prattis added that Churchill's most recent speech in Fulton, Missouri—his declaration that the Soviets erected an iron curtain from the Baltic to the Adriatic, which many scholars cite as the official start of the Cold War—supported Adamic's assertion that anticommunists were not champions of democracy but instead imperialists and racists.[43]

Aside from Prattis and other black journalists, Adamic had few supporters for his postwar antifascist politics. Most white reporters and later historians accepted the idea that his anti-Churchill animus or Anglophobia guided his critiques. These detractors ignored the fact that he regularly promoted Jawaharlal Nehru's *Discovery of India* in his writings and speeches. At that moment, Nehru led India's independence movement and then became that nation's first prime minister. Adamic typically reprinted articles from black newspapers about Nehru in his newsletter *T&T.*[44] During his 1947 lecture tour, Adamic juxtaposed discussions of events in Yugoslavia with celebrating India's drive for independence, opposing the segregationist practices of the Union of South Africa's prime minister Jan C. Smuts, and exposing fascist collaborators within the Greek monarchy.[45]

In addition to arguing that imperialism kept the fascist ethos alive and thereby denied the advance of democracy globally, Adamic also pointed out that anticommunists made the general public more susceptible to fascism by ratcheting up fears over communism. He insisted that in equating happiness with wealth, Americans never found satisfaction with their lives because they always needed to earn more money to consume more goods. Seeking fulfillment through unrestrained materialism deprived Americans of their humanity. To succeed, the average white American man "had to keep on the good side of all kinds of people," which fostered resentment toward those "who are in position to keep him from advancing." As a result, the typical white male projected his anger on others: "he hates Russia, the Jews, the Negroes; he hates the Slavs, the Reds, and all the other scapegoats that are invented for him to hate; and, sure, he's all for being 'tough' or 'firm,' and he's playing with the idea of joining the KKK," or some other reactionary group.[46] This fear and anger enlivened the fascist ethic and, according to Adamic, groups "who feel differently about our relations with the Russians" must help our neighbors reject the claims of red hunters.[47]

During this and a similar speech he had given, Adamic also pointed out Russian distortions of the United States. He was not advocating communism; he was trying to stop the spread of fascism by calling for a nuanced foreign policy and a revival of leftist politics animated by the masses' greatest hopes. Americans had to recognize that they were "ruled by a coalition of southern poll-tax reactionaries who call themselves Democrats and northern and Midwestern Republicans." To "rule" instead of "govern," this coalition of proto-fascists counted on the fact that "the people of the United States have next to nothing to do with the development of important public policy."[48]

Adamic then brought his speech back to foreign policy and articulated the links between imperialism, fascism, and anticolonialism. In recovering from the destruction of war, Britain could no "longer run the counter-revolution" and thus counted on the United States to "take over that job in Greece." Specifically, "Truman wants us to arm the fascist Greek army headed by King George . . . whom the British forcibly returned to Greece to fight the liberation army of the Greek people." Adamic speculated that "our American imperialist crowd already has immense interest in Middle Eastern oil. So it needs a military base and it thinks Greece will do." Truman, Adamic contended, "transforms the cause of Texas Oil Co. into a problem of our national interest, and he wants some hundreds of millions of dollars to arm the Greek fascists so they can try to kill off the upheaval of the Greek people, which is the same sort of upheaval that we tried to help Chiang Kai-shek kill off in China." Supporting the fascists in Greece, according to Adamic, meant that the Truman administration's "motives are counter-revolutionary" in that the president placed the interests of the oil companies above the advance of democracy for the "industrially underdeveloped peoples" who "want to get their resources out of the clutches of imperialism and begin to develop their industries in their own way."[49] The "get-tough-with-Russia policy" sought to confuse the "workingman" so "that he will not begin to see that his lot in America is related to the problems of peoples all over the world who are beginning to stir politically intent on improving their lot." The United States and the USSR had to "disentangle ourselves from the current tension" fueled by "a web of lies and fear—fear that distorts everything. And one of the chief factors, perhaps the chief factor, in all this is our 'tough' foreign policy which, again, isn't ours" but designed by the British and other corporate interests dictating to Truman.[50]

Anticommunism disguised US imperialism, he argued. It undermined US claims of being democratic and advanced fascism by committing the United States to racism and militarism. Adamic told those who gathered to hear him in 1947 not to "keep the dissent to yourself," not to allow the howl of anticommunists to succeed in "silencing you." When "these people get after you," do not doubt yourself. They belong to "the sick side of our society" that does not want the rest of the nation to recognize the absurdity "of spending 13 billion dollars a year for preparation for the next war" and promoting totalitarianism. The red-baiters, not those promoting antifascism, operated "subversively and aggressively in our national and international politics" because they championed imperialism and with it fascism. Opposing anticommunism meant advocating an authentic version of democracy.[51]

Adamic's militancy in the face of growing anticommunist attacks inspired other antifascists and they turned to him for reassurance and help. In May, for instance, journalist and editor Don Matchan wrote to Adamic and explained that he had started a newspaper, the *Valley City Times-Record,* in his little North Dakota town. By all accounts, Matchan did an excellent job of covering local government affairs and other community concerns. His circulation grew from 3,378 to 3,800 subscriptions in a town of 6,000 people. But he supported New Deal policies such as "farm cooperatives, [the] Missouri Valley Authority, price control[s], and Federal health insurance." Worse still in the minds of the businessmen in his town, Matchan had backed striking telephone workers and denounced the Truman Doctrine.[52] The business community labeled Matchan a communist because of his editorials and joined together to start a new paper. Both *Newsweek* and *Time* covered his story, but the Valley City conservatives refused to relent under national scrutiny.

By July, Matchan wrote, his paper would cease publication.[53] Adamic received similar letters and printed some of them in *T&T* in hopes of exposing businessmen's anticommunism as camouflage for their hatred of unions, uncritical embrace of free-market ideology, and oversimplified acceptance of a Manichean foreign policy.

As attacks mounted on both him and his fellow antifascists, Adamic became more strident in equating anticommunists with fascists. He went on another lecture tour from October through December to articulate this message. In November and December he shared stages with Robeson. At these engagements, Adamic contended that the "Negro-White situation here now is part of the color and colonial question in the world. We will not contribute to their solution if the American Negro remains, at best, a second-class citizen, forced to live in ghettoes and pick up the crumbs falling off the white man's table." The "counter-revolutionary efforts," Adamic's phrase for actions he considered guided by the fascist ethos, "directed from Washington at countries in Europe or Asia or Africa or Latin America *are tied up with the same sort of moves on the part of our counter-revolutionaries, our anti-equalitarians, at home*. . . . They spell WAR—several kinds of war."[54]

Adamic then directly tied racism and colonialism to anticommunism by attacking members of Truman's administration. He asserted that it was "no accident that Bernie Baruch [an adviser to Truman], Jimmy Byrnes [secretary of state], and Tom Connally [senator]—all three southerners, all three on record as racists—are three of the most important figures among the initiators of the United States' so-called 'tough policy' against the Soviet Union." Adamic found it no "accident that our white-supremacy politicians find" Winston Churchill and Jan Christian Smuts "natural" allies, for Churchill and Smuts are "the two greatest living champions of imperial colonialism." He concluded that "colored peoples here and in Asia, Africa and Latin America know this; so do white leaders of Russia and of countries in the Soviet orbit. But we Americans, as a people, are largely unaware of the significance of this important 'tough-policy' combination as it operates at home and abroad."[55]

By November, Adamic's words grew sharper. He told audiences that the House Committee on Un-American Activities (HUAC) would have investigated Jefferson and Lincoln for their radical ideas if they were alive today. Adamic then asserted that, by embracing a reactionary anticommunist vision, Truman and his administration, most of the commercial press, Churchill, Smuts, Chiang, Roxas of the Philippines, and de Gaulle of France forged a "counterrevolutionary international" combination. This "conspiracy disguised as patriotism" posed a great danger because it controlled atom bombs and shaped the media. He urged the crowds to reject fear by striving for world peace, industrial democracy, anticolonialism, and racial equality. He hammered home his point about racial equality by proclaiming that it "doesn't surprise me that many American Negro leaders and newspapers are recently becoming deeply interested in the colonial struggles between need and greed in Africa." If "the so-called 'Anglo-Saxon democracies' persist in their lack of democracy in the attitude toward the colored world, the colored world is bound to go fiercely pro-Soviet and Communist, if for no other reason, as a reaction against our and British racism; which will but further sharpen the tension between U.S.A. and U.S.S.R.; which, in turn, will increase the already too high likelihood of World War III."[56] Adamic long claimed that his antifascism resulted from blending his commitment to democracy with his acceptance of world political dynamics at the moment. Frequently, federal officials labeled him idealistic. He proclaimed himself a pragmatist and insisted that equality and peace seemed to be in his audience's own self-interest in order to avoid national and international tumult.

Adamic's confrontational approach failed to slow the decline of antifascism. He wrote his friend and fellow Tito supporter Janko Rogelj that in visiting Pittsburgh, Pennsylvania, and Manchester, New Hampshire, the last two cities on his October through December lecture tour, he faced "very rough" crowds. "The country is going nuts with hysteria. In Manchester, the Catholic bishop, the American Legion (of which I am a member!) and the Catholic Trade Union Alliance denounced me and the organization which engaged me." Then in "Pittsburgh the Press published 16 articles before Paul Robeson and I spoke. I think we're headed for something that won't be any good."[57] Adamic then reiterated to Rogelj that the current anticommunist "hysteria" he had just witnessed had spawned an American-style fascism.

With his speaking tours failing to generate the excitement that they had for pluralism during the 1930s, or for Tito and Yugoslavism during World War II, Adamic realized he had to find a different way to advance antifascism and anticolonialism. He determined that former vice president Henry Wallace's third-party bid for the presidency offered him the chance to reenergize the antifascist mood that dominated US politics from the mid-1930s through 1945. Adamic understood that Wallace and other Progressive Party candidates had little chance of winning. But establishing Progressive clubs and then keeping the members of those organizations united after the November election could lead to a reinvigorated left unafraid to confront anticommunists and dedicated to racial and ethnic equality, industrial democracy, and anticolonialism.

Reds, Red-Hunters, and Wallace

Wallace laid the foundation for the Progressive Party in a September 1946 speech at Madison Square Garden, where he asserted that peace should be the guiding principle for domestic and foreign relations. Domestically, peace meant challenging race hatred by enacting measures that undermined Jim Crow. Embracing peace in terms of international relations included negotiating with the Russians, agreeing to arms controls, challenging America's British allies to surrender their colonies, and allowing the peoples of Latin America, Asia, and Africa the right of self-determination. At that moment, Wallace served in the Truman administration as secretary of commerce. His views clashed with most of the president's positions and aligned with those on the left—ranging from New Deal liberals to communists—who believed that tensions with the Soviets would cause World War III. In a telling incident, Wallace elicited boos during his speech from communists in the crowd when he declared that promoting peace also included recognizing that "invasions" helped define "Russian character." Wallace promoted an honest dialogue between the United States and the USSR, not a "get tough with Russia" policy that would lead to the Soviets responding in kind. The next day, Truman demanded and received Wallace's resignation.[58]

From the end of 1946 through the spring of 1948, Wallace called for "peace and abundance," which harkened back to his 1942 appeal for a "century of the common man." His activism inspired leftists of all stripes whose politics had been forged by antifascism during the 1930s. For many on the American left in 1947, Wallace appeared a viable alternative to the Republicans and Democrats who both championed Cold War liberalism and animated the politics of fear, not to mention the reactionary Dixiecrat Party led by Strom Thurmond. In March 1948, architects of the New Deal, union leaders, champions of ethnic rights (especially from Slavic American organizations), NAACP activists, and CPUSA militants gathered in York, Pennsylvania, and formed the Progressive Party. They vowed to fight for racial and ethnic equality, labor rights, anticolonialism, and world peace.[59]

Adamic, who had long corresponded with Wallace and embraced his vision of the "Century of the Common Man," took to the campaign trail for the former vice president immediately, even though Wallace would not officially receive the party's nomination until July. After giving a speech in Northampton, Pennsylvania, in late April 1948, Adamic woke up the next morning to discover that Argues Begany, a Catholic priest, had denounced him as a communist agitator in the local paper, the *Cement News*. Adamic responded by challenging the tactics of anticommunist fear mongers, and then, as he had done many times before, pointed out the church's ties to fascism. Adamic chided Begany for trying to "give the impression that my background, views and activities are a deep, dark secret which I am carefully concealing" when instead they are clearly stated in the public record. True to his advice that one must adamantly confront anticommunist assertions, Adamic insisted that if anyone should explain himself it should be Begany. The priest belonged to the National Catholic Welfare Council, which Adamic claimed "is the central propaganda and pressure agency of the Roman Catholic Hierarchy in the U.S." That meant that it "is the agency here of a foreign state, the Vatican, whose main purpose for some years back has been, and is right now, a Counter-Reformation in the United States which will destroy this country's traditional character." Adamic then proclaimed that the Vatican was as "corrupt as any power in the world" and its leaders, including Pope Pius XII and New York's archbishop, Cardinal Francis Spellman, are just "high-level politicians operating in the world arena, reaching out for absolute power" because fascism animated their actions. They want a "Catholic empire which straddles the world from Italy through a DeGaullist France, a Franco Spain, a Salazar Portugal, a corporate Latin American, down to what has already become a clerical fascist Philippines."[60] As he had done in nearly all his attacks on Catholic officials, Adamic made a distinction between Catholicism as a religion, the faith he was raised in, and church leaders who manipulated the faithful to advance their political influence. Adamic concluded that they have "long been publicizing me as a 'Communist'" to deflect from their anti-Americanism. Adamic claimed that they opposed him "because I oppose anti-semitism and do not like people who hate Negroes. Because I am for Wallace. Because I am for people's governments wherever they exist. Because I know and say that most of the anti-Soviet and anti-Tito publicity in this country is a lie. Because I insist that Archbishop Stepinac is one of the worst war criminals of World War II in spite of the fact that the American Catholic Hierarchy chooses to glorify him. . . . Because I demand that those using the words 'Communist' and 'Communism' define them. And, above all else, because I don't want to see another war and the destruction of either the United States or the Soviet Union, to say nothing of the rest of the world."[61] Unfortunately for Adamic, his exchange with Begany marked an intensification of attacks by anticommunists against him and the Wallace campaign.

By serving on the Progressive Party's platform committee, Adamic helped to articulate the antifascist and anticolonial message he had been championing. Although he was just one of many platform authors—including Robeson, labor lawyer Lee Pressman, and economist and New Deal policymaker Rexford Tugwell—the section dealing with colonialized peoples repeated significant amounts of text that he had previously published in *T&T*.[62] Titled *Peace, Freedom and Abundance*, the Progressives' platform began by citing Franklin Roosevelt's assertion that when corporate power "becomes stronger" than the "democratic state," then "fascism" has arrived. It promised that a Wallace presidency would upend Jim Crow, encourage freedom of speech by removing loyalty oaths, promote unionization by repealing the Taft-Hartley Act, provide more government housing, enact rent controls, expand social security, and establish national health insurance. In regard to the international scene, Progressives promised to negotiate with the Soviets for arms control, advocate for world law, strengthen the UN, repudiate the Truman Doctrine, repeal the Displaced Persons Act of 1948, "which permits the entry into the United States of fascists and collaborators," and end intervention in China, Greece, Turkey, the Middle East, and Latin America. In addition, a Wallace administration would sever relations with Franco's Spain, cancel the Marshall Plan, and destroy existing atomic bombs. The platform committee also included a section on anticolonialism that condemned "the bipartisan policy of military and economic intervention to crush" the independence movements of "the peoples of Asia," which meant the "cessation of financial and military aid to the Chiang Kai-shek dictatorship." In emphasizing their commitment to abiding by the principle of self-determination, Progressives promised independence for Puerto Rico, the "abrogation" of "unequal trade treaties" with the Philippines and other "economically weaker peoples." Overall, they wanted the United States to work with other countries and the United Nations "to abolish the colonial system in all its forms and to realize the principle of self-determination for the peoples of Africa, Asia, the West Indies, and other colonial areas."[63]

Shortly after helping to author this aspirational document, Adamic started to fear that the Progressive Party would fail to revitalize antifascism. Internal fighting between independent leftists and communists became fierce, and red-baiting by the party's opponents reached new heights. CPUSA activists did not join the Wallace campaign with the intention of forging a united front of leftists, as noncommunists had hoped. They saw the Wallace movement as a vehicle to challenge the US anti-Soviet foreign policy. Communists won or coopted most of the leadership positions in state organizations and in the national campaign office. Their intransigence led most New Deal liberals and noncommunist radicals to abandon the campaign just as election season started to climax.[64] For instance, Thomas R. Amlie, an independent leftist working for Wallace's campaign in Wisconsin, wrote Adamic that as of "now, the Wallace movement in Wisconsin is generally considered to be 100% C.P. controlled." Those opposed to Stalinism stopped volunteering their time for the Progressives. Amlie believed that Wallace can get a "big vote next November, but he will have to demonstrate to people that he is entirely independent" from the CPUSA.[65] Adamic agreed.

That month, Adamic met with Wallace and asked him to expel CPUSA members from the Progressive Party. Adamic contended that the communists were destroying any chance to create an effective American left that would confront colonialism, segregation, and corporate control of the economy based on appeals to universal notions of liberty. Cold War liberalism and the politics of fear that emanated from it would go largely unchecked because the election results would extinguish the noncommunist left's willingness to maintain a progressive movement. Wallace disregarded Adamic's warnings.[66] Despite his disappointment at Wallace's decision, Adamic remained with the campaign because by the summer of 1948 he concluded that noncommunist antifascists had no other options. He now hoped that Wallace could somehow garner enough votes to sustain the fledging movement.

To aid Wallace at the polls, Adamic displayed the same temerity with which he propelled the South Slavic diaspora forward during World War II. He answered letters, wrote editorials, gave speeches, raised funds, and, in general, worked tirelessly on Wallace's behalf. Adamic's friend Nina Dexter, from Encino, California, wrote him after she had donated $5,000 to the campaign. She gave such a large sum because "there is nothing ahead for any of us if the progressive forces" do not stop "the advance of reaction and Fascism in this country."[67] Dexter abhorred Truman's Cold War liberalism. She wanted Americans to return to the "kind of Democracy which will stop this madness and the stupid attitude which is being taken by the present administration of an anti-Communist crusade."[68]

Progressives had witnessed Adamic succeed in convincing the majority of Americans to embrace Tito during World War II and play a vital role in advancing pluralism during the Depression. They expected him to be just as effective in gathering support for Wallace. But in addition to the social, political, and cultural dynamics changing drastically in the postwar period, divisions between Stalin and Tito further strained the already tenuous relationship between independent leftists and CPUSA activists within the progressive movement.

Immediately after World War II, the Soviets had refused to support Tito's claim to Trieste, and then they spurned the Greek Partisans' request for aid in fighting the monarchy. Tito favored Greek self-determination and even envisioned a communist Greece uniting with Yugoslavia in a Balkan federation. In an effort to calm tensions with the United States and Britain, Stalin agreed to back away from Greece. Although dissatisfied about Trieste and Greece, Tito remained loyal to Stalin. Then the Soviets attempted to control Yugoslavia's economy and military. By 1948, Stalin called for the creation of the Cominform, an organization that would coordinate actions between communist nations, and he announced his intention to locate it in Belgrade. Western powers pointed to this decision as evidence that Stalin and Tito remained close despite reported tensions. In reality, this was Stalin's attempt to place agents in Yugoslavia to pressure Tito to accept Soviet direction. When Tito opposed the effort to house the Cominform in Belgrade, Stalin expelled Yugoslavia from the Cominform in June 1948.[69]

After the Tito-Stalin split, the CPUSA encouraged South Slavic American communists to make statements "supporting the Cominform on its stand on Yugoslavia, especially since Louis Adamic" supported Tito. An FBI informant reported his July 21, 1948, conversation with the Croatian-born CPUSA official Steve Nelson. Nelson chaired "the Nationality Groups" section of the party. In his memoir, Nelson stated that, after hearing the Soviet version of Stalin's break with Tito, he and his fellow communists "reacted quite automatically in support of the Soviet position" and "felt obliged to ruthlessly attack the Titoist position, and I carried the ball among the Yugoslav members of the Party." At the time, Nelson condemned Tito as turning "reactionary" and seduced by the West.[70] He acknowledged that his opposition to Tito "must have been a difficult thing for some of these immigrant workers to accept." They grew up in "a bitterly poor" Yugoslavia defined by a "semifeudal collection of hostile ethnic groups." Tito changed that by fighting "the Nazis and the native fascists, but he now seemed to be successfully building a modern socialist nation." Nelson noted his regret that he and his fellow communists unquestioningly followed party dictates and had put their trust in Stalin ahead of their Yugoslavism. They came to realize that in reality Tito had refused to become Stalin's puppet.[71]

Tensions between Adamic and the communists came out in the open during the Progressive Party's July 1948 convention, when one delegate rose and offered a resolution to the platform supporting "self-determination for the Macedonian people." Macedonia served as a stronghold for the Greek

Partisans. The plank supported Tito's position of expanding communism in the Balkans. With few delegates in attendance at that moment, the amended position passed without notice. CPUSA members first recognized the anti-Stalinist plank after the official program had been printed. Agitated communists then held an emergency session to revise the platform, after which they grabbed pens and programs and scratched out the offending plank. Wallace's communist-affiliated campaign managers turned to Adamic as the leading voice of noncommunist Slavic Americans to restore unity. A pained Adamic took the stage and uncharacteristically delivered a rambling speech that offered little clarity on the issue of the Progressive Party's position on aid for the Greek Partisans. After the convention, he and CPUSA-controlled organizations distanced themselves from each other.[72]

When the Progressive Party convention ended, Adamic's problems compounded. Not only was he fighting a losing battle for control over the Progressive's message and future, anticommunists now accelerated their smear campaigns against him. HUAC started espionage hearings. On August 4, papers across the country reported that "author Louis Adamic and foreign-affairs expert Alger Hiss" were two "of the most prominent persons named in the current congressional investigations of asserted Communist espionage." Both men claimed that HUAC targeted them because of their involvement in Wallace's campaign.[73]

During these hearings, the "blond spy queen" Elizabeth Bentley, who had functioned as a courier for the leading Soviet intelligence-gathering network in the United States, claimed that Adamic had passed on secret information to a Moscow agent. Louis Budenz—who had edited the CPUSA's official newspaper the *Daily Worker* before becoming a government informant—added that he convinced Adamic to promote the "party line" in his 1943 *My Native Land*.[74] Adamic denied both claims. It is interesting to note that the press seemed more concerned with Budenz's assertion that Adamic allowed the former communist editor to approve the contents of *My Native Land* before it went to press. Adamic told the *Kansas City Times* that his views "were not altered in any way by Budenz," and the *New York Times* reported that Adamic called Budenz's testimony an "attempt to drag me in to the current spy scare."[75] Specifically, Budenz contended that he had convinced Adamic to switch his support from Mihailović to Tito. Adamic issued a press release declaring that it "may be true" that the Soviets assigned Budenz the task of corrupting him, but that effort would have been "superfluous." Adamic cited the *Native's Return* for proof that he had called for a federated Yugoslavia nine years "before I knew there was a Tito." That book and *Struggle* demonstrated that he had long favored a federation "attached on mutually acceptable terms to the Soviet Union or come within Soviet orbit. I saw no other choice for the Balkans in 1934 and I have not changed my mind on this point since." Adamic admitted that Budenz provided him with Partisan communiqués in 1942 but added that Budenz was only "one of my numerous sources of information. What he thought his role was in reference to me at the time was and is the height of irrelevance to me." Budenz likely had a copy of *My Native Land* and may have shared it with CPUSA head Earl Browder, but Adamic had provided copies to numerous people to get their feedback. Adamic then pointed out that he had "scores of letters from prominent Americans like the late Chief Justice Stone" and "several Senators thanking me for 'My Native Land' and expressing themselves favorably about the book." Congressional committees called upon Bentley and Budenz to repeatedly state their assertions about Adamic's communist ties, and newspapers continually reported their claims. It is important to note that FBI agents determined that Bentley's charges had no merit. In her allegation that Adamic had passed on secrets to the Soviets, she stated that he did so when he worked for the Office of Strategic Services (OSS) during World War II. She said that she learned of his treasonous act from Budenz. In an interview with the FBI, Budenz stated that he never told Bentley this story. Adamic never worked for the OSS, and so he never had access to records Bentley accused him of handing over to the Soviets. FBI agents expressed their skepticism of Budenz's story.[76] Since FBI files remained confidential, anticommunists could attack Adamic without fear of being contradicted.

Despite the growing divisions between noncommunist leftists and communists, and the heightened attacks he endured from red hunters, Adamic continued to battle on Wallace's behalf. He spoke at rallies, wrote editorials and articles, and answered letters from Wallace's supporters. In response to a Progressive Party activist who asked whether the campaign was falling apart, Adamic avoided the question. Instead, he asserted that the "two old parties" are supported by those who profited from wartime inflation, rejected a national housing program, accepted segregation, and contested a national health program. "They are responsible, as agents of profit-hungry, power-mad corporate-clerical interests, for the moves toward war." Candidates from the mainstream parties and their supporters, he added, "smear" Wallace and others seeking peace and democracy "with the word 'Communism.'" Adamic asserted that most people do not really know the meaning of communism, and if they did, "they would not be scared;" they would recognize that in many nations communist revolutionaries represent the only force capable of establishing "equality among men, education, peace, old age security, medical protection for every citizen, [and] universal material well-being."[77] In light of the problems Adamic faced from CPUSA members at that moment, his response seemed surprising. But by this point in the campaign he recognized that contrasting Soviet communists, whom he increasingly viewed as imperialists, with Chinese, Greek, and Yugoslav communists, whom he saw as slowly advancing democracy by overthrowing autocratic monarchies, would only confuse voters. Thus, he reiterated the themes of Wallace's "Century of the Common Man" speech.

In a letter he wrote during the campaign, Adamic outlined how the politics of fear as practiced by the anticommunists operated. "It infects all levels, all strata of our society, from the press or radio correspondent or the preacher who knows better, but repeats the lie because his job depends on it, to the grocery clerk who thinks Wallace is right but won't stand up for him because 'the family must eat.'" This refusal to listen stemmed from the fact that the Republicans and Democrats will not debate issues, but "only smear."[78] The politics of fear functioned by making most of the citizenry worry about being accused of behaviors that would deprive them of work and damage their relationships with friends and family.

Thomas G. Robischon of Bozeman, Montana, sent a letter to Adamic in September 1948 to thank him for keeping antifascist politics alive through *T&T* and to offer another example of how the politics of fear functioned. Robischon wrote advertising copy for a radio station, and he wore his "Wallace for President" button when meeting with clients. Some of the "'prominent' citizens" whose accounts he handled pressured the station manager to fire him, and the manager complied. Robischon concluded, "What in hell did I spend 44 months in the Navy—in Sicily, Tarwa" during World War II for now "I [no longer could] exercise a basic constitutional privilege?"[79] Because Adamic now fought on multiple fronts—against the communists trying to control the Progressive Party for their own ends, and against the red-baiters attempting to smear the Wallace campaign and him—he could do little except respond with empathetic letters and use *T&T* to print Robischon's story and others like it.

As the election neared, the divisions between independent leftists and communists within the Wallace campaign threatened to unravel any future progressive project. On November 1, Adamic's ally Lee Fryer traveled through Montana, Idaho, Washington, and Oregon and explained that communists were now the biggest "obstacle to Progressive Party success" in this region that once appeared promising for a large Wallace turnout. A frustrated Fryer proclaimed that "the Communist Party in the United States has not yet attained the sense of responsibility and maturity which entitles it to any special consideration," and he wanted Adamic to continue to join him in urging Wallace to denounce the communists who failed to recognize that "time is short and the danger of fascism great."[80] Adamic had no influence left. Wallace came in a disappointing fourth. Progressives could not even finish ahead of the Dixiecrats, who garnered 1,169,021 popular votes and thirty-nine ballots in the Electoral College. The Progressives won no states and Wallace received only 1,156,103 votes.

Immediately after the election, Adamic participated in meetings organized by Progressive Party leaders aimed at assessing why the campaign failed so miserably and strategizing ways to advance the progressive vision over the next four years. Those assembled attempted to ignore the glaring divisions between communists and noncommunists.[81] The most promising solution offered at these gatherings was to construct Progressive Party community centers. These buildings would bring people together for a night's entertainment by holding plays and showing movies and at other times hosting lecturers and political debates. They could also act as sites for community assistance, and people could come and obtain legal advice, get referrals for doctors, or meet with those who could help them with housing issues. The final report also recommended that these centers hold a "Labor Week, a Minorities Week, a Women's Week, [and] a Youth Week" as ways to energize the progressive agenda. The centers would be venues for "working people to express their ways, not for some to make what's real abstract." Progressive centers had to prioritize social experiences because "RED-BAITING BECOMES LESS EFFECTIVE IN A SITUATION WHERE PEOPLE ARE TALKING OR WORKING TOGETHER." This model was to make democracy a lived experience and build solidarity as a consequence.[82] After this gathering, Adamic attended a meeting on how to increase the African American vote for future Progressive candidates. When that discussion ended, his participation in electoral politics ceased.

After the 1948 election, *T&T* was the only consistent platform Adamic had to express his views. In the first issue of his newsletter after Wallace's sound defeat, Adamic urged his readers to view global tensions in terms of colonizers and their resisters, not communists and anticommunists. He explained that Stalin and Churchill shared a lack of "respect for small nations." Stalin, he stressed, "has no faith in the progressive potentialities of peoples other than the Russians" and could achieve only "what passes for socialism in the USSR" by engaging in "conquest." Tito and Yugoslav communists, conversely, practiced "Socialist principles of international cooperation, of mutual aid according to their respective needs and abilities, rather than on secret-police domination and exploitation of small or less developed states by the big or better developed ones."[83] Adamic painted far too favorable a picture of life under Tito's government, but the fact that he criticized Cold War liberalism and the Soviets simultaneously placed him, along with DuBois, in a limited group of outspoken noncommunist leftists challenging Americans and the rest of the world to adopt a far different version of democracy than proponents of the Cold War consensus offered.

Adamic wrote this *T&T* piece as he planned to see the new Yugoslavia for himself. While traveling, he hoped to stop in Russia to gain a full understanding of the Tito-Stalin split, as well as compare the expansionism of the Soviets and the United States by touring the "Asian Soviet republics." He wanted to witness firsthand how Stalin's government "handled the nationality or minority problem" because the Russians were as responsible as the Americans for "the making of peace." Soviet officials refused to grant him a visa.[84]

Conclusion

In trying to revive antifascism through anticolonialism, Adamic discovered that he had lost his influence over US public opinion. Adamic became a prominent immigrant voice in the culture wars of the 1920s, a noted labor reporter during the revival of unionism in the 1930s, the most recognized advocate of pluralism in the New Deal era, and the diasporic leader who convinced Americans to support a communist guerrilla fighter during World War II. He succeeded in these endeavors because he was a master storyteller. Adamic's enemies neutralized his political efficacy by robbing him of the power to narrate and reinvent the meaning of democratic politics. In an era of extreme nationalism, anticommunists used Adamic's transnationalism against him. They, with the help of some of his fellow Slavs who saw red-baiting as a conduit to Americanization, turned Adamic from an immigrant success story into a foreigner trying to subvert the American way of life.

Adamic and other anticolonial antifascists have received little to no attention from scholars. Most studies concerned with the politics of this period focus on Cold War liberalism's coming to fruition, American communists' decline from relevance, and anticommunism's domination of political culture. Historians portray Adamic in this period as some combination of Tito's leading propagandist in the United States, a fellow traveler, and a victim of red-hunters. Some truth exists in each of these categorizations, but their application neglects the reality that antifascism was once the dominant political culture of the United States. Adamic belonged to a group of globally conscious leftists, which included key figures from Roosevelt's administration such as Tugwell, Wallace, Ickes, and even Eleanor Roosevelt, who refused to trade in the social democratic impulses of New Deal politics for the Cold War consensus. In a 1946 letter to Adamic, Ickes exclaimed, "I have the same uneasy feeling about the world situation today that you seem to have. It is so difficult in this country to try to persuade the people to be reasonable when a carefully worked out speech or statement or book can be effectually met by the one devastating word 'Communism.'" Ickes added, "It is not the Communists in this country that I worry about, it is the Fascists."[85] Ickes and other New Deal leftists, being native-born and possessing significant political power, could overcome anticommunist attacks. Adamic could not.

As anticommunists increasingly harassed Adamic, African American journalists, especially the *Pittsburgh Courier*'s P. L. Prattis, came to his defense. Prattis proclaimed Adamic a "small 'd' democrat," not a communist. He then explained that at first Adamic "was a Yugo-Slav," but then he broadened his vision of liberty and produced "the most stirring and thought provoking books to promote the democratic cause." Adamic wrote about Tito, but his politics were not tethered to his homeland. Prattis understood that Adamic viewed imperialism as a form of fascism and that he wanted to forge a coalition of leftists to fight "the forces at work in the world today." On the Tito-Stalin split, Prattis asked his readers whether democracy was better served, as Adamic argued, by a US-Yugoslav alliance or Yugoslav-USSR friendship?[86] Adamic's detractors cared little what Prattis had to say, since white supremacists served as an essential constituency within the larger anticommunist movement. Being an antifascist in an anticommunist America meant that Adamic had become essentially incoherent to all but the black anticolonialists who were also relegated to the margins of the emerging civil-rights movement. For instance, the National Association for the Advancement of Colored People (NAACP) reversed course on linking Jim Crow to imperialism and demanding that the US government use its influence to help all colonized peoples secure the right of self-determination. In 1948, NAACP head Walter White expelled DuBois for maintaining this stance. NAACP leaders abandoned their anticolonialist positions in hopes that the Truman administration would aid the fight against Jim Crow by taking executive action. They also counted on Congress and Supreme Court decisions.[87] DuBois went into exile, black journalists turned their attention to the civil-rights movement, and Adamic either committed suicide or was murdered.

5

Anticommunists and Death Narratives

Beginning in 1949, former Ustaši soldiers (Croatian fascists), fearing that they would be persecuted under Josip Broz Tito's communist regime, gained entry into the United States as displaced persons and started threatening Louis Adamic's life. Soviet agents did too, but Adamic, according to witnesses interviewed by the Federal Bureau of Investigation (FBI), considered Hitler's former allies a far greater threat than Stalin's spies.[1] Both groups wanted Adamic to stop writing what became his posthumously published thirteenth book, *The Eagle and the Roots*, an account of his visit to Yugoslavia that year. Despite the threats on his life, Adamic continued to write. He took the precaution of leaving his Milford, New Jersey, farmhouse and moving around to various hotels. During a stay at the Shelton Hotel in New York City, he wrote to his brother France and reiterated his concern that former Ustaši troops wanted him dead.[2] By the fall of 1951, Adamic felt safe enough to return home.

On September 4, 1951, the farmer living closest to Adamic's house smelled smoke at 4 AM. He called the fire department after seeing flames at Adamic's property from his window. After putting out the blaze, firefighters walked into the upstairs bedroom that Adamic used as an office and found him dead, apparently from a gunshot wound to his head. Firefighters called the New Jersey state police, and investigators wondered whether someone had murdered Adamic because the rifle that killed him curiously lay by his side with smudged fingerprints on it. Despite their suspicions of foul play, police closed the case after the coroner ruled Adamic's death a suicide.[3] Reporters writing for papers throughout the country initially accepted the coroner's ruling, especially after Louis's estranged wife Stella said that he could have taken his own life because of stress he experienced trying to complete *The Eagle and the Roots*.[4]

The morning after Adamic died, many papers around the country printed the Associated Press obituary that mentioned his most popular books and reported the coroner's ruling.[5] By September 6, reporters for the major newspapers depicted Adamic as a communist apostate likely assassinated on orders from Soviet premier Joseph Stalin. Two communists-turned-professional-witnesses fed this speculation: Louis Budenz (who had edited the leading procommunist newspaper in the United States, *The Daily Worker*) and Elizabeth Bentley (who carried messages between contacts in a Soviet spy ring).[6] Anticommunists contended that Stalin established sleeper cells throughout the United States to advance his project for world domination. Whenever the Kremlin ordered these Soviet spies into action, they would commit murder, perform acts of terror, or engage in sabotage.[7] Plays and popular novels helped root these tropes of Soviet mayhem and assassination in American popular culture.[8] Various members of the anticommunist network that included ex-communist professional witnesses, politicians, reporters, government bureaucrats, and self-appointed patriots saw Adamic's death as an opportunity to offer their own version of his life.

Politicians and federal bureaucrats who spearheaded the anticommunist movement feared Adamic because, in addition to remaining steadfast in his efforts to advance a progressive vision of democracy, he repeatedly succeeded in shaping public opinion. During World War II, he convinced lawmakers, members of the Roosevelt administration, military officers, and most Americans to see Josip Broz Tito, a communist guerrilla fighter, as the embodiment of the antifascist spirit guiding the Allied effort. In the aftermath of the war, Adamic's support for Tito called into question the anticommunists' claim that Stalin led a monolithic conspiracy for global hegemony. In 1948, Tito refused to follow Stalin's dictates, and Stalin expelled Yugoslavia from the Communist Information Bureau (Cominform), the organization intended to unite the world's Communist parties. Adamic continued to back Tito's government because he viewed it as a successful example of a pluralist cultural revolution. Adamic insisted that in adopting ethnic equality as a founding principle, the new Yugoslavia would evolve into a democracy. If Adamic succeeded in explaining the Tito-Stalin split to the American people, he would expose anticommunists' erroneous assertion that all communists were automatons unquestioningly carrying out the wishes of the Kremlin. That realization would in turn open a host of domestic and foreign policies to public scrutiny.

Instead, former communists, fellow travelers, and leftists capitulating to the climate of fear of the late 1940s and early 1950s entered a collaborative relationship with red-hunting politicians and policymakers to demonize critics of racial, ethnic, and economic inequality as subversives. Witnesses such as Budenz and Bentley would impugn a congressional committee's target to gain notoriety and financial gain. Other witnesses, as in the case of Adamic's former South Slavic activist colleagues, saw testifying as means of assimilating. Their appearance before Congress signified a formal renunciation of their former foreign radicalism and an embrace of their Americanness.[9]

Cary McWilliams unintentionally aided the anticommunists' effort to demonize Adamic's politics. He wrote an obituary about his friend for *The Nation* in which he presented Adamic's writings about cultural pluralism and Tito's Partisans as separate phases in Adamic's life.[10] McWilliams's assertion fueled the claim that Adamic had abandoned cultural pluralism and embraced communism. McWilliams's "two Adamics" formulation—cultural pluralist and Tito supporter—helps to keep the debate over whether Adamic was a communist central to defining his legacy.[11]

We should recognize that Adamic, like anticolonial writers in Asia, Africa, and Latin America, advocated a radical version of cultural pluralism. Global democracy included allowing "Third World" peoples the right to govern themselves instead of being pressured to align with one of the superpowers.[12] By 1944, Adamic had linked Yugoslavia to colonized nations in the global south and argued that the leftist uprisings in "underdeveloped" nations had more to do with fighting colonialism than it did with inhabitants' desires for a dictatorship of the proletariat. After the Tito-Stalin split, he drew more parallels between Yugoslavia and Asian, African, and Latin American independence movements. Adamic contended that many people throughout the world shared the idea that independence meant creating a new set of human relationships guided by an ethic that placed the recognition of each individual's dignity above economic gain. In a chapter that his editors excluded from *The Eagle and the Roots*, Adamic argued that the conception of progress shared by governments of the United States, its European allies, and the Soviets justified imperialism.[13]

Had Adamic lived another decade, he would have enthusiastically supported the Bandung Conference in April 1955 that saw Third World leaders meet to discuss an alliance so that they could remain independent from global superpowers. Then he would have been ecstatic when Tito, along with the leaders of Algeria, Egypt, Ghana, India, and Indonesia, met in Belgrade in 1961 to organize the Nonaligned Movement, which rapidly expanded across the Third World.[14]

Adamic *connected* discussions of what a new humanism meant to criticisms of the anticommunist's politics of fear, and to the imperial policies and practices of the United States and the Soviet Union in *The Eagle and the Roots*. The book, however, was dense and suffered from poor editing. As a result, his last book did not compel readers to reevaluate their beliefs and it failed to challenge the status quo the way his other works had. Anticommunists' success in convincing the public to ask whether Stalin had Adamic killed meant that his enemies stole his most powerful weapon, storytelling, and used it against him to obscure both his legacy and the progressive antifascist politics he advocated.

Establishing the "Adamic as Communist" Narrative

Before 1948, anticommunists had little success in hurting Adamic's public image. They attacked him in the press as a subversive after the release of his first book, *Dynamite* (1931). Then, during World War II, his pro-Tito activism led Justice Department lawyers and FBI agents to investigate him as a possible foreign agent. His antifascist message resonated widely as military officers, politicians, Roosevelt administration bureaucrats, and wide swaths of the public found his arguments convincing and turned to him for insights on events occurring in Yugoslavia. The FBI decided to end their investigation into his alleged subversive activities that summer, and Justice Department attorneys stopped pressuring him to register as a foreign agent.

Unlike his counterparts in the executive branch, J. B. (Joseph Brown) Matthews, a former communist who became director of research for the House Committee on Un-American Activities (HUAC), continued to target Adamic for investigation that year. On October 5, 1944, Matthews, who cared more about headlines than facts, reported to the committee that Adamic had "a long Communist record." As evidence for his claim, Matthews listed the twenty-five "front" organizations, or allegedly communist-controlled groups, that Adamic had joined. Then Matthews cited quotes from Adamic's media interviews, books, and articles as further proof of Adamic's subversive behavior. Matthews presented Adamic's 1934 claim that the ideals that guided the Russian Revolution "are the highest promise and hope that humanity has today" and his assertion that the Roosevelt administration practiced "New Deal imperialism" in deciding to remain neutral during the Spanish Civil War as particularly damning.[15]

Matthews exemplified how red-baiters operated. He correctly identified the organizations Adamic belonged to, but, like most anticommunists, he disingenuously claimed that these groups operated as communist fronts to advance Moscow's interests. In a posthumously published July 1952 *Nation* article, Adamic responded to criticisms of his affiliations by declaring that if "I weren't a subversive, I couldn't endure myself." In that piece, he explained that he helped to start and joined organizations that battled for greater rights for immigrants and African Americans and that challenged foreign policy efforts that enriched corporations at the expense of people's well-being. Adamic sarcastically concluded the piece by wondering why anticommunists never mentioned in their biographies of him that he had fought in World War I or that he belonged to the American Legion.[16]

In regard to Matthews's other evidence, Adamic did indeed praise the Russian Revolution, but he viewed it as a movement forward in a political trajectory that would eventually result in the creation of a democracy. By the time Matthews testified, Adamic routinely voiced his agreement with Vice President Henry Wallace's claim that the American and Russian revolutions illuminated the global desire of the "common man" for independence and equality from colonial and monarchical powers. Matthews likely included Adamic's reference to "New Deal imperialism" in his findings in an effort to win liberals over to his position. He got sloppy in cherry-picking his evidence, however, as he included Adamic's prediction that a second world war would happen if the United States did not intervene to stop the fascist coup in Spain. Adamic clearly wanted to prevent fascism's advance, not promote the Soviets' agenda. The rest of the report was composed of Adamic's quotes that Matthews had taken out of context. The public largely ignored HUAC's initial attack on Adamic, but future congressional committees recycled the evidence Matthews presented. Matthews also shared his "research" with a number of columnists who wrote for the leading red-baiting media outlets.[17]

Although Winston Churchill formally declared the Cold War's existence on March 5, 1946, anticommunists did not dominate US culture and politics until 1948. The shift occurred because scores of New Deal liberals abandoned antifascism as they grew fearful of the consequences of being linked to progressives and communists. Concerns over losing jobs, being blacklisted, and being ostracized by friends drove many former leftists into an alliance with anticommunists. In part, President Harry Truman's 1947 federal loyalty program spread these fears. Truman created the program to mollify conservative Democrats and Republicans who claimed that during the New Deal communists had infiltrated the federal government by taking civil-service jobs. Between 1947 and 1956, FBI agents interviewed more than five million federal employees. Out of those, twenty-five thousand received intense scrutiny, twenty-seven hundred were fired, and twelve thousand quit. The vast majority of these federal employees were not left liberals, let alone communists, or spies for Stalin. Having supported the New Deal, calling for peace abroad, or advocating racial equality in the United States typically triggered an investigation into one's patriotism. The loyalty program encouraged federal employees to leave government service.[18]

New Deal liberals at one point counted themselves among Adamic's most vocal supporters, but by aligning with his conservative enemies they played a key role in making his politics incomprehensible in our historical memories. With Truman willing to appease conservative anticommunists, Adamic and his fellow progressives asserted that the United States moved closer to fascism than democracy.[19] With the Nazis defeated, a barrage of warnings about Soviet aggression encouraged those who transitioned from New Deal liberalism to Cold War liberalism found Adamic's concerns about fascism in America easy to ignore.

As the anticommunists grew more aggressive in targeting Adamic, it became even easier for former supporters to distance themselves from the activist writer they once admired. In 1948, Adamic's enemies counted on Louis Budenz to lead the charge against him. Testifying before HUAC, Budenz claimed that during World War II he brought Adamic into the Communist Party's orbit.[20] After the hearing, reporters questioned Adamic repeatedly about his politics. By that point, the archconservative syndicated columnist Westbrook Pegler was regularly attacking Adamic in his editorials.[21] Editors of high-profile magazines stopped asking Adamic for article submissions and fewer and fewer organizations invited him to speak.

Between May and September 1949, the attacks on Adamic had intensified. Nevada's ardent anticommunist Democratic senator Patrick A. McCarran chaired a subcommittee created to expose Soviet sympathizers within US ethnic communities, and he focused on Adamic. Bogdan Raditsa, a one-time friend of Adamic and Tito supporter, aided McCarran. Raditsa left the United States to serve in Tito's government, but he returned to the United States after seeing firsthand Tito's rule through "terror." Raditsa identified Adamic as the "brain trust of the American-Slav movement in this country" and added that "he is in all of the Slav-Communist movements." Then Otto J. Dekom, a staff member hired to investigate suspected subversives on the subcommittee's behalf, interrupted Raditsa's testimony and declared that, according to his research, Adamic "has the longest record of Communist-front affiliations of any person we have studied so far." Dekom, building on Matthews's research, claimed that Adamic belonged to more than fifty organizations affiliated with or controlled by the Communist Party.[22] Raditsa treated testifying before Congress as an act of confession. Instead of gaining absolution for his sins, he received "Americanness" from the anticommunists now claiming to be the arbiters of national identity.

William H. Smyth followed Raditsa. He had run a business in Yugoslavia until 1941, and the committee called him to testify about conversations he had overheard in Belgrade coffeehouses about Adamic. According to Smyth, Adamic's critiques of Serbian irredentist and autocratic monarch Alexander were the result of Adamic feeling slighted because Alexander had made Adamic wait an extraordinarily long time to see him. The members of McCarran's subcommittee let Smyth's innuendo stand as fact. No one thought to ask whether Alexander's use of torture, which Adamic detailed for the English-speaking world in 1934, could have been the actual reason Adamic criticized the Serbian king. Also, none of the senators inquired why groups such as the prodemocratic noncommunist Croatian Peasant Party joined with the various South Slavic Communist parties to advocate a federation government of Slovenes, Croats, and Serbs to replace Alexander.[23] In addition, Smyth rejected the idea that the Tito-Stalin split actually occurred. He suspected that the two dictators fabricated Yugoslavia's break from Cominform to advance some communist scheme that he never explained.[24]

Smyth concluded his testimony by urging Congress to amend the 1918 Immigration Act in order to make penalties against immigrant subversives more severe. In making this recommendation, he insisted that most immigrant organizations were in actuality communist cells. "We" need to keep out the "people who have no business being here," and if they get in, and "we" find out, "we can throw them out right on their necks."[25] In referring to "we" and "they," Smyth asserted that "American" meant white and that immigrants needed to accept Anglo cultural practices, embrace free market capitalism, and support the anticommunist movement.

Adamic's anticommunist enemies failed to point out that his views on Yugoslavia usually aligned with official US policy both during World War II and after the Tito-Stalin split. Acknowledging these facts would have undermined the overlapping efforts by politicians, journalists, and professional patriots to neutralize Adamic's antifascist message. McCarran further illustrated this point by calling Elizabeth Bentley and Budenz to testify after Raditsa and Smyth. Bentley had appeared before HUAC in 1948 and claimed that Adamic had spied for the USSR during World War II.[26] She repeated this assertion. Budenz again stated that he "nursed" Adamic along until Adamic promoted the communist line. When asked why Adamic now sided with Tito, Budenz replied that Communist Party leaders always feared Adamic's Slovene roots "would overshadow the concepts he was developing."[27] Not one of the senators on the subcommittee asked a follow-up question. They all understood that the Tito-Stalin split undermined the assertion that communism was a monolithic movement.

As McCarran gathered his evidence, in June HUAC released a report on the American Slav Congress (ASC) that included an entire section on Adamic even though he never officially belonged to that body. Formed during the war, early ASC leaders wanted to create a pro-Allied antifascist organization that linked the concerns of members' homelands and their adopted land. The FBI, some State Department officials, and conservative Slavic American associations worried that the Soviets would control the group. After Secretary of State Cordell Hull gave tentative support to the formation of the ASC, more conservative ethnic leaders, especially among the Polish and Serbian American communities, agreed to join. For roughly a year, the ASC sold war bonds and collected food, clothing, and money.[28] Divisions among Polish Americans spurred conservatives to renounce their affiliation, and communists eventually took control of the ASC.

By 1949, HUAC was proclaiming Adamic a "tower of strength" for the ASC because he allowed its leaders to use his notoriety as a popular writer and his contacts within the Slav community to advance its communist agenda. The report identified Adamic as "the spokesman of various Communist-front organizations operating among the Slavic population in America," noted that he switched his support from Mihailović to Tito at the same time the Russian press did, and credited Budenz with "poisoning" Adamic's mind.[29] The committee claimed that Adamic's "consistently hostile" opposition to US foreign policy most clearly illustrated his pro-Soviet beliefs. Examples of his anti-American attitude, according to HUAC, included the fact that he signed an April 1948 petition condemning the arrest of "Chilean Communist poet" Pablo Neruda, along with his membership in the following organizations: American Council for a Democratic Greece, the American Committee for Spanish Freedom, and the American League against War and Fascism. These groups indeed overlapped with or explicitly supported Soviet foreign-policy objectives. But they also opposed fascist regimes that the United States funded. At this point, a year had passed since the Tito-Stalin split. The fact that Adamic still opposed US and Soviet imperialism while siding with the Yugoslav leader and not the Soviets escaped comment. So, too, did the fact that the Truman administration funneled money to Tito in hopes of maintaining a crack in the Iron Curtain.[30]

Like Raditsa in his testimony before McCarran's subcommittee, former ASC activist Mark Basic appeared before HUAC and smeared Adamic as a way to claim an American identity. HUAC members credited Basic's book *It Happened in Yugoslavia, It Must not Happen Here* as exposing how the ASC promoted the Soviets' agenda.[31] Basic made sure to mention learning his catechism from his village priest at thirteen, working hard, saving, and going to night school in the United States in order to become "more thoroughly Americanized." Then he remarked on a trip he made to his homeland during the early 1930s. Unlike Adamic's migration tale of seeking to escape Austrian colonialism, Basic recalled "that living conditions in America were better than in Yugoslavia, yet the peasants enjoyed a certain degree of prosperity and freedom; in comparison, that is, with what they have today." After couching his life story in an Algeresque narrative, Basic then sought to correct the falsehoods that had been spread in the American press about Yugoslavia. As a delegate representing the ASC at the 1947 All Slav Congress in Yugoslavia, he discovered that in promoting atheism the communists had alienated much of the citizenry. He also explained that Tito shot Chetnik leader Draža Mihailović, the Serbian general who fought the Partisans in hopes of reinstalling the monarchy after World War II, because the promonarchist general was becoming "too popular and too honest a nationalist." This trip had instilled in Basic a "hatred for the police state" and, as he left Yugoslavia, he could recall the line from the Gettysburg Address: "That this nation, under God, shall have a new birth of freedom."[32] In conclusion, Basic proclaimed that the Tito-Stalin split was "a beautiful scheme Uncle Joe has invented for gullible and wishful thinking Americans." He hoped that Americans would not "fall for this Communistic delusion."[33]

Basic illustrated why Adamic's antifascism became incomprehensible to a public marginally aware or purposefully forgetting Yugoslavia's recent history. Basic turned Mihailović, a Serbian irredentist general who collaborated with fascists in hopes of reinstalling a monarchy, into a champion of pan-Slavism and a proponent of a democratic Yugoslavia that fell victim to Tito's totalitarianism. HUAC entered Basic's book into the record without questioning assertions such as that peasants were happier under the monarchy, and that he thought about the Gettysburg Address while witnessing the destruction communism had done to his homeland. And, by 1949, the members of HUAC knew that the Tito-Stalin split was real.

HUAC's espionage hearing, McCarran's subcommittee to expose radical immigrants, and HUAC's investigation of the ASC combined to fashion a narrative of Adamic as a subversive foreigner undermining American ideals. These congressional groups depended on the unreliable testimony of Budenz, Bentley, and former immigrant radicals, all of whom agreed to identify Adamic as a subversive in order to prove their own Americanness. These anticommunists proclaimed that Adamic's critiques of US, British, and Soviet imperialism were not the result of his genuine concerns for a better world, but instead evidence of his duplicity. Adamic, they insisted, wanted to distract attention from his real aim of spreading communism throughout the world.

The FBI also targeted Adamic as a security risk. Unlike their congressional counterparts, however, bureau agents did not prioritize sensational headlines. The FBI had begun investigating Adamic in 1941 and concluded its report on March 15, 1951. D. Milton Ladd, head of domestic intelligence, created the category "A pro-Tito Communist" just for Adamic. As with congressional anticommunists, Adamic's support for Tito confounded the FBI's belief that Stalin led a monolithic global conspiracy.[34] FBI agents, like congressional staffers, presented Adamic's leftist affiliations in their reports as if they had uncovered clandestine materials that proved he belonged to their imagined communist conspiracy. Adamic had proudly and publicly declared his involvement in relief organizations, groups that promoted industrial democracy, championed racial equality, opposed war, and most especially challenged fascism. FBI agents simply had to read his editorials and look at the letterhead of organizations he belonged to acquire a list of his affiliations. By opposing fascism in Spain, signing a petition opposing the renewal of the House Un-American Activities Committee, supporting the partisans in Greece, and advocating for more amicable relations with the Soviets, the FBI concluded that Adamic threatened US security. Special agent Robert C. Blount ordered FBI personnel to investigate Adamic's finances and had confidential informants sort through his garbage. Blount noted that after interviewing Adamic, the famous writer "expressed himself as being in favor of certain phases of Communism but stated he was not a Communist." Blount also talked to informants who said that Adamic "was a proponent of unity between the Communists and non-Communists."[35]

After the Tito-Stalin split, members of the Truman administration and the FBI believed that Russian leaders and Communists loyal to the Soviet Union feared Adamic's ability to persuade leftists worldwide to support Yugoslavia and undermine Cold War liberalism. For instance, in a report to Secretary of State Dean Acheson, William A. Fowler, first secretary for the Yugoslav chargé d'affaires, explained that Tito knows that foreign communists remain "undivided" in their loyalty to the USSR. Therefore, Tito's regime "is at present seeking support from leftist and fellow-traveler intellectuals whose influence is felt within the communist movement. In this respect the value of Louis Adamic's support is probably regarded . . . as second only to that of the French author Jean Cassou," a leading antifascist resistance fighter during World War II. Fowler noted that Adamic called upon "all honest anti-imperialistically inclined Americans" to support Tito's government.[36] Adamic continued to frame his politics as antifascist, and he viewed anticolonialism as the central characteristic of antifascism. Fowler observed that Adamic stressed the "federal principle," Tito's commitment to ethnic equality, as the most important feature of Yugoslavia's revolution because it demonstrated to the whole world that "progressive movements" could succeed.[37] Fowler's report, which ended up in Adamic's FBI file, made it clear that he did not consider Adamic a communist.

The politics of fear shaping the mood of the late 1940s and early 1950s allowed innuendo and unchallenged assertions to become the basis of a narrative that turned Adamic from an anticolonialist into an agent of Stalin. By making people afraid that journalists and politicians would question their commitment to democracy if they invited Adamic to speak or contribute articles to their periodicals, the overlapping voices of anticommunism convinced leaders of civic groups, faculty at universities, employees at government agencies, and editors of mainstream periodicals to silence him. His newsletter became the only platform he had to express his views, and it was an inadequate means of swaying public opinion, especially because red-hunting politicians acquired celebrity with the dawn of television.

Communists as Murderers

In 1919, thousands of newspaper stories warned against communist plots (with "communist" referring loosely to any radical) to assassinate world leaders, including President Woodrow Wilson. The media stressed that murder was a defining characteristic of the Bolshevik ethos.[38] Even after the Red Scare of 1919 through 1921 died down, articles in major daily newspapers repeated rumors of conspiracies designed by Lenin that would soon be carried out by his secret agents. In June 1925, a *Los Angeles Times* piece claimed that "an active terrorist campaign in France" aimed at assassinating any enemy of the Soviet Union was afoot.[39] The next year, the same paper compared the rule of Lenin and Trotsky to the "atrocities" of Nero and Caligula and asserted that these "criminal conspirators" violated accepted morals in that they, like Herod, ordered the "slaying of children."[40]

In 1930, German playwright and Marxist Bertolt Brecht helped cement the communist assassination motif with his production of *The Measures Taken*, which American anticommunists regularly cited as evidence of Soviet bloodlust. This play promulgated the idea that, at times, maintaining the Soviet experiment might require the murder of those whose revolutionary discipline faltered. Brecht's critics argued that he first voiced the logic that Stalinists would later employ to justify the Great Terror that began six years later. From 1936 through 1938, Stalin's agents arbitrarily jailed or killed those they labeled political enemies. Brecht's play focused on three Soviet communists on a secret mission to China to foster revolution. Their guide, a dedicated revolutionary, continually acted on his enthusiasm for the cause, but each time his efforts impede the group's work. After he broke protocol and revealed his true identity to his comrades, they determined that they had to kill the guide. The guide, after hearing their reasoning, submitted to his own murder. HUAC, in 1947, pointed to the play as evidence of how communists think and called Brecht, who moved to the United States in 1941 to escape the Nazis, to testify. On October 30, 1947, he explained to the House committee members who subpoenaed him that in 1930 he had wanted audiences to examine the choices revolutionaries faced in challenging fascists for control of Europe and Asia. The German writer did not fathom that the Great Terror would happen. When he wrote the play, he wanted radicals to abandon their emotional views of revolution and embrace a "new objectivity" predicated on discipline.[41]

In 1941, Hungarian-born communist dissident Arthur Koestler further inserted the assassination narrative into the larger story of international communist tactics by contending that to Stalinists death represented the only suitable punishment for apostasy. Koestler's 1941 novel about Stalin's terror and show trials, *Darkness at Noon*, declared that the Communist Party "knew only one crime: to swerve from the course laid out; and only one punishment: death."[42] Koestler's main character, Nicholas Salmanovitch Rubashov, explained that, in "the Party," death "had no romantic aspect," it simply meant the "cessation of political activity."[43] *Darkness at Noon* proved so popular in the United States that it became a Broadway play performed from January 1950 through June 1951 (which Adamic saw). The novel served as the backdrop for reporters covering the deaths of anyone directly or indirectly tied to the Communist Party, including Adamic.

On September 6, two days after Adamic's death, both the *Chicago Tribune* and its sister paper the *Washington Tribune-Herald* ran the same story that proclaimed that—of the "long list of people in and about the New Deal who played around with communism"—Adamic "is the latest to die by violent means." A pattern existed, the story asserted, "in most of these violent deaths among the leftists." Adamic "was an ideological curiosity" because he "leaned toward Stalinism until Tito split with Stalin. Then his Yugoslav nationalism became predominant and inclined him toward Titoism." The piece concluded by bringing up the suspicious deaths of six others with ties to the Communist Party.[44]

Reporters purposefully distorted Adamic's politics. In magazine and newspaper articles, books, and speeches he had repeatedly and clearly distinguished between working with communists and affiliating with the Communist Party. During the New Deal period, he consistently criticized party leaders as undemocratic and beholden to Moscow, dismissed proletarian literature as propaganda, and in the postwar period attacked "red imperialism." From 1938 on, he did argue that under oppressive regimes communist revolutions could function as a means of moving a society forward. When Vice President Henry Wallace articulated this point more clearly in his 1942 "Century of the Common Man" speech, Adamic cited Wallace's words and maintained Wallace's position. He had never been a Stalinist, and he championed Tito because Tito advanced a revolutionary notion of pluralism. Reporters refused to present Adamic's politics as they had before and during World War II, turning him into a stock character in their unimaginative narrative of communists versus anticommunists.

On September 7, the *Washington Post* ran an editorial more explicitly focused on how Adamic's death connected to a host of other "former" communists who renounced Stalin. The piece began by pointing out that the rushed police report resembled the "lamentable haste" of the work done by "police here in Washington more than 10 years ago in closing the case of Gen. Walter Krivitsky." Krivitsky, a Soviet defector, also died of an apparent self-inflicted gunshot wound to his head in a Washington, DC, hotel room.[45] The story then proclaimed that Adamic had no "apparent reason" to "destroy himself," since his current manuscript, a "glorification of Marshal Tito," was not finished. "But to suppose that the Kremlin decreed his death, for the sole purpose of preventing publication is to attach an astonishing importance to the book."[46] Echoing Koestler, the writer suggested that "no resignations are permitted" from "the Communist espionage 'apparatus.'" Therefore, Adamic must have been a spy, and his act of disloyalty, like Krivitsky's defection, appeared a more plausible reason for Stalin to order Adamic's death than retribution for a pro-Tito book.[47]

In November, the *Los Angeles Times* ran a story pointing to Adamic as the most recent example of the Soviets' use of murder to quiet dissenters.

Words such as *alleged* and *possible* no longer appeared before *assassination* and *murder*. The only nuance to the *Los Angeles Times* story was that it cited the murder of Leon Trotsky, not Krivitsky, as the starting point for Soviet agents killing deviationists in North America.[48]

The press and much of the public believed that Stalin had ordered Adamic's death because they assumed that political assassinations were standard operating procedure for the Soviets. Reporters functioning within the anticommunist network had to link Adamic to the Soviets. Politicians and the mainstream press did so by turning to the dubious testimonies of Bentley and Budenz. After Adamic's death, reporters began their stories with these charges and turned to Bentley and Budenz for comment. Both told a *New York Times* reporter, the morning police found Adamic's body, that "a very strong possibility" existed that Soviet agents killed the famous writer.[49]

As previous chapters have repeatedly shown, the FBI had cleared Adamic of espionage,[50] and Bentley's claim that Adamic passed on secret information to the Russians while working for the OSS did not hold water—FBI agents noted that Adamic had never worked for the OSS. And as for Budenz, the FBI did not regard him as a reliable witness.[51] He testified before congressional committees thirty-three times in twelve years and usually tailored his responses to the desired outcome the committee that called him wanted to hear.[52] Ladd, in May 1948, wrote J. Edgar Hoover that "Budenz apparently is inclined to make sensational charges which the press interprets as startling new information when, in fact, the information is old and not completely substantiated."[53] The FBI kept a record of the discrepancies in Budenz's statements but did not reveal them because he was the key witness in so many congressional hearings and court cases.[54]

As for Budenz's specific charges against Adamic, we can turn to a 1948 press release Adamic wrote after Budenz named him, and incidentally Alger Hiss, as a communist before HUAC. Budenz claimed that he had convinced Adamic to follow the party line in 1942. Budenz pointed to Adamic's *My Native Land*, published that year, as proof. Allegedly, Adamic permitted Budenz and other Communist Party officials to scrutinize the final draft of the book in order to make sure it advanced party interests. *My Native Land* championed Tito's Partisans, denounced fascists, condemned the once popular promonarchical Chetniks as fascist collaborators, and called for a federated Yugoslavia of ethnic equals after the war. Adamic had been advocating both the communists' efforts to undermine the Serbian monarchy and the creation of a federated Yugoslavia since 1934.[55] Congressional red hunters and journalists never asked Budenz why the US and British governments reached the same conclusion about Tito that Adamic had around the same time in 1942. Again, looking at Adamic's support for Tito closely reveals that he never abandoned his pluralist sensibilities. Tito wanted a Yugoslavia of ethnic equals, not one where fascism or Serbian ethnocentrism defined social, political, and cultural relations.

As Bentley and Budenz's interviews with the *New York Times* fueled speculation that the Soviets killed Adamic, Raditsa published a remembrance of Adamic's life that advanced the communist assassination narrative. Raditsa declared "that the Cominform did Adamic in, as Stalin's gunmen have eliminated so many others."[56] The piece began by acknowledging that whether they "admired or hated" Adamic, all "Yugoslavs were in agreement that he was the most powerful journalistic voice their small country had" produced. Raditsa credited Adamic with inspiring ethnic Americans to realize that, like the "Mayflower stock," they "had a right to participation and leadership." He proclaimed that "Adamic was not content to rest with the Jeffersonian philosophy of tolerance." Raditsa held Adamic responsible for Tito's ascendency to power in Yugoslavia and claimed that he wanted to advance the Soviet agenda in the United States.[57]

Raditsa also contended that Adamic would never have killed himself before finishing his book on Tito because his "ambitious, money loving, fame-obsessed" nature meant he would never have forgone the book royalties and recognition.[58] Then, forgetting that he too supported Tito's Yugoslavism during World War II, Raditsa asserted that Adamic's limited intellect, ignorance of European history and culture, and psychosis that befalls all radicals led to his embrace of Stalinism.[59] Raditsa argued that in being a "second-rate intellectual" Adamic had become part of a "generation of sad little boys" looking to "Moscow as a father, as a prophet, as a deliverer."[60] Adamic failed to see, Raditsa asserted, that "real revolution in East Europe can only be brought about by a flexible emulation of the American experience" because "Communism—official or unofficial . . . is, a brutal tyranny."[61] Raditsa concluded that Adamic "was restless," America had been nice to him, but "he did not feel American." He had become a man without a country because "he had also lost his European heritage."[62] Raditsa and other émigrés from Eastern Europe recalibrated what it meant to be an American during the Cold War as they supported anticommunist narratives with seemingly endless examples of the horrors suffered under Communist totalitarianism.[63]

The social climate for Eastern Europeans had changed since the post–World War I Red Scare, and many anticommunist Anglo-Saxon Protestants came to view Eastern European Catholics and Jews as valuable allies in the fight against communism.[64] The Anglo majority's acceptance of Raditsa and other "new" immigrants signified a recalibration of what it meant to be an American. In post–World War II America, Catholics and Jews were accepted by Protestants as long as they helped advance the notion that being anticommunist was a crucial component of being American.

In proclaiming that Adamic chose communism over Jeffersonian values, Raditsa employed demagoguery to sidestep three difficult discussions. First, he did not engage Adamic's claims that the pervasiveness of Jim Crow suggested that a current of fascism flowed through US political culture. Second, he avoided explaining why Yugoslavs, Slavic Americans, Allied governments, and Raditsa himself had joined Adamic in supporting Tito during the war. Third, Raditsa evaded any recognition of the Tito-Stalin split. Acknowledging this break would have required the anticommunist convert to defend his claim that communism was a monolithic international conspiracy and justify why the US government now grudgingly backed Tito. In praising Adamic's early work and then presenting him as a communist caricature, Raditsa also helped to advance McWilliams's two-Adamics thesis that continues to shape scholars' outlook today. Raditsa's account mattered because he left journalism for the academy. As a history professor at Fairleigh Dickson University, he laid the foundation for our current scholarly understanding of Yugoslavia and Adamic's life.

Possible Alternatives

Understanding the "Stalin assassinated Adamic" narrative as a political tactic employed by conservative anticommunists to obscure the political message of an influential opponent, the question then becomes, who did kill Adamic? The two most likely scenarios for Adamic's death are a revenge killing by Croatian fascists or a suicide resulting largely from his growing despondency over his failing marriage. The journalists who reported on Adamic's potential suicide did not investigate the fact that Louis and Stella lived apart. They repeated Stella's claim that the stress Louis exhibited while writing *The Eagle and the Roots* led him into a state of depression so intense that he took his own life. Reporters also noted that when police searched his body, they found a newspaper clipping in his pocket reporting on Bentley's testimony calling him a spy and the fact that he would soon be subpoenaed to answer the charge.[65] Journalists made no effort to question these competing claims in any depth.

In his private letters, Adamic expressed few worries over testifying before HUAC, but he repeatedly noted concerns over his failing marriage. As Louis became more involved in the war effort in 1942, both in helping to sell war bonds for the US government and then championing Tito and the Partisans, Stella warned him to consider the consequences of his actions. She stated that "it's important that you keep a non-warlike state of mind, that you keep yourself as free as possible."[66] In 1946, Louis wrote a friend, "I'm in a hell of a mess personally myself: I'm dead tired, my wife is tired and insists we sell our farm and move to New Mexico or some such remote place where I won't be expected to go to Wash. or N.Y. every couple of days. This matter is really serious, for Stella is convinced—as are the doctor friends with whom I talked—that I can't keep up this way and stay alive."[67] FBI agents who monitored Adamic's life through numerous informants reported to their superiors that his support for Tito had increasingly strained his marriage.[68]

Ultimately, Louis remained politically active and his relationship suffered. Stella went for an extended stay in California at some point after World War II while Louis continued to live in Milford. In one of the few surviving correspondences with Stella, dated June 22, 1951, Louis wrote while traveling to apologize for any pain he had caused Stella and declared, "I'm going home. I hope you will come too."[69] She did not. Louis died three months later.

In a letter to Ross Wills, a mutual friend of Carey McWilliams and the Adamics, McWilliams explained that he visited with Stella right after Louis' death. McWilliams wrote that "she is convinced that it was suicide. . . . When Louis returned to the East late in July they had agreed to a permanent separation and she had not heard from him since." McWilliams added that "she tells me also that these moods of dark despair had become recurrent." Then he concluded that the "papers, of course, would like to make it a case of murder by the Communists" and "certain Yugoslavs seem to be encouraging this theory. . . . At Milford the coroner and the detective-lt. in charge of the case told me that while the facts were somewhat ambiguous, the anatomical findings tended to support the theory of suicide."[70] That McWilliams referred to Louis and Stella's marriage and not politics, especially in conjunction with Louis's letter to Stella, adds support to despondency over his marriage as a motivator.

Adamic may have killed himself, as the coroner and his wife concluded. Yet the conflicting evidence at the scene of his death, combined with Louis's correspondence with France (noted earlier in this chapter), the recollections of his acquaintances, and interviews in his FBI file suggest that he was murdered. Investigators had concerns about the position of the rifle and the smudged fingerprints on it. In addition, his house was set on fire, and investigators determined that his clothes did not smell of kerosene or gasoline, the accelerants used to start the blaze. Why would a despondent man set his home, especially his files, on fire if he was about to shoot himself? Just before his death, he had borrowed a large sum of money from a friend that was later discovered in the walls of his farmhouse when it was sold in the 1970s. Why would he borrow it, hide it, and then attempt to burn it up?[71]

In his interview with the New Jersey State Police, Anton Smole, a friend of Adamic's who worked for the Yugoslav News Agency, stated that in 1949 Adamic had begun to receive constant death threats and at times encountered violence. Earlier that year, Smole remembered, a group of men attacked Adamic and beat him unconscious outside a California beach cottage he had rented. Adamic kept the first incident hidden from Stella. In an interview with reporters, Ethel Sharp, Adamic's typist, recounted that in 1950, he had told her of a visit he received from four men who, "somewhat threateningly, inquired into the direction the [Tito] book was following." He had shared the same story with his publisher and Yugoslav diplomat to the United Nations Aleš Bebler.[72]

Vladimir Dedijer, a partisan fighter in Tito's army turned dissident, wrote in his memoir about a four-and-a-half-hour conversation he had with Adamic on July 17, 1951. Dedijer and Adamic had become friends in July 1945 when Adamic hosted Dedijer at his New Jersey farm. Dedijer was on official business for his newly liberated Yugoslavia but took the time to express Tito's gratitude to Adamic for the writer's support on behalf of the Partisans during the war. Then, in 1949, Dedijer helped arrange interviews between Adamic and top communist officials, including Tito, during Adamic's 1949 visit to Yugoslavia.[73] During their July 17 conversation, Adamic told Dedijer that a Cominform agent had warned him twice, in 1949 and again in 1950, that "he [Adamic] would become an enemy of the people if he supported Tito." But Adamic doubted this agent would do him harm. He concerned himself more with the four men in a car with Michigan license plates—whom Smole and Sharp mentioned to investigators and reporters—who visited Adamic in October 1950 and asked him about his manuscript on Tito. It became clear to Dedijer that "Adamic is living in constant fear that someone is going to assassinate him." He added that "Adamic feels the threats originate with the extreme right-wing[,] the Ustasi."[74]

Dedijer's account overlapped with much of the information the FBI gathered while conducting interviews about Adamic's death. One person, whose name censors redacted, told the agent interviewing him that Adamic received a number of death threats. He identified two groups: Cominform agents in the United States who "feared the effects of his book [about Tito] in Soviet lands" and former "Ustashi [sic] members" who "came from Yugoslavia during 1946 and 1947 as displaced persons," and now "violently opposed" any "friendly cooperation between the United States and Yugoslavia."[75] It is worth noting that despite the fact that the press and politicians at that moment claimed the Tito-Stalin split was a communist ruse to confuse the West, the Truman and Eisenhower administrations were providing some funds to Tito in order to maintain the schism in the communist bloc. Eight days after Adamic's death, Chicago agent Nicholas Wultich reported to J. Edgar Hoover "that two men were at Adamic's place for the purpose of killing him." Wultich's informant claimed that Adamic's "death may have been caused by the Ustashi [sic]" and resulted from their opposition to Adamic's forthcoming pro-Tito book.[76]

Another special agent, A. H. Belmont, reported to Ladd that one of his informants believed that someone "associated with Cominform agents in the United States" who also had ties to CPUSA threatened Adamic. The informant told Ladd that "I am threatened" by the same "elements." This communist warned Adamic that "there would be 'a bad ending'" if Adamic published a book on Tito. Belmont's informant also knew the story of the four men from Michigan and offered details beyond what the press had reported. For instance, the informant told Belmont that Ante Pavelić, the leader of Hitler's puppet government in Croatia, had fled to Argentina after the war and become a security adviser to reactionary president Juan Perón. Pavelić maintained an organization that "violently opposed" any "friendly cooperation between the United States and Yugoslavia."[77]

Although the FBI publicly claimed to have never investigated Adamic's death, they maintained an active file that questioned the finding of suicide at least through 1957 and then added newspaper clippings in the 1970s after the discovery of the hidden money. Although they noted other possible assassins, informants most frequently cited Croatian fascists as the most likely suspects. If indeed Adamic was murdered, the killers had to have been professional enough to provide the coroner with evidence to rule Adamic's death a suicide.[78]

Soviet agents would have known that Adamic had lost his influence with the American public and that the US government viewed assisting Tito as a strategic advantage regardless of what Adamic wrote. Adamic had never spied for the Soviets and had no knowledge to share with the US government that would have made him a threat to KGB operations. For the Croatian fascists, however, Adamic's support of the Partisans helped undermine their nationalist aspirations, and they wanted revenge. Anticommunists had no desire to acknowledge that Adamic either killed himself in part because of a failing marriage or was killed by Croatian fascist assassins who wanted him dead because he championed revolutionary antifascism. Portraying Adamic as the most recent victim of the KGB's standard practice of killing defectors allowed anticommunists to avoid addressing Adamic's charge that US officials masked their imperialistic intentions by insisting that they rooted their foreign policy choices in concerns for national security.

The Eagle and the Roots

The Eagle and the Roots appeared nine months after Adamic's death, and it provided Adamic with one last chance to remind the world that he favored an antifascist revolution focused on abolishing racism, ethnocentrism, and colonialism and promoting industrial democracy. To him, antifascism was cultural pluralism on a global scale, and it encompassed a nation's right to self-determination over colonialism. He pointed to Yugoslavia as a successful example of a people committed to overthrowing their colonial past and fighting fascism because of their devotion to a new humanism.

Adamic wrote *The Eagle and the Roots* after visiting his homeland from January through August 1949. During the trip, he saw family members in Slovenia, toured the country, and met with former rank-and-file Partisan soldiers as well as Yugoslavia's leaders. On June 9, Tito granted him a seven-hour interview.[79] These meetings convinced him that, above all else, the Yugoslav revolution was "a popular anti-imperialist move."[80] Adamic argued that Austrian colonization and Serbian irredentism made Yugoslavia "a mainstay of technological backwardness" and its people found themselves in "an ever deepening political-diplomatic-military hole." Trying to make a collectivist system work appeared their only way forward.[81] Seeking to establish a new Yugoslavia independent from the major world powers "was utopianism," but it had also been idealistic to believe that the Partisans could defeat both the Nazis and the Chetniks during the war.[82]

The Partisans' improbable victory and Tito's break from Stalin, Adamic claimed, inspired South Slavs to turn their revolutionary pluralism into the spirit that animated the new Yugoslavia. Early in the book, Adamic emphasized this point by recounting a conversation with his youngest brother,

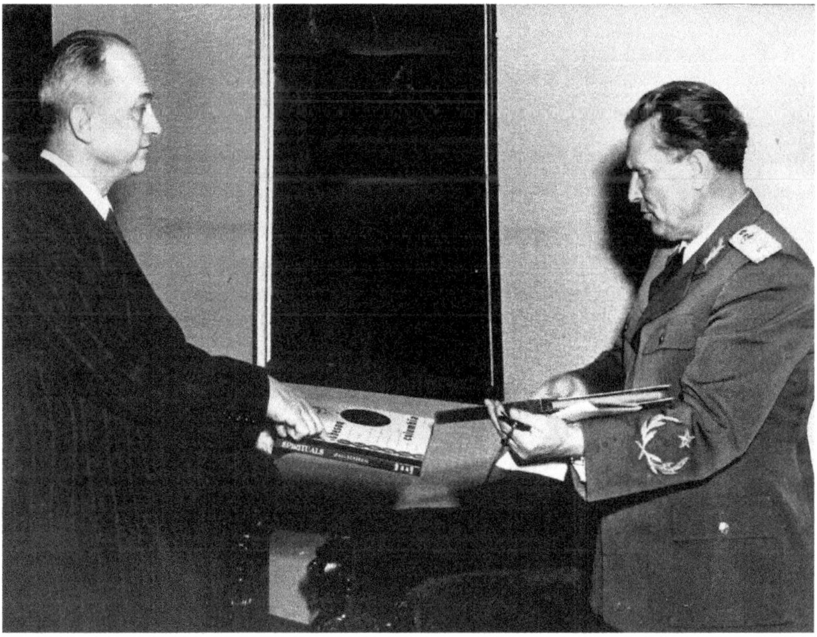

Visit to Josip Broz Tito, president of Yugoslavia, Belgrade, January 19, 1949. Courtesy of Združenje Slovenska izseljenska matica (Slovene Emigrant Association), Ljubljana, Slovenia.

France, about why throughout Yugoslavia people painted "Tito" and the slogan "Brotherhood and Unity" on walls, chimneys, and buildings. France explained to Louis that "the masses of people feel" that "Tito represents Liberation in the Yugoslav sense." Liberation meant "every-day things," such as "more schools, theaters, and cinemas" and "newspapers, more electric lights, highways," and railroad tracks and getting a new home with a bathroom, a job, and "three months' vacation." Previously, only elites loyal to the Austrian and then Serbian monarchies had regular access to education, culture, and modern conveniences. Now all could have such experiences. France pointed out the important point that, to some, Tito meant "the direct opposite," including the execution of one's "oldest son as a war criminal" and government seizure of the factory that you once owned.[83] France concluded that "Tito isn't so much the man as the symbol: and, more than a symbol, a surging idea. Most of us can't articulate it, so we say 'Tito' or paint his name on walls and buildings."[84] Tito represented a centuries-long desire among most South Slavs to live in a federated state of their own making.

Adamic considered himself a progressive, an independent leftist who would align with anyone from communists to conservatives who committed to moving democracy forward everywhere in the world. As a result, he viewed Tito's communist Yugoslavia as a stage in a larger political evolution toward democracy rather than as an end in itself. Making this point in *The Eagle and the Roots* could explain why Tito banned the book. Yugoslavism had mobilized Tito's revolution and was a defining feature of the nation, but Adamic understated the dictator's commitment to communism.

Adamic's message was lost on all but a few reviewers already sympathetic to his worldview. Anticommunist portrayals of Adamic as a pro-Soviet-mouthpiece-turned-Tito-apostle predisposed a fearful public to read their preconceptions into *The Eagle and the Roots*. Namely, they viewed the book as propaganda. Adamic's failure to examine acts of repression and brutality, including the executions of alleged war criminals, carried out by Tito's government certainly hurt Adamic's case with his critics. In addition, the book overwhelmed readers with details and digressions that blurred Adamic's points, and the editing contributed to this problem. Upon his return from Yugoslavia in the fall of 1949, Doubleday acquired the rights to the book and Adamic completed a draft by the spring of 1950. Concerned about the political climate, editors at the press put the project on hold. As relations between the United States and Yugoslavia strengthened, Doubleday's interest resumed and Adamic returned to writing and finished a second draft in the spring of 1951.[85] Numbering well over a thousand typed pages, the book required another round of revisions that never happened because of Adamic's untimely death. Stella returned from California to the couple's farmhouse in New Jersey and worked with Adamic's editor Timothy Seldes to cut the manuscript's size by one-third.[86]

Stella and Seldes removed Louis's original second chapter, "Old Yugoslavia: 1918–1940," mostly because it regurgitated his overview of Yugoslav history from *My Native Land*. Excising it meant losing evidence of the corrupt practices of the police and other government officials under the Serbian monarchy as well as a portrait of the life of peasants under semifeudal conditions. These stories had helped to highlight why establishing a new society based on "brotherhood and unity" meant so much.[87] A more significant but completely understandable omission was Adamic's 439 typescript pages of the chapter "A Game of Chess in an Earthquake." It focused on the relationship between domestic and foreign policy in the United States between 1950 and 1951. He argued that because World War II pulled the United States out of the Great

Depression, champions of the free enterprise system associated prosperity with war. As Americans returned to their consumerist ethic, which linked white middle-class suburban abundance with fighting communism, Adamic implied that Americans reverted to their "shadow" identities. Throughout the 1930s he considered most Americans shadows because they embraced conformity through a consumerist ethos. What they bought and what they wanted to purchase defined their identities. In the process, they lost their humanness and thus an appreciation for meaningful cultural exchanges that framed notions of democracy and community. He had argued in the 1930s that this shallowness made Americans ripe for a fascist movement. Adamic pointed to the Korean War as evidence that the United States now rooted its economic growth in military conflicts and that the majority of Americans accepted this new reality because it underpinned the culture of abundance. Adamic warned that Indochina might be the next theater of battle.[88]

Even if Stella and Seldes would have concentrated on his message and kept only the examples from those two chapters necessary to illustrate Adamic's antifascist anti-imperialism, it is unlikely that *The Eagle and the Roots* would have swayed the public as his earlier works had. Anticommunists had already succeeded in getting Americans to associate buying new cars, homes, televisions, and washing machines as helping to defeat communism and advance democracy.[89] Furthermore, Adamic's assertions that the tenets of fascism now underpinned US imperialist policies, and that policymakers' and pundits' calls for military action to contain communism masked this imperialism, would have been considered communist propaganda. Most Americans believed that fascism had been defeated and now viewed the Soviets as exemplars of totalitarianism. To the vast majority of people who accepted the Cold War liberal framing of the postwar world, Adamic's arguments were abstruse. Combined with the constant smears of Adamic by journalists, professional witnesses, and politicians, it became easy for the average person to conclude that Adamic was a subversive.

Newspapers, leading magazines, and academic journals reviewed *The Eagle and the Roots*. Pieces in the *New Republic*, the *Saturday Review*, and *The Nation* challenged the anticommunist narrative about Adamic. Noting that he first witnessed red-hunting politicians' efforts to smear Adamic when he covered congressional hearings in 1948 for the *New York Star*, Alexander H. Uhl, writing for the *New Republic*, declared that Adamic was neither a communist nor Tito's lackey. Although noting that *The Eagle and the Roots* was difficult to read, Uhl asserted that Adamic clearly wanted to promote a more humane world. In the

Saturday Review, Adamic's friend Shaemas O'Sheel praised Adamic as a champion of justice. Journalist Mark Gayn—a Jewish-Russian born in China and educated in Vladivostok before emigrating to the United States—had battled anticommunists during his personal and professional life simply because of his upbringing. He proved to be Adamic's most sympathetic reviewer. Writing for *The Nation*, he found *The Eagle and the Roots* "the story of an American liberal, distressed by the illiberal trends he saw at home, repelled by Soviet tactics, and seeking in loneness and anguish new freedom and spiritual reformation in the Yugoslavia where he was born."[90]

Unfortunately for Adamic's legacy, most reviews of *The Eagle and the Roots* reinforced the obituaries that presented him as a communist apostate who remained loyal to Tito because he had never truly assimilated as an American. The *Pittsfield (MA) Berkshire Eagle*, for instance, acknowledged that Adamic wrote "this book in a state of queer political ambivalence. . . . It is a paean to Tito's Yugoslavia tinged with only half-concealed bitterness to America and Britain. Adamic couldn't or wouldn't forget the time when the door was shut against him." This "book makes it clear (to this reviewer, at least) that, for all the 40 years he lived in this country, Adamic never really became an American. His heart remained in Yugoslavia."[91] The reviewer for the *Saint Louis Post-Dispatch* considered the book a "valuable step in understanding Yugoslavia," but he claimed that Adamic once saw the Soviets as "the hope of mankind."[92]

The reception of *The Eagle and the Roots* highlighted the fact that the anticommunists' narrative of Adamic's life and death had taken hold among the general public. People willingly forgot why they had praised his work from the 1930s through 1948. A poorly edited unfinished draft mired in excessive details and some redundancies undermined the slim chance that his antifascist message could resurface and affect public opinion.

Legacy

Anticommunists' version of Adamic's life and death continue to shape our current misunderstanding of him, in part, because some of the anticommunists who attacked him became scholars. Raditsa, for instance, went on to become a professor of European history at Fairleigh Dickinson University from 1950 to 1975. He joined both Bogdan Novak (University of Toledo) and George J. Prpic (John Carroll University) in writing some of the first scholarly accounts in the United States that dealt with Adamic and Yugoslav communism. Novak and Prpic had fled Tito's Yugoslavia and helped establish the traditionalist school of Cold War history. Traditionalists rejected the portrayal of American communists and fellow travelers as social idealists who romanticized the Russian Revolution and instead considered them agents of Soviet aggression who advanced Moscow's agenda in the United States.[93] Novak asserted that Adamic came "to support Tito, perhaps on orders from the Comintern."[94] Likewise, Prpic declared that when the Slovenian refugees who escaped Yugoslavia in 1945 "learned about massacres of many of their relatives" by the communists, "the blame was put on Adamic and his men."[95]

Henry Christian and Rudolph Vecoli wrote about Adamic in the same period as Novak and Prpic, and they rejected the assertion that Adamic embraced communism. But Christian and Vecoli repeated Adamic's friend and long-time *Nation* editor Carey McWilliams's assertion that, although not a communist, Adamic had gotten too caught up in the politics of his homeland.[96] Christian, Vecoli, McWilliams, and the most recent scholars of American identity have accepted the idea that Adamic stopped championing pluralism in 1942 and thus limited his antifascist activism. They failed to recognize that Adamic did not abandon pluralism for Titoism, but instead articulated a far more dynamic vision of ethnic and racial equality that eventually embraced anticolonialism led by black intellectuals and political activists. Misrepresenting Adamic's politics bogs us down in debates over whether he was a communist. And regardless of one's conclusion, the debate itself obscures how he revised and then globalized cultural pluralism and bridged it to black radicalism, and then worked with black activists and journalists to promote a new humanism.

With the opening of the Soviet archives, fights between the traditionalists and revisionists have heated up in the past two decades, and the importance of antifascism was further marginalized. In offering evidence of espionage and Soviet-funded front groups, traditionalists have asserted that anticommunists, while "excessive" at moments, were correct in seeing American communists as agents of Soviet aggression.[97] Some traditionalists have even gone as far as to try and revive the reputations of Budenz and Bentley. In Adamic's case, that has meant that the two leading traditionalists, John Earl Haynes and Harvey Klehr, have repeated Bentley's baseless accusation—which Raditsa, Novak, and Prpic gave credence to—that Adamic acted as an agent of the Soviet Union.[98]

Since the 1990s, a number of books have appeared demanding that we rethink anticommunism in more nuanced terms and by recognizing that a range of anticommunists existed from the dangerous and demagogic to the pragmatic. Most of these works acknowledge that independent leftists such as Adamic were victims of the politics of fear. A small number of those targeted by red hunters committed suicide, most lost jobs and then faced blacklists for about a decade, some went to jail, and all experienced various degrees of harassment.[99] Many scholars offer laments for such outcomes but then contend that concerns for national security (although overstated) were real and that liberal anticommunists could win economic and political reforms only by distancing themselves from communists. An uneasy synthesis has emerged that differentiates between "pragmatic" liberal anticommunists and their reactionary counterparts. The pragmatists supported the civil-rights movement, envisioned unions primarily as laborers' representatives in contract negotiations, and accepted containment as the guiding principle of US foreign policy. Reactionaries, in contrast, used anticommunism simply to advance their political ambitions and to shield their race hatred, xenophobia, antiunionism, and imperialist outlook.[100] Regardless of the interpretation one favors, scholars of anticommunism present the end of the Cold War as the conclusion of their stories. In doing so, they erase the politics of antifascism.

Adamic's lifelong project to define and advocate democracy led him to become an intellectual bridge between the cultural pluralists of the Progressive Era and the anticolonial activists who increasingly gained influence in the post–World War II years. He wanted his contemporaries to look beyond the communist-anticommunist dichotomy to focus on expanding workers' rights and on battling racism, nativism, and imperialism. Although a range of anticommunists certainly existed, liberal anticommunists ultimately accepted an alliance, no matter how uneasy, with reactionaries. For instance, Lyndon Johnson's administration promoted civil-rights legislation while simultaneously allowing Hoover and the FBI to expand surveillance operations on Martin Luther King Jr., Malcom X, and the Black Panthers because they feared communist influences in the African American community. Like other antifascists, Adamic, by the 1930s, recognized that anticommunists held an Anglocentric view of US history. Those who subscribed to this outlook promoted assimilation and thus undermined cultural pluralism, even if they supported aspects of pluralism.

To truly appreciate Adamic's legacy, we need to recognize that fascists and anticommunists both embraced militarism, accepted racial and ethnic hierarchies, and opposed militant working-class activism. By intervening in the Greek Civil War to aid an unpopular monarch and defeat the Greek partisans, Adamic argued that Truman advanced imperialism, underpinned by these fascist characteristics, in the name of anticommunism. Both Democratic and Republican administrations employed this approach to foreign policy from the 1950s through the 1990s in Southeast Asia and Latin America. As Historian Greg Grandin explained, the death squads in Vietnam and Central America not only sought to kill those they "thought to be working with the enemy but" they also wanted "to limit the actions of rebels or potential rebels by keeping them in a state of fear and anxiety."[101] Anticommunist death squads trained by the US military and aided by the Central Intelligence Agency used the containment of communism as an excuse to murder leftists of all stripes and install right-wing totalitarian governments in Asia and Latin America. Obviously, the principle of self-determination was never really a consideration in US foreign relations during the Cold War or after. On the domestic front, racial injustice and rising xenophobia defined the postwar United States, and the concerted effort by the anticommunist network to weaken unions validates the concerns of antifascists. With Soviet communism a distant memory, we continue to live in an America plagued by nativism, racism, and corporate hegemony, as well as a foreign policy that champions an economic colonialism. With deportations at an all-time high, frequent incidents of police attacks on people of color, and a president who panders to the richest Americans and white supremacists, recovering Adamic's legacy so that we can better understand our antifascist past is vital to our future.

Epilogue

Antifascism Today

Since 2016, public interest in antifascism has swelled as world politics have taken a hard right turn. In the United States, discussions and debates about fascism's reemergence have been directly connected to Donald Trump's campaign for president and subsequent victory in November 2016. On the campaign trail, Trump made racist, xenophobic, misogynistic, and homophobic statements, mocked a physically disabled reporter, promised to advance corporate hegemony by repealing labor and environmental regulations, encouraged his supporters to use violence against protestors, and expressed a passion for militarism. Pundits predicted that he had no chance at victory. When Trump won the general election, journalists and scholars began debating the meaning of fascism and what a US-style fascism would look like.[1] On August 12, 2017, concerns about fascism in the United States grew more palpable after white supremacists organized a "Unite the Right" rally in Charlottesville, Virginia. The white nationalists opposed city leaders' decision to take down a statue of Robert E. Lee. Counterprotesters mobilized their own demonstration in support of the monument's removal. A white nationalist drove his car into a gathering of the civil-rights supporters, killing activist Heather Heyer. Trump responded to the incident by saying both the white nationalists and civil-rights advocates deserved blame for the violence that occurred and insisted that "you have some very fine people on both sides."[2] Some journalists and scholars have compared Trump to Hitler, and others have argued that he is more like Mussolini. Still others assert that Trump's administration has accelerated the erosion of democratic norms that started in the 1990s and he could serve as a conduit to authoritarian rule in the United States.[3]

As I write this epilogue, the migrant children being separated from their parents and put into holding cells are added to the top of the very long list that public figures recite when they compare Trump's policies to fascism, which includes proposals to build a wall between the United States and Mexico to stop "illegals" and trying to ban Muslims from entry into the United States. Added to growing concerns about fascism's resurgence is the fact that reactionaries are gaining influence in France, the United Kingdom, Germany, and the Netherlands, and—as in the United States—have won office in Brazil, Italy, Hungary, Russia, Turkey, India, and the Philippines. It is possible that, over the next two years, this angst will dissipate as liberals and leftists mobilize into coalitions and elect new leaders. Obviously, the opposite possibility that the hard right will acquire even more power also exists.

Looking to Louis Adamic's legacy of progressive antifascism for insights about how to deal with our current moment has less to do with confronting specific policies and mobilizing for elections than it does with recognizing the importance of the stories we tell. Adamic knew that the way people understand their past reflects their values and their aspirations of the future. Seeing America as a melting pot, for instance, includes having a static idea of culture as white and Protestant. Adamic used narratives as political weapons to get the public to empathize with immigrants' feelings of exile, working-class anger, Japanese and African Americans' experiences with racial injustices, and Yugoslav revolutionary motivations. He advocated for visions such as the cultural pluralists' "beloved community" and the black radical image of "new humanism" that viewed identity making as a continuous process and true democracy as the spirit that guided the making and remaking of collective identities. Adamic admitted that the visions he fought for were utopian but then argued that the only way a new society could emerge was through such imagined futures.

Adamic's fight to kill fascism also included his determination to deliver his message regardless of the consequences, which for him included constant harassment by red-baiters, blacklisting by most newspapers and magazines, and likely his murder. After World War II, Adamic continued to argue that fascism had not ended with the Nazi's defeat because the same spirit of hatred that energized the brown shirts and black shirts animated colonialism. Included among his unfinished work was a chapter in which he argued that colonialism grew out of the "greatest subversive force in history . . . the Industrial Revolution." As McCarthyism enveloped the United States, Adamic intended to publish a piece that further asserted that financiers, not radicals, were the real subversives because they portrayed capitalism as progress and justified imperialism by claiming that they were helping "industrially backward areas of the world" advance. He criticized the Soviets for sharing their Western European and American rivals' belief that industrialization equaled development. Great Britain, France, the United States, and the Soviet Union sent troops into India, Nigeria, Vietnam, Guatemala, the Philippines, and Central Asia under the pretense of modernizing them but instead polluted streams, befouled the air, and disrupted cultural patterns.[4] At the moment Adamic died, he was pinning his hopes for the creation of a new humanism on the burgeoning anticolonial movements in Asian, Latin American, and African countries, as well as on the people in the new Yugoslavia who refused to become a client state of the Soviets. Adamic wanted his readers to view anticolonial uprisings as battles for a new morality that would bring death to the fascist ethos by placing equality above exploitation and thus build a society founded on true democracy.

His time and ours are different, but they are connected by what he identified as the persistence of a fascist ethos that linked white supremacy and a thirst for violence. Whether we are living through a moment in which that spirit has generated a short-lived ebb that will soon recede or whether the ebb will become a tsunami that overwhelms our liberal institutions and throws us into political chaos (as some predict), or something in between these two possibilities, remains to be seen. Adamic would tell us that as long as we let the fascist idea live, as long as we fail to build a society that seeks a beloved community and a new humanism that would include attitudes and policies that foster racial and ethnic equality, economic justice, and peace, we will continue to face iterations of fascism.

As the fascist ethos has survived, so too has the tradition of progressive antifascism, most noticeably in the form of Black Lives Matter.[5] Black Lives Matter activists operate locally, nationally, and globally "to change the terms of the debate on Blackness around the world" and to transform cultural dynamics "with an eye toward the dangerous impacts of anti-Blackness." Black Lives Matter began in 2012 after vigilante white supremacist George Zimmerman shot and killed seventeen-year-old Trayvon Martin in Florida. Taking stock of our current moment on what would have been Martin's twenty-third birthday, Patrisse Cullors, a cofounder of Black Lives Matter, declared that we "need to fight for a new human rights movement that recognizes and values Black life. Our fight must challenge white supremacist and state violence; otherwise, we will face the complete erosion of American democracy." Cullors then firmly placed Black Lives Matter in the antifascist tradition when she asserted, "Trayvon sparked a movement that stands up to fascism, that challenges the Trump administration and its Muslim ban, border wall and desecration of humanity; we must continue to remember Trayvon in our fight for Black lives."[6] Cullors and her fellow Black Lives Matter activists want to "build and nurture a beloved community that is bonded together through a beautiful struggle that is restorative, not depleting." In citing the idea of the "beloved community," Cullors harkened back to Randolph Bourne's argument that for democracy to flourish, marginalized people had to be at the center of defining rights and justice. For Cullors, building a beloved community means putting the black radical tradition and its focus on creating a new humanity at the center of our understanding of US history in order to create a future where blackness is "decriminalized."[7]

Currently, Black Lives Matter chapters are seeking to change discriminatory laws and increase black political power through the Electoral Justice Project and the Black Futures Lab. Leaders Jessica Byrd and Alicia Garza explained that these efforts have less to do with President Trump than they do with the Democrats. The organization wants Democrats to come to the aid of their base.[8] Speaking at the University of California–Berkeley in October 2017, Garza proclaimed that in "a fight against fascism, we need every tool we can get," including moments of direct confrontation, as happened in Charlottesville.[9] By this she means finding lawyers to assist those stopped by police and other means of nonviolent direct action that force a rethinking of black people's existence.[10]

Today's antifascist movement also seeks to confront far-right ideologues and fascists in the streets, and they are willing to engage in violence if they see it as necessary. What today is known as antifa is a decentralized organization with local chapters throughout the world whose members align themselves with the most radical end of the antifascist spectrum, "at the intersection of pan-socialist politics and direct-action strategy."[11] Antifa activists prefer to shape public discourse through meetings, writing articles, making movies, giving speeches, and protesting, but they do at times "punch Nazis in the face and don't apologize for it."[12] Antifa activists contend that violence in the name of "white supremacy, patriarchy, and authoritarianism" is a central feature of fascism and thus requires various forms of resistance, including "collective self-defense."[13]

Adamic and other progressive antifascists considered revolution to be one option among many, and he called revolutions a "method of progress" in 1938.[14] But Adamic also insisted that revolutions were a last resort, such as when the Nazis and Italian fascists invaded Yugoslavia. Antifa activists, for the most part, see Adamic's generation as failing to recognize that with the onset of fascism in Europe they were dealing with reactionary hypernationalists dedicated to advancing authoritarianism through violence. Antifa contends that to prevent a reemergence of fascist regimes, those seeking a beloved community have to view responding in kind, or even being more aggressive, as reasonable.[15]

We live in a moment when juries will rarely convict police officers and vigilantes for killing black people, and where most Americans accept or feel powerless to stop the social ills resulting from policies promoting stock-market growth over people's most basic needs, labor rights, and infrastructure. This reality existed before Trump's inauguration. As in Adamic's time, dealing a death blow to fascism clearly requires more than voting. People must directly confront white supremacy, xenophobia, corporate hegemony, and imperialism for democracy to truly exist.

Notes

Introduction

1. *Wilkes-Barre Record*, February 11, 1947, 13.

2. Ibid.

3. Historian Robert O. Paxton has offered a definition of fascism similar to the one Adamic provided. Paxton asserts that in its earliest stage fascism is a political mindset where adherents proclaim themselves victims of outsiders who have put their country in peril by threatening the purity of their national identity. See Paxton, "The Five Stages of Fascism" *Journal of Modern History* 70 (March 1998): 1–23; Paxton, *The Anatomy of Fascism* (New York: Knopf, 2004), 10–23; Richard Steigmann-Gall, "Star-Spangled Fascism: American Interwar Political Extremism in Comparative Perspective," *Social History* 42 (June 2017): 98–100.

4. Noticeably absent from Adamic's formulation of antifascism was the role of feminism. When making broad pronouncements, Adamic called for gender equality, and many of his writings included important female characters. But, for the most part, women remained in the background of his stories as an unexamined masculinity informed his politics.

5. Dejan Djokic, "'After One Hundred Years': The Yugoslav Idea in Historical Perspective," *Historically Speaking* 5 (November 2003): 18–19; Ervin Dolenc, "'The Generation at a Closed Door': Slovenian Intellectual Issues between the Two World Wars," *Slovene Studies* 23, nos. 1–2 (2001): 15–25, esp. 16.

6. Gerald Meyer, "The Cultural Pluralist Response to Americanization: Horace Kallen, Randolph Bourne, Louis Adamic, and Leonard Covello," *Socialism and Democracy* 22 (November 2008), online edition at http://sdonline.org/48/the-cultural-pluralist-response-to-americanization-horace-kallen-randolph-bourne-louis-adamic-and-leonard-covello/, 1, 8–10; Gary Gerstle, *American Crucible: Race and Nation in*

the Twentieth Century (Princeton, NJ: Princeton University Press, 2001), 3–13, 85–89, 186–96; Paul Spickard, *Almost All Aliens: Immigration, Race, and Colonialism in American History and Identity* (New York: Verso, 2007), 19–25; Nikhil Pal Singh, *Race and America's Long War* (Oakland: University of California Press, 2017), 35–53. It is important to note that immigrants did not passively submit to Americanizers' efforts and often found their own American identities through forms of everyday resistance to Americanization efforts. See James R. Barrett, "Americanization from the Bottom Up: Immigration and the Remaking of the Working Class in the United States, 1880–1930," *Journal of American History* (December 1992): 998. I would contend that the examples of "Americanization from the bottom up" that Barrett identified represented instances of cultural pluralist activism.

7. Louis Adamic, *My America, 1928–1938* (New York: Harper and Brothers, 1938), 207. Janja Žitnik Serafin, "Louis Adamic's Role in the Prehistory of Multiculturalism," *Association of European Migration Institution Journal* 11 (2012): 75–81; Meyer, "Cultural Pluralist Response"; Dan Shiffman, *Rooting Multiculturalism: The Work of Louis Adamic* (Madison, NJ: Fairleigh Dickinson University Press, 2003), 14–16, 142–65.

8. Randolph Bourne, "Trans-National America," *Atlantic Monthly*, July 1916, 93–97. Also see Everett Helmut Akam, *Transnational America: Cultural Pluralist Thought in the Twentieth Century* (New York: Rowman and Littlefield, 2002), 61–65; Casey Nelson Blake, *Beloved Community: The Cultural Criticism of Randolph Bourne, Van Wyck Brooks, Waldo Frank, and Lewis Mumford* (Chapel Hill: University of North Carolina Press, 1990), 118–21; Leslie J. Vaughn, "Cosmopolitanism, Ethnicity and American Identity: Randolph Bourne's 'Trans-national America,'" *Journal of American Studies* 25 (December 1991): 452–58.

9. Adamic, *My America*, 207. Historian Lizabeth Cohen later referred to the CIO's embrace of cultural pluralism as the culture of unity. See her *Making a New Deal: Industrial Workers in Chicago, 1919–1939* (New York: Cambridge University Press, 1990), 333–55.

10. Louis Adamic to Carey McWilliams, May 11, 1932, box 83, folder 8, Carey McWilliams Papers, 1894–1982, Collection 1319, Charles E. Young Research Library, Department of Special Collections, University of California–Los Angeles.

11. Louis Adamic, *The Native's Return: An American Immigrant Visits Yugoslavia and Discovers His Old Country* (New York: Harper and Brothers, 1934), 351; *Nation*, April 17, 1936, 457.

12. Louis Adamic to Carlton [last name illegible], October 30, 1931, box 51, folder 5, Louis Adamic Papers, Rare Books and Special Collections Department, Firestone Library, Princeton University (hereafter, Firestone).

13. Louis Adamic, "'America' Is a Magic Name," *Journal of Educational Sociology* 16 (February 1943): 327–28.

14. Janja Žitnik, "Louis Adamic, a Slovene, an American, an Observer, a Fighter, a 'Poet,'" *Dve domovini/Two Homelands* 9 (1998): 97; Dejan Djokic, "'After One Hundred Years': The Yugoslav Idea in Historical Perspective," *Historically Speaking* 5 (November 2003): 18–19; Dolenc, "'Slovenian Intellectuals," 16.

15. Louis Adamic, *A Nation of Nations* (New York: Harper and Brothers, 1945), 202–7.

16. W. E. B. DuBois, "The Souls of White Folk," in *Darkwater: Voices from Within the Veil* (New York: Harcourt, Brace and Howe, 1920), 31.

17. DuBois, "Souls of White Folk," 37.

18. DuBois quoted in Nikhil Pal Singh, "Culture/Wars: Recoding Empire in an Age of Democracy," *American Quarterly* 50 (September 1998): 484. On DuBois and black anticolonialism in general, see Nikhil Pal Singh, *Black Is a Country: Race and the Unfinished Struggle for Democracy* (Cambridge, MA: Harvard University Press, 2004), 101–73. On links between Adamic and DuBois, see Louis Adamic to W. E. B. DuBois, July 7, 1947; DuBois to Adamic, October 28, 1947, W. E. B. DuBois Papers (MS 312), Special Collections and University Archives, University of Massachusetts Amherst Libraries; *New York Amsterdam Star-News*, December 13, 1941, 17; *New York Amsterdam Star-News*, October 16, 1948, 23; *El Paso Herald-Post*, January 22, 1948, 14; *Courier-News* (Bridgewater, New Jersey), February 21, 1949, 4; *Terre Haute (IN) Tribune*, April 5, 1951, 6.

19. *War and Post-war* 3 (January–February 1944): 6. On his critiques of communists, see Louis Adamic, "What the Proletariat Reads: Conclusions Based on a Year's Study among Hundreds of Workers in the United States," *Saturday Review of Literature* 11 (December 1, 1934), 321–22; Adamic, "The Great 'Bootleg Coal' Industry," *Nation* (January 9, 1935), 46. Adamic, *My America*, 70, 82–84, 650–51. On "progressive," see Doug Rossinow, *Visions of Progress: The Left-Liberal Tradition in America* (Philadelphia: University of Pennsylvania Press, 2008), 147.

20. Michael Denning, *The Cultural Front: The Laboring of American Culture in the Twentieth Century* (London: Verso, 1997), 4–11, 454. Denning's quote calling Adamic a leading "theorist" is on page 11. For more on antifascism dominating that period, see Wendy L. Wall, *Inventing the "American Way": The Politics of Consensus from the New Deal to the Civil Rights Movement* (New York: Oxford University Press, 2008), 43–48; Christopher Vials, *Haunted by Hitler: Liberals, the Left, and the Fight against Fascism in the United States* (Amherst: University of Massachusetts Press, 2014), 72–79; Daniel Geary, "Carey McWilliams and Antifascism, 1934–43," *Journal of American History* 90 (December 2003): 912–34.

21. Carey McWilliams, *Louis Adamic and Shadow-America* (Los Angeles: Arthur Whipple, 1935), 42, 40, 53.

22. Louis Adamic, *Laughing in the Jungle* (New York: Arno and the New York Times, 1969), 25–37.

23. John L. Modic, "Laughing in the Jungle: The Writer as Hero" *Slovene Studies Journal* 4, no. 2 (1982): 113–22; Jerneja Petrič, "The Strenuous Business of Creating a New World: The Literary Radicalism of Louis Adamic," *Slovenski Izseljenski Kolendar* 1994. It should be noted that some scholars have repeated this story as fact, leading to misperceptions about Adamic's connection to his homeland.

24. Louis Adamic, *What's Your Name?* (New York: Harper and Brothers, 1942), 11–12.

25. Gerstle, *American Crucible*, 128–86; Paul Spickard, *Almost All Aliens*, 291–339.

26. Louis Adamic, "America and Yugoslavia," 1947, folder 2, box 37, Firestone.

27. Report from New York Office to J. Edgar Hoover, May 2, 1957, and Report Newark Office to Director FBI, May 3, 1957, FBI, Department of Justice, Washington, DC, FOIA/FBI Adamic file 100–63670–1; *Chicago Tribune*, September 6, 1951, 14; *Los Angeles Times*, November 4, 1951, 32.

28. In the late 1990s, Michael Denning and Gerald Horne pointed out that by calling progressive organizations and individuals "front groups" and "dupes of Moscow," anticommunists not only blunted the effectiveness of those activists trying to advance their social justice agenda from the Great Depression through the Cold War, they also influenced the historical record. Too often scholars have concerned themselves more with investigating whether progressives had ties to the Communist Party than with focusing on the work that they did. Adamic distrusted Communist Party leaders because he found them too committed to the party line. But he worked with party members who shared his antifascist beliefs. Although Denning and Horne made such distinctions and focused on activism over affiliation, traditionalist scholars, those who identify all communists as working first and foremost for Stalin, have kept the anticommunist version of this period influential, if not dominant. Recently, Landon R. Y. Storrs and Nick Fischer, building on Denning, Horne, and other works on progressives, convincingly challenge the traditionalists' insistence that responsible anticommunists should be separated from their more extreme associates. Extreme anticommunists held power and created the policies that undermined efforts to advance true democratic projects by building the surveillance state, militarizing police forces, and presenting dissent as un-American and therefore illegitimate. My work joins Rachel Ida Buff's study of the American Committee for the Protection of the Foreign Born (which Adamic belonged to) and Robert Zecker's examination of the International Workers Order (which Adamic worked with) to build on Denning and Horne's search to better understand the progressive project for racial and ethnic equality, anticolonialism, and economic justice. Denning, *Cultural Front*, xiii–50; Gerald Horne, *Communist Front? The Civil Rights Congress, 1946–1956* (Rutherford, NJ: Fairleigh Dickinson University Press, 1988), 13–21; Landon R. Y. Storrs, *The Second Red Scare and the Unmaking of the New Deal Left* (Princeton, NJ: Princeton University Press, 2013), 4–15; Nick Fischer, *Spider Web: The Birth of American Anticommunism* (Urbana: University of Illinois Press, 2016), 256–82; Rachel Ida Buff, *Against the Deportation Terror: Organizing for Immigrant Rights in the Twentieth Century* (Philadelphia: Temple University Press, 2018), 1–77; Robert Zecker, *"A Road to Peace and Freedom": The International Workers' Order and the Struggle for Economic Justice and Civil Rights, 1930–1954* (Philadelphia: Temple University Press, 2018), 1–18.

29. Benjamin Balthaser, *Anti-imperialist Modernism: Race and Transnational Radical Culture from the Great Depression to the Cold War* (Ann Arbor, MI: University of Michigan Press, 2016), 1–37, 188–49; Rachel A. Batch, "Ethnic Unity and Class Struggle: Croatian-Americans, Transnationalism, and Political Action in Depres-

sion and War," paper presented at Pennsylvania Labor History Workshop, February 2012, in author's possession; Keisha N. Blain, *Set the World on Fire: Black Nationalist Women and the Global Struggle for Freedom* (Philadelphia: University of Pennsylvania Press, 2018), 133–65; Mark Bray, *Antifa: The Anti-fascist Handbook* (New York: Melville House, 2017), xiii–37; Buff, *Against the Deportation Terror*, 1–77; Joseph Fronczak, "Local People's Global Politics: A Transnational History of the Hands off Ethiopia Movement of 1935." *Diplomatic History* 39, no. 2 (2015): 245–74; Barbara Ransby, *Eslanda: The Large and Unconventional Life of Mrs. Paul Robeson* (New Haven, CT: Yale University Press, 2014), 7–8, 122–58; Vials, *Haunted by Hitler*, 1–89; Zecker, "*Road to Peace and Freedom*," 166–212.

Chapter 1. Modernism and Exile: The Origins of Louis Adamic's Politics

1. Louis Adamic, *Laughing in the Jungle* (New York: Arno, 1969), 293.

2. David R. Roediger, *Working toward Whiteness: How America's Immigrants Became White* (New York: Basic, 2005), 37–51, 59, 72–92.

3. Adamic, *Laughing*, 26.

4. Ibid., 12.

5. Irena Avsenik Nabergoj, *Mirror of Reality and Dreams: Stories and Confession by Ivan Cankar* (Frankfurt: Peter Lang, 2008), 24–26. For more on Cankar's importance to Adamic, see Jerneja Petrič, "Mediator between Two Cultures: Louis Adamic's Translation of Alojz Kraigher's Short Story into English," *Dve domovini/Two Homelands* 9 (1998): 85–87; Henry A. Christian, "Louis Adamic: Immigrant and American Liberal" (PhD diss., Brown University, 1968), 18–20; France Adamič, "The Links between Louis Adamič and Slovene Journalists and Literary Figures (1921–1941)," *Dve domovini/Two Homelands* 9 (1998): 56. For feelings of exile in this era, see George Cotkin, *Existential America* (Baltimore, MD: Johns Hopkins University Press, 2003), 5.

6. James R. Barrett, "Americanization from the Bottom Up: Immigration and the Remaking of the Working Class in the United States, 1880–1930," *Journal of American History* (December 1992): 998; Homi K. Bhabha, *The Location of Culture* (New York: Routledge, 2010), 1–2, 7; Bhabha, "Culture's In-Between," in *Questions of Cultural Identity*, ed. Stuart Hall and Paul Du Gay (London: Sage, 1996), 53–60; Ien Ang, "Together-in-Difference: Beyond Diaspora, into Hybridity," *Asian Studies Review* 27 (June 2003): 149–50; Henry R. Cooper Jr., "Are Louis Adamic's Novels Slovene Novels?," in *Slovenski roman: Mednarodni simpozij Obdobja—Metode in zvrsti*, ed. Miran Hladnik and Gregor Kocijan (Ljubljana: Univerza v Ljubljani, 2003), 623–24.

7. Scrapbook, box 1, Dr. Tine Kurent Collection (uncatalogued as of May–June 2014), Narodna in Univerzitetna Knjižnica Ljubljana (hereafter, NUK). Henry A. Christian, *Louis Adamic: A Checklist* (Kent, OH: Kent State University Press, 1971), xxviii; Dan Shiffman, *Rooting Multiculturalism: The Work of Louis Adamic* (Madison, NJ: Fairleigh Dickinson University Press, 2003), 27–30.

8. The dates of Adamic's departure from Slovenia and arrival in the United States have been a matter of debate, because Adamic referred to different dates at different points in his life. Aljoša Pelhan of the National and University Library of Slovenia found the manifest from the ship Adamic took and confirmed that he left in the fall of 1912 and arrived at Ellis Island in December of that year. Scrapbook, box 1, Dr. Tine Kurent Collection, NUK. Christian, *Louis Adamic*, xxviii; Shiffman, *Rooting Multiculturalism*, 27–30.

9. Matjaž Klemenčič, "Slovenes and Slovene Americans, 1870–1940," *Immigration in American History: Arrival, Adaptation, and Integration*, ed. Elliott Robert Barkan (Santa Barbara, CA: ABC-CLIO, 2013), 2: 619.

10. Scrapbook, box 1, Dr. Tine Kurent Collection, NUK. Shiffman, *Rooting Multiculturalism*, 27–45; Dale E. Peterson, "The American Adamic: Immigrant Bard of Diversity," *Massachusetts Review* 44 (Spring 2003): 235.

11. Scrapbook, box 1, Dr. Tine Kurent Collection (uncatalogued as of May–June 2014), NUK. Christian, "Louis Adamic," 1–14; Shiffman, *Rooting Multiculturalism*, 27–45; Peterson, "American Adamic," 235.

12. Kevin Starr, *Material Dreams: Southern California through the 1920s* (New York: Oxford University Press, 1990), 348; Michael Denning, *The Cultural Front: The Laboring of American Culture in the Twentieth Century* (London: Verso, 1997), 237.

13. Christian, "Louis Adamic," 1–14.

14. Peterson, "American Adamic," 235; Christian, *Louis Adamic*, xxii–xxiii; Shiffman, *Rooting Multiculturalism*, 42–43.

15. Christian, "Louis Adamic," 48–49, 66.

16. Ibid., 48–49, 66.

17. Louis and Stella Adamic radio interview transcript on WLZ on March 9, 1934, gradivo 6, mapa 23, Louis Adamič M.S. 1858 (hereafter, Adamič M.S.), NUK.

18. Louis Adamic, "The Land of Laughs," *American Mercury* 16, no. 64 (April 1929): 482–83.

19. Cotkin, *Existential America*, 5, 31–32; James R. Barrett, "Americanization from the Bottom Up: Immigration and the Remaking of the Working Class in the United States, 1880–1930," *Journal of American History*, December 1992, 997–1000, 1006–7.

20. Louis Adamic, "The Passing of American Individualism," *American Scholar* 1 (October 1932): 423.

21. Carl E. Schorske, *Fin-de-Siècle Vienna: Politics and Culture* (New York: Knopf, 1979), xvii–xxvii, 12.

22. Friedrich Nietzsche, *On the Genealogy of Morals*, trans. Walter Kaufmann and R. J. Hollingdale (New York: Vintage, 1989), 152.

23. Friedrich Nietzsche, *Ecce Homo*, trans. Walter Kaufmann (New York: Vintage, 1989), 218.

24. Friedrich Nietzsche, *Beyond Good and Evil*, trans. R. J. Hollingdale (New York: Penguin, 2003), 194–202; Jennifer Ratner-Rosenhagen, *American Nietzsche: A History of an Icon and His Ideas* (Chicago: University of Chicago Press, 2012), 22, 109–16.

25. On Adamic's Nietzschean point of view, see Louis Adamic to Ivan Molek, March 9, 1926, folder 2, box 1, Ivan Molek Papers, Chicago History Museum, Chicago (hereafter, Molek Papers). Adamic misdated the letter 1925, but it is clearly 1926. It should be noted that most modern scholars do not view Nietzsche as a nihilist, as writers in the early twentieth century did. Nietzsche argued that catharsis followed one's coming to terms with absurdity and despair. See Cotkin, *Existential America*, 5.

26. Christian, "Louis Adamic," 37, 41.

27. Nabergoj, *Mirror*, 24–26. For more on Cankar's importance to Adamic, see Petrič, "Mediator," 85–87; Christian, "Louis Adamic," 18–20. It should be noted that Adamic's translations of Cankar were criticized by Slovene intellectuals. See Adamič, "Links," 56.

28. Henry R. Cooper Jr., "Oton Župančič and Slovene Modernism," *Slovene Studies* 13, no. 1 (1991): 7–9; Irena Avsenik Nabergoj, *Justice and Redemption: Anthropological Realities and Literary Visions by Ivan Cankar* (Frankfurt: Peter Lang, 2014), 118, 303–17.

29. Josef Svatopluk Machar, "Superman," *Living Age*, December 8, 1923, 467–73, trans. Louis Adamic. Thomas Ort, *Art and Life in Modernist Prague: Karel Čapek and His Generation, 1911–1938* (New York: Palgrave Macmillan, 2013), 49–50. In addition to Machar, for the February 2, 1924, issue of *Living Age*, Adamic also translated the Slovenian writer Alojz Kraigher's story of a peasant king who experienced the tragedies of a superman. Petrič, "Mediator," 88.

30. Adamic, *Laughing*, 186.

31. Christian, "Louis Adamic," 1–14.

32. Matthew Avery Sutton, *Aimee Semple McPherson and the Resurrection of Christian America* (Cambridge, MA: Harvard University Press, 2007), 1–4, 120–22.

33. Starr, *Material Dreams*, 142–43; Sutton, *Aimee Semple McPherson*, 94–143.

34. Sutton, *Aimee Semple McPherson*, 115.

35. Louis Adamic, "Was Aimee McPherson's 'Shack' in the Grove of Aphrodite?" *Haldeman-Julius Monthly* 4 (October 1926): 18–20.

36. Adamic, "Aimee McPherson's 'Shack,'" 23, 24.

37. Adamic, *Laughing*, 118. For the Burton story, see Louis Adamic, "The Crusader," *American Parade* 1 (July 1926): 72–77; *Laughing*, 116–22.

38. Adamic, "Crusader," 72.

39. Adamic, "Crusader," 74–77. Adamic, *Laughing*, 237, 239. Others have used the Lonie Burton example to illustrate Adamic's skepticism of socialism. See Carey McWilliams, *Louis Adamic and Shadow-America* (Los Angeles: Arthur Whipple, 1935), 21–22; Christian, "Louis Adamic," 20–25.

40. Matjaž Klemenčič, "American Slovenes and the Leftist Movements in the United States in the First Half of the Twentieth Century," *Journal of American Ethnic History* 15 (Spring 1996): 33; Joseph Petro Stipanovich, "'In Unity Is Strength': Immigrant Workers and Immigrant Intellectuals in Progressive America: A History of the South Slav"

(PhD diss., University of Minnesota, 1978), 1–35; Federal Bureau of Investigation/FOIA Etbin Kristan file 105–16532.

41. Adamic to Molek, March 9, 1926, box 1, folder 2, Molek Papers.

42. Klemenčič, "American Slovenes," 33; Stipanovich, "In Unity Is Strength," 1–35, 149–51; Ivan Čizmič, "Yugoslav Immigrants in the U.S. Labor Movement, 1880–1920," in *American Labor and Immigration History, 1877–1920s: Recent European Research*, ed. Dirk Hoerder (Urbana: University of Illinois Press, 1983), 188–89; Frank Petrich, "The South Slavic Socialist Activities in the United States" in *The American Labor Year-Book, 1916* (New York: Rand School Press, 1916), 142–43; Federal Bureau of Investigation/FOIA Etbin Kristan file 105–16532.

43. Mirko Jurak, "'The New World' in Etbin Kristan's Plays," *MELUS* 12 (Winter 1985): 53–54; Federal Bureau of Investigation/FOIA Etbin Kristan file 105–16532.

44. Stipanovich, "In Unity Is Strength," 15–30; Čizmič, "Yugoslav Immigrants," 185–89.

45. Adamic to Molek, February 26, 1926, box 1, file 2, Molek Papers.

46. Ibid.

47. Ivan Cankar, *Yerney's Justice*, trans. Louis Adamic (New York: Vanguard, 1926), iv.

48. Cankar, *Yerney's Justice*, 15.

49. Cankar, *Yerney's Justice*. For an analysis of Cankar's influence on Adamic and of his translation of *Yerney's Justice*, see James Gow and Cathie Carmichael, *Slovenia and the Slovenes: A Small State and the New Europe* (Bloomington: Indiana University Press, 2000), 71–73; Louis Adamic, *My America, 1928–1938* (New York: Harper and Brothers, 1938), 131; Christian, *Louis Adamic*, xxii; Petrič, "Mediator," 85–87; Christian, "Louis Adamic," 18–20.

50. Adamic to Molek, March 9, 1926, box 1, folder 2, Molek Papers.

51. Ibid.

52. Upton Sinclair to Louis Adamic, July 28, 1926, box 49, folder 9, Louis Adamic Papers, Rare Books and Special Collections Department, Firestone Library, Princeton University, Princeton, NJ (hereafter, Firestone).

53. Adamic to Sinclair, July 30, 1926; Sinclair to Adamic, July 31, 1926, both in box 49, folder 9, Firestone.

54. Adamic to Sinclair, July 30, 1926, box 7, file July 16–31, Upton Sinclair Papers, Lilly Library, University of Indiana, Bloomington.

55. Philip Gleason, "American Identity and Americanization," *Harvard Encyclopedia of American Ethnic Groups*, ed. Stephan Thernstrom, Ann Orlov, and Oscar Handlin (Cambridge, MA: Harvard University Press, 1980), 40–41; Gary Gerstle, "Liberty, Coercion, and the Making of Americans," *Journal of American History* 84 (September 1997): 525; Russell A. Kazal, "Revisiting Assimilation: The Rise, Fall, and Reappraisal of a Concept in American Ethnic History," *American Historical Review* 100 (April 1995): 437–40; Gerald Meyer, "The Cultural Pluralist Response to Americanization: Horace Kallen, Randolph Bourne, Louis Adamic, and Leonard

Covello," *Socialism and Democracy* 22 (November 2008), online edition at http://sdonline.org/48/the-cultural-pluralist-response-to-americanization-horace-kallen-randolph-bourne-louis-adamic-and-leonard-covello/, 1, 8–10. For a slightly different perspective, see Christina A. Ziegler-McPherson, *Americanization in the States: Immigrant Social Welfare Policy, Citizenship, and National Identity in the United States, 1908–1929* (Gainesville: University of Florida Press, 2009), 1–15.

56. Adamic, "Land of Laughs," 482.

57. Ibid., 482–83.

58. Ibid., 486.

59. Louis Adamic, "The 'Assassin' of Wilson," *American Mercury* 21 (October 1930): 146.

60. H. L. Mencken, "On Being an American," in *Prejudices: First, Second, and Third Series* (New York: Library of America, 2010), 303, 309.

61. Mencken, "On Being an American," 309.

62. Mencken, "On Being an American," 311.

63. Christian, "Louis Adamic," 48–49, 66.

64. Adamic, *Laughing*, 333, and Kevin Piper, "The Making of an American: Counternarration in Louis Adamic's *Laughing in the Jungle* and Anzia Yezierska's *Bread Givers*," *MELUS* 35 (Spring 2010): 99–109.

65. Adamic, *Laughing*, 14–15, 20.

66. Ibid., 81–90.

67. Ibid., 95–96.

68. Ibid., 310–15.

69. Ibid., 323–24.

70. Ibid., 270.

71. Louis Adamic, "Case History," *American Mercury* (November 1928): 290–92; Adamic, *Laughing*, 270–80.

72. Adamic, "Case History," 293–95; Adamic, *Laughing*, 281–83.

73. Adamic, *Laughing*, 288–91.

74. Ibid., 118.

75. Norman Foerster to Adamic, October 29, 1934, korespondenca 4, mapa 12, Adamič M.S., NUK.

76. Louis Adamic, "Dynamite Explained," *Contempo* 1 (June 1931), 3–4; Louis Adamic, *Dynamite: The Story of Class Violence in America*, repr. (New York: Chelsea House, 1983), ix.

77. Rudolph J. Vecoli, "*Dynamite*: Adamic and Working Class America" in *Louis Adamic: Simpozij/Symposium* (Ljubljana: Univerza Edvarda Kardelja, 1981), 155.

78. Adamic, *Dynamite*, 380–93.

79. Ibid., viii, 350–51.

80. Adamic, "Dynamite Explained," 3–4.

81. Adamic, *Dynamite*, 202. On rank and file workers, see Adamic, "Dynamite Explained," 3–4.

82. Adamic, *Dynamite*, 7–8.

83. Ibid., 5.

84. Ibid., 135.

85. Ibid., 156.

86. Christian, "Louis Adamic," 57.

87. Austin Lewis to Adamic, May 1, 1931, box 47, folder 5, Firestone.

88. Christian, "Louis Adamic," 57–59. William Z. Foster is quoted on page 58.

89. I appreciate Jon-Christian Suggs's sharing his knowledge of James McCann with me in a series of email exchanges. James McCann to Adamic, April 1, 1930, box 48, folder 4, Firestone.

90. McCann to Adamic, April 24, 1931, box 48, folder 4, Firestone.

91. McCann to Adamic, July 31, 1932, box 48, folder 4, Firestone.

92. Adamic, "Dynamite Explained," 4.

93. Slovenian intellectuals took notice of Adamic after his translation of *Yerney's Justice*. Literary critic Josip Vidmar credited Adamic with capturing the spirit of Cankar's work but rebuked him for eliminating complex passages and thus failing to provide English-language readers with an appreciation of the book's nuances. Then, in 1931, Adamic received more positive press from Mile Klopčič, a poet and journalist, who reported from Slovenia for Molek's *Prosveta* as well as the Ljubljana newspaper *Jutro* ("Morning"). Eventually, Klopčič introduced Adamic to the writer Juš Kozak, who translated some of Adamic's articles for inclusion in edited collections of Slovene literature. See F. Adamič, "Links," 56–57.

94. Ervin Dolenc, "Culture, Politics, and Slovene Identity," in *Independent Slovenia: Origins, Movements, Prospects*, ed. Jill Benderly and Evan Kraft (New York: St. Martin's, 1994), 69–80.

95. Gow and Carmichael, *Slovenia*, 61–62.

96. Župančič quoted in Janja Žitnik, "Louis Adamic, a Slovene, an American, an Observer, a Fighter, a 'Poet,'" *Dve domovini/Two Homelands* 9 (1998): 98, 100.

97. Žitnik, "Louis Adamic," 96–105; Henry R. Cooper Jr., "Are Louis Adamic's Novels Slovene Novels?," in *Slovenski roman*, Mednarodni simpozij Obdobja—Metode in zvrsti, Ljubljana, December 5–7, 2002, ed. Miran Hladnik and Gregor Kocijan, 623–24 (Ljubljana: Univerza v Ljubljani, 2003).

98. Louis and Stella Adamic radio interview transcript on WLZ on March 9, 1934, gradivo 6, mapa 23, Adamič M.S., NUK.

99. Adamic, *Native's Return*, 6.

100. Adamic's nephew, Tine Kurent, has some of his uncle's letters to his mother and grandmother. See box 1, Dr. Tine Kurent Collection, NUK.

101. Louis Adamic, *Grandsons* (New York: Harper and Brothers, 1935), 81.

102. Dejan Djokic, "'After One Hundred Years': The Yugoslav Idea in Historical Perspective," *Historically Speaking* 5 (November 2003): 18–19; Sabrina P. Ramet, "The Meaning of Yugoslav History," *Slovene Studies* 31, no. 2 (2009): 141–42; Carole Rogel, *The Slovenes and Yugoslavism, 1890–1914* (New York: Columbia University Press,

1977), v–vii, 14–27, 75–89; Ivo Banac, "Historiography of the Countries of Eastern Europe: Yugoslavia," *American Historical Review* 97, no. 4 (October 1992): 1084–1104.

103. Dolenc, "Generation at a Closed Door," 19.

104. Ibid., 20.

105. Ibid.

106. Henry A. Christian, "Adamic's *Struggle*: The International History of a 'Radical' Pamphlet," in *Louis Adamic: Simpozij/Symposium*, 323–30.

107. Adamic, *Struggle*, 3–5. Brigit Farley, "Aleksandar Karadjordjević and the Royal Dictatorship of Yugoslavia," in *Balkan Strongmen: Dictators and Authoritarian Rulers of South Eastern Europe*, ed. Bernard J. Fischer, 60–86 (West Lafayette, IN: Purdue University Press, 2007).

108. Adamic to Molek, March 24, 1933, box 1, folder 4; Molek to Adamic, April 11, 1933, box 1, folder 4; Molek to Adamic, April 19, 1933, box 1, folder 4, all in Molek Papers.

109. Adamic, *Struggle*, 3–5. Farley, "Aleksandar Karadjordjević," 60–86; Lorraine M. Lees, *Yugoslav-Americans and National Security during World War II* (Urbana, IL: University of Illinois Press, 2007), 55.

Chapter 2. Liberating "Shadow" America: Antifascism, Pluralism, and Democracy

1. Louis Adamic, *Grandsons* (New York: Harper and Brothers, 1935), 30, 326.

2. Michael Denning, *The Cultural Front: The Laboring of American Culture in the Twentieth Century* (London: Verso, 1997), 11.

3. On Adamic and pluralism, see Janja Žitnik Serafin, "Louis Adamic's Role in the Prehistory of Multiculturalism," *Association of European Migration Institution Journal* 11 (2012): 75–81; Gerald Meyer, "The Cultural Pluralist Response to Americanization: Horace Kallen, Randolph Bourne, Louis Adamic, and Leonard Covello," *Socialism and Democracy* 22 (November 2008), online edition at http://sdonline.org/48/the-cultural-pluralist-response-to-americanization-horace-kallen-randolph-bourne-louis-adamic-and-leonard-covello/, 1, 8–10; Dan Shiffman, *Rooting Multiculturalism: The Work of Louis Adamic* (Madison, NJ: Fairleigh Dickinson University Press, 2003), 14–16, 142–65. For other views of Slavic immigrants synthesizing radical visions and cultural values, see Robert M. Zecker, "'Not Communists Exactly, but Sort of like Non-believers': The Hidden Radical Transcript of Slovak Immigrants in Philadelphia, 1890–1954," *Oral History Review* 29, no. 1 (Winter–Spring 2002): 1–37; Rachel A. Batch, "Ethnic Unity and Class Struggle: Croatian-Americans, Transnationalism, and Political Action in Depression and War," paper presented at Pennsylvania Labor History Workshop, Harrisburg, PA, February 2012, in author's possession. On pluralism, see Jonathan Hansen, "True Americanism: Progressive Intellectuals and the Problem of Liberal Nationalism," in *Americanism: New Perspectives on the History of an Ideal*, ed. Michael Kazin and Joseph A. McCartin, 73–89 (Chapel Hill, NC: University of North

Carolina Press, 2006); Russell A. Kazal, "The Lost World of Pennsylvania Pluralism: Immigrants, Regions, and the Early Origins of Pluralist Ideologies in America," *Journal of American Ethnic History* 27, no. 3 (Spring 2008): 7–11; Matthew Frye Jacobson, "A Ghetto to Look Back To: *World of Our Fathers*, Ethnic Revival, and the Arc of Multiculturalism," *American Jewish History* 88, no. 4 (December 2000): 463–74. On civic and racial nationalism, see Gary Gerstle, *American Crucible: Race and Nation in the Twentieth Century* (Princeton, NJ: Princeton University Press, 2001), 3–13, 85–89, 186–96; David Gutiérrez, "Migration, Emergent Ethnicity, and the 'Third Space': The Shifting Politics of Nationalism in Greater Mexico," *Journal of American History* 86, no. 2 (September 1999): 498–504. On immigrants and being "white," see David R. Roediger, *Working toward Whiteness: How America's Immigrants Became White* (New York: Basic, 2005), 3–34, 199–234; Mae M. Ngai, *Impossible Subjects: Illegal Aliens and the Making of Modern America* (Princeton, NJ: Princeton University Press, 2004), 3–10; William Preston Jr., *Aliens and Dissenters: Federal Suppression of Radicals, 1903–1933*, repr. (Urbana, IL: University of Illinois Press, 1994), 2–4.

4. Randolph Bourne, "Trans-national America," *Atlantic Monthly*, July 1916, 97. Louis Adamic, "The Passing of American Individualism," *American Scholar* 1 (October 1932): 423–29. Everett Helmut Akam, *Transnational America: Cultural Pluralist Thought in the Twentieth Century* (New York: Rowman and Littlefield, 2002), 4, 32–33; Casey Nelson Blake, *Beloved Community: The Cultural Criticism of Randolph Bourne, Van Wyck Brooks, Waldo Frank, and Lewis Mumford* (Chapel Hill: University of North Carolina Press, 1990), 51–52, 115–21; James Livingston, *Pragmatism and the Political Economy of Cultural Revolution, 1850–1940* (Chapel Hill: University of North Carolina Press, 1997), 65–82, 129–31; Jeffrey Sklansky, *The Soul's Economy: Market Society and Selfhood in American Thought, 1820–1920* (Chapel Hill: University of North Carolina Press, 2002), 3–6, 205–23; Richard Schneirov and Gaston A. Fernandez, *Democracy as a Way of Life in America* (New York: Routledge, 2014), 48–67.

5. Denning, *Cultural Front*, 237–43.

6. Louis Adamic, *My America, 1928–1938* (New York: Harper and Brothers, 1938), 134–35; Adamic, *On Unity and Uniformity* (Cleveland, OH: Cleveland Council for American Unity, 1941), 2–3, 9.

7. Nelson Lichtenstein, *State of the Union: A Century of American Labor* (Princeton, NJ: Princeton University Press, 2002), 30–32; Joseph A. McCartin, *Labor's Great War: The Struggle for Industrial Democracy and the Origins of Modern American Labor Relations, 1912–1921* (Chapel Hill: University of North Carolina Press, 1997), 1–10, 38–40; Lizabeth Cohen, *Making a New Deal: Industrial Workers in Chicago, 1919—1939* (Cambridge: Cambridge University Press, 1990), 333–49.

8. Sinclair Lewis, "Seeing Red," in *The Man from Main Street: Selected Essays and Other Writings, 1904–1950*, ed. Harry E. Maule and Melville H. Cane (New York: Random House, 1953), 30.

9. Fraser M. Ottanelli, *The Communist Party of the United States: From the Depression to World War II* (New Brunswick, NJ: Rutgers University Press, 1991), 49–105;

Mark Naison, "Remaking America: Communists and Liberals in the Popular Front," in *New Studies in the Politics of Culture of U.S. Communism*, ed. Michael E. Brown, Randy Martin, Frank Rosengarten, and George Snedeker, 45–70 (New York: Monthly Review Press, 1993); John Gerassi, "The Comintern, the Fronts, and the CPUSA," in *New Studies*, ed. Brown et al., 75–90. For a better understanding of independent leftists, see Doug Rossinow, *Visions of Progress: The Left-Liberal Tradition in America* (Philadelphia: University of Pennsylvania Press, 2008), 143–94.

10. Adamic, *My America*, 90–107, 328–31; Carrie McWilliams, interview by Joel Gardner, UCLA Oral History Project, tape 2, side 2, July 12, 1978, xx, http://oralhistory.library.ucla.edu/viewItem.do?ark=21198/zz0009n15n&fileSeq=null&xsl=null.

11. Adamic, *My America*, 329–31.

12. Ibid., 94. For his overall view, see 91–95, 328–38.

13. Barbara Foley, *Radical Representations: Politics and Form in U.S. Proletarian Fiction, 1929–1941* (Durham, NC: Duke University Press, 1993), ix, 87; Eric Homberger, "Proletarian Literature and the John Reed Clubs," *Journal of American Studies* 13 (August 1979): 222, 232, 237, 241.

14. Granville Hicks to Adamic, April 3, 1932, box 48, folder 1, Louis Adamic Papers, Rare Books and Special Collections Department, Firestone Library, Princeton University, Princeton, NJ (hereafter, Firestone).

15. Adamic to Granville Hicks, April 4, 1932, box 48, folder 1, Firestone.

16. Louis Adamic, *Laughing in the Jungle* (New York: Arno, 1969), 14–15, 20.

17. Adamic, *My America*, 337.

18. Ibid., 94. For his overall view, see 91–95, 328–38.

19. Louis Adamic, *The Native's Return: An American Immigrant Visits Yugoslavia and Discovers His Old Country* (New York: Harper and Brothers, 1934), 351.

20. Louis Adamic to Ivan Molek, March 24, 1933, box 1, folder 4; Ivan Molek to Louis Adamic, April 11, 1933, box 1, folder 4; Ivan Molek to Louis Adamic, April 19, 1933, box 1, folder 4, all in Ivan Molek Papers, Chicago History Museum, Chicago (hereafter, Molek Papers).

21. Louis Adamic to Ivan Molek, April 22, 1933, box 1, folder 4, Molek Papers.

22. *St. Paul Dispatch*, April 24, 1934, clipping in box 4, folder 5, Immigration and Refugee Services of America, 1918–1985 Collection, Immigration History Research Center, Elmer L. Andersen Library, University of Minnesota, Minneapolis (hereafter, Immigration and Refugee Services).

23. Louis Adamic, "Where We Stand," *International Literature*, July 1934, 6; Adamic to Secretariat, International Union of Revolutionary Writers, January 23, 1932, box 47, folder 1, Firestone.

24. *Pittsburgh Post-Gazette*, March 27, 1934, clipping in box 4, folder 5, Immigration and Refugee Services.

25. Louis Adamic, "Who Built America?: Profiteers, Professional Patriots, or 'Vile Immigrants,'" *Common Sense* (April 1934), typed copy in box 4, file 3, Immigration and Refugee Services.

26. William C. Beyer, "Louis Adamic and *Common Ground*, 1940–1949," in *Louis Adamic: Simpozij/Symposium* (Ljubljana: Univerza Edvarda Kardelja, 1981), 226; Daniel E. Weinberg, "The Ethnic Technician and the Foreign-Born: Another Look at Americanization Ideology and Goals," *Societas* 7, no. 3 (1977): 219; Wendy L. Wall, *Inventing the "American Way": The Politics of Consensus from the New Deal to the Civil Rights Movement* (New York: Oxford University Press, 2008), 70.

27. Louis Adamic, "Thirty Million New Americans," *Harper's Weekly*, November 1934, 687.

28. Ibid., 688.

29. Ibid., 694.

30. Ibid., 689.

31. Ibid., 687. Parts of this article appeared in a speech Adamic gave. It is unclear which came first. See "Talk at Progressive Education Association Conference," n.p., n.d., 6–7, box 37, folder 12, Firestone.

32. Adamic, "Thirty Million," 691.

33. Ibid., 692.

34. Diana Selig, *Americans All: The Cultural Gifts Movement* (Cambridge, MA: Harvard University Press, 2008), 187–91.

35. Louis Adamic, "What the Proletariat Reads: Conclusions Based on a Year's Study among Hundreds of Workers in the United States," *Saturday Review of Literature* 11 (December 1, 1934), 321–22.

36. Adamic, *Grandsons*, 246.

37. Ibid., 214–15.

38. Ibid., 325–26.

39. Kevin Starr, *Endangered Dreams: The Great Depression in California* (New York: Oxford University Press, 1996), 172–73.

40. Norman Mini to Louis Adamic, May 27, 1935, box 48, folder 2, Firestone.

41. Louis Adamic, "The Great 'Bootleg Coal' Industry," *Nation*, January 9, 1935, 46.

42. Louis Adamic, "Sitdown," *Nation*, December 5, 1936, 654.

43. Louis Adamic, "John L. Lewis' Push to Power," *Forum* 97 (March 1937): 133–36.

44. Adamic, "Lewis' Push," 137.

45. Louis Adamic, "The Truth about the C.I.O.," *Forum* 98 (November 1937): 232.

46. Ibid., 233.

47. Wall, *Inventing the "American Way,"* 43–48.

48. Adamic, "Truth about C.I.O.," 233.

49. Ibid., 237.

50. On the CIO's culture of unity, see Cohen, *Making a New Deal*, 333–55. On the limits of equality, see Roediger, *Working toward Whiteness*, 207–24; Michael Honey, "Racism, Organized Labor, and the Black Freedom Struggle," *Contours* 1 (Spring 2003): 57–81.

51. Louis Adamic, "Shall We Send Them Back to Hitler?" *Nation*, March 25, 1936, 377–78.

52. Ibid.

53. Alan M. Kraut, Richard Breitman, and Thomas W. Imhoof, "The State Department, the Labor Department, and German Jewish Immigration, 1930–1940," *Journal of American Ethnic History* 3, no. 2 (Spring 1984): 7 9.

54. Louis Adamic, *America and the Refugees* (New York: Public Affairs Committee, 1939), 2, 30–31.

55. Louis Adamic, "Aliens and Alien-Baiters," *Harper's Magazine*, November 1936, 562–63, 572–73.

56. Adamic, *My America*, 337; Adamic, "Lewis' Push," 133–36; Adamic, "Truth about C.I.O.," 232–37.

57. Nick Fischer, *Spider Web: The Birth of American Anticommunism* (Urbana: University of Illinois Press, 2016), 95–98.

58. Fischer, *Spider Web*, 69–81.

59. Ngai, *Impossible Subjects*, 3, 7–8; Fischer, *Spider Web*, 116–23.

60. Fischer, *Spider Web*, 86.

61. Adamic, "Aliens and Alien-Baiters," *Harper's Magazine*, November 1936, 562–63.

62. Ibid., 567, 566.

63. Ibid., 571.

64. Jacob L. Halevi to Adamic April 20, 1939, box 61, folder 6, Firestone. For letters from Jewish Americans in general, see folders 5 and 6 of box 61. Also, much of boxes 62 and 63 contains correspondence with Jewish American organizations and letters and articles citing instances of anti-Semitism.

65. *In Re: Two Way Passage*, August–September 1942, 3.

66. Adamic to Read Lewis, November 19, 1936, with an enclosed letter from N. W. Rogers to Adamic, November 10, 1936, box 3, folder 15, Immigration and Refugee Services.

67. C. H. Palmer to Louis Adamic, June 13, 1939, box 49, folder 8, Firestone.

68. For examples of exposé literature, see *The Hour* (a newsletter published by the New York–based American Council against Nazi Propaganda from 1939 to 1941); John Spivak, *Anti-Semitism Exposed: Plotting America's Pogroms* (New York: New Masses, 1934); Harold Lavine, *Fifth Column in America* (New York: Doubleday, Doran, 1940); George Seldes, *You Can't Do That* (New York: Modern Age, 1938); John Roy Carlson, *Under Cover* (New York: World, 1943). For an overview of fears of fascism, see Rebecca Hill, "The History of the Smith Act and the Hatch Act: Anti-communism and the Rise of the Conservative Coalition in Congress," in *Little Red Scares*, ed. Robert Justin Goldstein (New York: Ashgate, 2014), 315–46; Leo P. Ribuffo, *The Old Christian Right: The Protestant Far Right from the Great Depression to the Cold War* (Philadelphia: Temple University Press, 1983), 178–224; Philip Jenkins, *Hoods and Shirts: The Extreme Right in Pennsylvania, 1925–1950* (Chapel Hill: University of North Carolina Press, 1997), 1–5. On fifth columnists in particular, see Francis MacDonnell, *Insidious Foes: The Axis Fifth Column and the American Home Front* (New York: Oxford University Press, 1995), 7–8, 137–83.

69. Walter Goodman, *The Committee: The Extraordinary Career of the House Committee on Un-American Activities* (New York: Farrar, Straus and Giroux, 1964), 3–20; Phillip Deery, *Red Apple: Communism and McCarthyism in Cold War New York* (New York: Fordham University Press, 2014), 1–37; Hill, "History of the Smith Act," 315–46.

70. Adamic to Lewis, September 18, 1939, box 3, folder 14, Immigration and Refugee Services.

71. Adamic to Read Lewis, September 3, 1939, box 3, folder 14, Immigration and Refugee Services of America.

72. Adamic to Read Lewis, September 7, 1939, box 3, folder 14, Immigration and Refugee Services.

73. Wall, *Inventing the "American Way,"* 70–71.

74. Adamic to Lewis, October 26, 1936, box 3, folder 16; Adamic to Lewis, September 30, 1937, box 3, folder 15, both in Immigration and Refugee Services. Lewis to Adamic, October 8, 1937; Philip H. Cohen to Adamic, July 29, 1938, Adamic to Lewis, October 28, 1938, all in box 3, folder 15, Immigration and Refugee Services.

75. Shiffman offers an excellent literature review of these critiques of Adamic; see Shiffman, *Rooting Multiculturalism*, 16, 30, 68–69, 151–57.

76. Robert Forsythe, "Ben's Little Boy, Louie," *New Masses*, June 14, 1938, 13.

77. Wall, *Inventing the "American Way,"* 67–100; Rachel Ida Buff, *Against the Deportation Terror: Organizing for Immigrant Rights in the Twentieth Century* (Philadelphia: Temple University Press, 2018), 27–52; Robert Zecker, *"A Road to Peace and Freedom": The International Workers' Order and the Struggle for Economic Justice and Civil Rights, 1930–1954* (Philadelphia: Temple University Press, 2018), 19–54.

78. Ivan Molek to Adamic, May 11, 1938, box 1, file folder 3, Molek Papers.

79. *Proletarec*, June 8, 1938, 1.

80. Ibid.

81. The editors of New York's *Socialist Call* accepted Adamic's expertise on Yugoslav and immigrant matters but found that *My America* failed to adequately comprehend working-class politics. An editorial proclaimed Adamic as "unquestionably one of the most gifted and honest of the literary radicals, or labor journalists, writing today" and applauded him for refusing to simply parrot the Communist Party line as most "literary fellow-travelers" did. But, the piece continued, despite "his proletarian and peasant background," Adamic was clearly "a literary dilettante in the labor movement." They advised him to stick to writing about Yugoslavia and immigrant issues. *Socialist Call*, September 3, 1938, 10.

82. Fred M. Butzel to Adamic, August 17, 1939, box 3, folder 14, Immigration and Refugee Services.

83. Adamic, "On Unity and Uniformity," 2–3, 9.

84. Larry Ceplair, *Anti-communism in Twentieth-Century America: A Critical History* (Santa Barbara, CA: Praeger, 2011), 53–57.

85. Hill, "History of the Smith Act," 315–46; Ceplair, *Anti-communism*, 53–57.

86. "Aliens and Alien-Baiting," box 70, folders 1–4, Firestone. These folders con-

tain notes between Adamic and Lewis and others at the FLIS. Also, they hold all the newsletters and memos of the FLIS and Common Council for American Unity about alien baiting. Adamic wrote some of them and used them for speeches that he gave. Also see *Louisville (KY) Courier Journal*, December 4, 1939, 4; *Ames (IA) Daily Tribune*, January 13, 1942, 2.

87. Adamic to Lewis, September 30, 1939, box 3, folder 14, Immigration and Refugee Services.

88. Louis Adamic, *From Many Lands* (New York: Harper and Brothers, 1940), 309–10.

89. Ibid., 291, 298, 293.

90. Adamic to Lewis, October 26, 1939, box 3, folder 14, Immigration and Refugee Services.

91. Adamic to Lewis, October 23, 1939, box 3, folder 14, Immigration and Refugee Services.

92. Beyer, "Louis Adamic and *Common Ground*, 1940–1949," 225.

93. *Common Ground* 1, no. 1 (Autumn 1940): 2. For more on *Common Ground*, see Richard W. Steele, "The War on Intolerance: The Reformulation of American Nationalism, 1939–1941," *Journal of American Ethnic History* 9, no. 1 (Fall 1989): 15–18; William C. Beyer, "Creating 'Common Ground' on the Home Front: Race, Class, and Ethnicity in a 1940s Quarterly Magazine," in *The Home-Front War: World War II and American Society*, ed. Kenneth Paul O'Brien and Lynn Hudson Parsons (Westport, CT: Greenwood, 1995), 41–55.

94. John L. Modic, "Louis Adamic and the Story of *Common Ground*," and Beyer, "Louis Adamic and *Common Ground*, 1940–1949," both in *Louis Adamic: Simpozij/ Symposium* (Ljubljana: Univerza Edvarda Kardelja, 1981), 243–47, 223.

95. *Saint Louis Post-Dispatch*, October 13, 1939, 2E.

96. *Rochester (NY) Democrat and Chronicle*, December 29, 1940, 2E.

97. *New York Times Sunday Magazine*, February 15, 1942, 38.

Chapter 3. *Smrt Fašizmu, Svoboda Narodu!* The Life of a Diasporic Leader

1. Adamic to Clifton Fadiman, August 11, 1944, pisma 3, mapa 7, Louis Adamič M.S. 1858, Narodna in Univerzitetna Knjižnica Ljubljana (hereafter, Adamič M.S.).

2. John R. Lampe, *Yugoslavia as History: Twice There Was a Country* (Cambridge: Cambridge University Press, 1996), 197–207; Hilde Katrine Haug, *Creating a Socialist Yugoslavia: Tito, Communist Leadership and the National Question* (London: I. B. Tauris, 2012), 1–6; Dejan Jović, "Yugoslavism and Yugoslav Communism: From Tito to Kardelj," in *Yugoslavism: Histories of a Failed Idea 1918–1922*, ed. Dejan Djokić (Madison: University of Wisconsin Press, 2003), 158–60; Stevan K. Pavlowitch, "Serbia, Montenegro and Yugoslavia," in *Yugoslavism: Histories of a Failed Idea 1918–1922*, ed. Dejan Djokić (Madison: University of Wisconsin Press, 2003), 65; John V. A. Fine,

"Strongmen Can Be Beneficial: The Exceptional Case of Josip Broz Tito," in *Balkan Strongmen: Dictators and Authoritarian Rulers of South Eastern Europe,* ed. Bernard J. Fischer (West Lafayette, IN: Purdue University Press, 2007), 272. On pre-Tito notions of Yugoslavism, see Branka Prpa-Jovanović, "The Making of Yugoslavia: 1830–1945," in *Burn This House: The Making and Unmaking of Yugoslavia,* ed. Jasminka Udovički and James Ridgeway (Durham, NC: Duke University Press, 2000), 48–49; Brigit Farley, "Aleksandar Karadjordjević and the Royal Dictatorship of Yugoslavia," in *Balkan Strongmen: Dictators and Authoritarian Rules of South Eastern Europe,* ed. Bernard J. Fischer (West Lafayette, IN: Purdue University Press, 2007), 61–63.

3. Louis Adamic, *My Native Land* (New York: Harper and Brothers, 1943), 109, 467–68.

4. Henry A. Wallace, "The Price of Free World Victory," in *Democracy Reborn,* ed. Russell Lord (New York: Reynal and Hitchcock, 1944), 190–96. Also see Wendy L. Wall, *Inventing the "American Way": The Politics of Consensus from the New Deal to the Civil Rights Movement* (New York: Oxford University Press, 2008), 112–13.

5. Franklin Delano Roosevelt, "The 'Four Freedoms,'" annual address to Congress, January 6, 1941, FDR Library website, http://docs.fdrlibrary.marist.edu:8000/od4frees.html, accessed July 16, 2010. Elizabeth Borgwardt, *A New Deal for the World: America's Vision for Human Rights* (Cambridge, MA: Harvard University Press, 2005), 4–6, 50, 135–36.

6. *War and Post-war* 3, January and February 1944, 1.

7. Ibid., 4.

8. Ibid.

9. *Two Way Passage,* February 1942, 1–4, and March 1942, 2–3.

10. Christopher Vials, *Haunted by Hitler: Liberals, the Left, and the Fight against Fascism in the United States* (Amherst: University of Massachusetts Press, 2014), 59–69; Nikhil Pal Singh, *Black Is a Country: Race and the Unfinished Struggle for Democracy* (Cambridge, MA: Harvard University Press, 2004), 111; Ronald Takaki, *Double V: A Multi-cultural History of America in World War II* (New York: Back Bay, 2000), 22–57; Lauren Rebecca Sklaroff, "Constructing G.I. Joe Louis: Cultural Solutions to the 'Negro Problem' during World War II," *Journal of American History* 89 (December 2002): 958–83.

11. Adamic, *My Native Land,* 140.

12. Brent Hayes Edwards, "The Uses of Diaspora," *Social Text* 19 (Spring 2001): 45–73; Kevin Kenny, *Diaspora: A Very Short Introduction* (New York: Oxford University Press, 2013), 1–15.

13. On defining diasporas as historical events, see Kenny, *Diaspora,* 1–15; Ewa Morawska, "'Diaspora' Diasporas' Representations of Their Homelands: Exploring the Polymorphs," *Ethnic and Racial Studies* 34 (June 2011): 1029–40; Stéphane Dufoix, *Diasporas,* trans. William Roadarmor (Berkeley: University of California Press, 2003), xv–34; Stuart Hall, "Cultural Identity and Diaspora," in *Identity: Community, Culture and Difference,* ed. Jonathan Rutherford (London: Lawrence and Wishart,

1990): 223–35; Donna R. Gabaccia, *Italy's Many Diasporas* (New York: Routledge, 2005), 1–11.

14. Louis Adamic, *Two-Way Passage* (New York: Harper and Brothers, 1941), 266. Czech nationalist Tomáš Masaryk inspired Adamic's idea that ethnic and immigrant Americans should take a passage back across the Atlantic because they or their families had honed their vision of democracy on two continents. In an oversimplified version of events, Adamic explained that while in exile, Masaryk and his ethnic and immigrant supporters in the United States met in Pittsburgh and created an inde pendent Czechoslovakia. *In Re: Two-Way Passage*, January 1942, 1.

15. Louis Adamic, "Memorandum for Mrs. Roosevelt," January 25, 1942, box 35, folder 18, Louis Adamic Papers, Rare Books and Special Collections Department, Firestone Library, Princeton University (hereafter, Firestone).

16. *In Re: Two-Way Passage*, January 1942, 1–3; *In Re: Two-Way Passage*, February 1942, 1–3; *In Re: Two-Way Passage*, March 1942, 2.

17. *In Re: Two-Way Passage*, June 1942, 4; July 1942, 1, 2; August–September 1942, 2, 3; January 1943, 4.

18. November 17, 1942, memorandum to Lanning MacFarland, November 17, 1942, Office of Strategic Services Manuscript Collection, Record Group 226, box 166, folder 36, National Archives II, College Park, Maryland. Adamic's letter to President Roosevelt, February 3, 1942, which outlines this example, is copied and contained in this memo.

19. Louis Adamic, *Dinner at the White House* (New York: Harper and Brothers, 1946), 43–44.

20. Matthew M. Briones, *Jim and Jap Crow: A Cultural History of 1940s Interracial America* (Princeton, NJ: Princeton University Press, 2012), 50–52; Erika Lee, *The Making of Asian America: A History* (New York: Simon and Schuster, 2015), 229–51.

21. Adamic, *Dinner at the White House*, 45.

22. In writing about Adamic's relationship with Japanese Americans, Yuji Ichioka collected all Adamic's correspondence and other materials relating to Japanese Americans. One can find most of them in Adamic's papers at Princeton, but Professor Ichioka's efforts provide a much more comprehensive understanding by including newspaper articles and other documents. For Adamic's exchanges with Kikuchi, see Yuji Ichioka Papers, ca. 1880–2002, Collection 242, box 88, folder 2, Charles E. Young Research Library, Department of Special Collections, UCLA. For a clear understanding of Adamic and Japanese Americans, see boxes 88, 109, and 147. Also see Briones, *Jim and Jap Crow*, 52–60. Briones importantly pointed out that although we must remember Adamic as being "one of the most reliable, allies whom people of color and immigrants could trust," his stories often "reinforced Orientalism." As a consequence, Kikuchi faced some criticism and resentment in Gila, the camp where he was imprisoned, because of Adamic's writings. See pages 60–65 for more on their relationship.

23. Mary Oyama, "After Pearl Harbor: Los Angeles," *Common Ground* 2 (Spring

1942): 13. For more analysis of *Common Ground* and the Japanese American community, see Briones, *Jim and Jap Crow*, 66.

24. Roi Ottley, "A White Folk's War?," *Common Ground* 2 (Spring 1942): 30, 31.

25. Robert L. Brown, "Manzanar—Relocation Center," *Common Ground* 3 (Autumn 1942): 27–32. For an excellent critique of Brown's essay and praise for Margaret Anderson's skillful editing in highlighting Brown's effort to mislead readers on the conditions at Manzanar, see Briones, *Jim and Jap Crow*, 69.

26. M. Margaret Anderson, "Democracy Begins at Home—II: Get the Evacuees Out!," *Common Ground* 3 (Summer 1943): 65.

27. John L. Modic, "Louis Adamic and the Story of *Common Ground*," in *Louis Adamic: Simpozij/Symposium* (Ljubljana: Univerza Edvarda Kardelja, 1981), 245–46.

28. Modic, "Louis Adamic and the Story of *Common Ground*," 241–53, and William C. Beyer, "Louis Adamic and *Common Ground*, 1940–1949," 223–39, both in *Louis Adamic: Simpozij/Symposium* (Ljubljana: Univerza Edvarda Kardelja, 1981).

29. Modic, "Louis Adamic," 245–46.

30. Modic, "Louis Adamic," 250–51; Briones, *Jim and Jap Crow*, 69.

31. Adamic, *My Native Land*, 136, 138–39.

32. Lampe, *Yugoslavia as History*, 197–207.

33. Franc Snoj to Adamic, February 4, 1942, korespondenca 4, mapa 17, Adamič M.S., NUK; Louis Adamic, "The Liberation Front in Yugoslavia," *Nation*, October 30, 1943, 500; Bogdan C. Novak, "Louis Adamic's Work for the Official Recognition of Tito and the National Liberation Movement of Yugoslavia by the United States Government," *Dve domovini/Two Homelands* 9 (1998), 69–70.

34. Lorraine M. Lees, *Yugoslav-Americans and National Security during World War II* (Urbana: University of Illinois Press, 2007), 271–74.

35. Mihailović appeared on the cover of the May 25, 1942, issue of *Time*. In 1943, 20th Century Fox released *Chetniks! The Fighting Guerrillas*. That same year Istvan Tamas's *Sergeant Nikola: A Novel of the Chetnik Brigades* and Frederich Heydenau's *The Wrath of Eagles: A Novel of the Chetniks* appeared. Among the comics that celebrated Mihailović and the Chetniks were "The Chetniks," *Prize Comics*, March 1942; "Chief of the 'Chetniks,'" *Real Heroes Comics*, September 1942; "Draja Mihailovitch, the Yugoslav MacArthur," *Real Life Comics*, November 1942; "Mission to Yugoslavia," and "The Chumps and the Chetniks," *Military Comics: Stories of the Army and Navy*, December 1942; "Liberty for the Chetniks," *Master Comics, Captain Marvel Jr.*, February 1943; "The American Crusader Joins the Chetniks," *Thrilling Comics, American Crusader*, May 1943. See Alexander Mirkovic, "Grey Falcon and the Union Man: Miloje Sokić Collection of the Clippings from the American Press 1941–1945," *Balcanica* 43 (2012): 227–32.

36. On depopulation, see Milovan Djilas, *Wartime* (New York: Harcourt, Brace, Jovanovich, 1977), 94; Louis Adamic, "Mikhailovitch Is Pro-Axis!" n.d., box 35, folder 19, Firestone.

37. Adamic, "Mikhailovitch Is Pro-Axis!"

38. Ivan (John) Molek, *Slovene Immigrant History 1900–1950: Autobiographical Sketches*, translated by Mary Molek (Dover, DE: Mary Molek, 1979), 251, 257, 269; Matjaž Klemenčič, *Slovenes of Cleveland: The Creation of a New Nation and a New World Community Slovenia and the Slovenes of Cleveland, Ohio* (Novo Mesto, Slovenia: Dolenjska, 1995), 365–66; Matjaž Klemenčič, "American Slovenes and the Leftist Movements in the United States in the First Half of the Twentieth Century," *Journal of American Ethnic History* 15 (Spring 1996): 34; Novak, "Louis Adamic's Work," 74.

39. Lees, *Yugoslav-Americans*, 99–105; Molek, *Slovene Immigrant History*, 45.

40. Adamic to Rev. Kazimir Zakrajsek, January 18, 1943, pisma 3, mapa 9, Adamič M.S.

41. Vincent Cainkar to Adamic, February 6, 1943, korespondenca 4, mapa 11, Adamič M.S.

42. Ibid.

43. Alan Cranston to Adamic, February 6, 1943, korespondenca 4, mapa 11, Adamič M.S. Cranston was one of the officials the Catholic activists notified, and he informed Adamic of their opposition to his leadership.

44. Adamic to DeWitt C. Poole, May 9, 1943, pisma 3, mapa 9, Adamič M.S., NUK; Adamic, *My Native Land*, 464; *In Re: Two-Way Passage* 2 (February–March 1943): 8.

45. Adamic, *Two-Way Passage*, 266.

46. See the *Los Angeles Times*, *New York Times*, and *Washington Post* on March 28, 1943, for the stories that LaGuardia and Adamic were headed to North Africa to oversee Italian reconstruction and then Roosevelt's denial in the same papers on April 7, 1943.

47. All of folder 7 in box 51, Firestone, deals with Adamic serving as LaGuardia's aid in North Africa.

48. Adamic to Fiorello LaGuardia, n.d., folder 7, box 51, Firestone.

49. *American Srbobran*, April 7, 1943.

50. "Slovene Press Clippings," Immigration and Refugee Services of America, 1918–1985 Collection, box 151, folder 3, Immigration History Research Center, University of Minnesota.

51. Lampe, *Yugoslavia as History*, 215–17.

52. Ibid.; Franklin Lindsay, *Beacons in the Night: With the OSS and Tito's Partisans in Wartime Yugoslavia* (Stanford, CA: Stanford University Press, 1993), 272–75. For more on collaboration, see Jozo Tomasevich, *War and Revolution in Yugoslavia, 1941–1945: Occupation and Collaboration* (Stanford, CA: Stanford University Press, 2001), 140–48.

53. Adamic to Franklin Roosevelt, July 26, 1943, pisma 3, mapa 9, Adamič M.S.

54. *Bulletin of the United Committee of South-Slavic Americans*, January 15, 1944, 1–2.

55. Matjaž Klemenčič, "American Slovenes," 36–37, and Novak, "Louis Adamic's Work," 74–76.

56. Adamic, *My Native Land*, 109, 467–68.

57. For two recent examples of the relationship between the Vatican and fascism, see David I. Kertzer, *The Pope and Mussolini: The Secret History of Pius XI and the Rise of Fascism in Europe* (New York: Random House, 2014); Pino Adriano and Giorgio Cingolanai, *Nationalism and Terror: Ante Pavelić and Ustasha Terrorism from Fascism to the Cold War* (Budapest: Central European University Press, 2018), 186–87.

58. Adamic, *My Native Land*, 463.

59. Ibid., 464.

60. Louis Adamic, "Death in Front of the Church," *Harper's*, September 1943, 365.

61. Ibid., 372, 374.

62. Adamic, "Death," 368, 370.

63. Lee White to Adamic, August 26, 1943, korespondenca 4, mapa 18, Adamič M.S.

64. Ibid.

65. Victor E. Devereaux to Adamic, October 20, 1943, and Karl Detzer to Adamic, October 21, 1943, both in korespondenca 4, mapa 11, Adamič M.S.

66. J. J. Kuharic to Adamic, n.d., korespondenca 4, mapa 13, Adamič M.S. Also see Paul Michael Chuchic to Adamic, June 4, 1944, korespondenca 4, mapa 11, Adamič M.S.

67. Adamic to Mr. Jones, May 19, 1944, pisma 3, mapa 8, Adamič M.S.

68. G. M. Trunk to Adamic, December 13, 1943, korespondenca 4, mapa 17, Adamič M.S.

69. *War and Post-war* 2, October 1943, 4.

70. Bernard Ambrožič, *Shall Slovenia Be Sovietized?: A Rebuttal to Louis Adamic* (Cleveland, OH: Union of Slovenian Parishes of America, 1944), 4–5.

71. S. H. Cross to Adamic, March 18, 1944, korespondenca 4, mapa 11, Adamič M.S.

72. Novak, "Louis Adamic's Work," 67–69.

73. Lees, *Yugoslav-Americans*, 73, 81.

74. SNDC quoted in Lees, *Yugoslav-Americans*, 62. For the FNB's report, see page 82.

75. Brown quoted in Lees, *Yugoslav-Americans*, 82. For Peter's visit, see pages 82–85.

76. Lee White to Adamic, August 26, 1943, korespondenca 4, mapa 18, Adamič M.S.

77. Adamic to Simms, August 27, 1944, pisma 3, mapa 9; and, for another example, see Adamic to Mr. Gaeth, August 27, 1944, pisma 3, mapa 8, both in Adamič M.S.

78. White to Adamic, August 26, 1943, korespondenca 4, mapa 18, Adamič M.S.

79. Mirko G. Kuhel to Adamic, July 1, 1943, korespondenca 4, mapa 13; Mirko G. Kuhel to *Chicago Sunday Times*, July 7, 1943, tuja korespondenca 5, mapa 21, Adamič M.S.

80. Adamic to Mr. [S. Burton] Heath, n.d., pisma 3, mapa 8, Adamič M.S. Heath was a syndicated columnist and wrote a story that circulated around the country that misquoted Adamic. For two examples of Heath's column, see *Ithaca (NY) Journal*, December 18, 1943, 6; *Odessa (TX) American*, December 23, 1943, 4.

81. M. R. Humble to Adamic, November 4, 1943, korespondenca 4, mapa 12, Adamič M.S. Humble sent Adamic a clipping from the *Detroit News*.

82. Adamic to Saul Mills, date illegible, 1943, pisma 3, mapa 8, Adamič M.S.

83. Among the unions that went on record supporting the Partisans was the International Fishermen and Allied Workers of America (Waterfront Workers History Project, Harry Bridges Center for Labor Studies, University of Washington, http://depts.washington.edu/dock/IFAWA_pt4.shtml, accessed July 15, 2016). See also Robert Zecker, *"A Road to Peace and Freedom": The International Workers' Order and the Struggle for Economic Justice and Civil Rights, 1930–1954* (Philadelphia: Temple University Press, 2018), 166–212.

84. Frank Lausche to Adamic, June 26, 1943, korespondenca 4, mapa 13, Adamič M.S.

85. Thomas J. Sugrue, *The Origins of the Urban Crisis: Race and Inequality in Postwar Detroit* (Princeton, NJ: Princeton University Press, 2005), 29.

86. Adamic to Frank Lausche, n.d, pisma 3, mapa 8; Frank Lausche to Adamic, August 11, 1943, korespondenca 4, mapa 13, Adamič M.S.

87. Estelle M. Sternberger to Adamic, December 13, 1943, korespondenca 4, mapa 17, Adamič M.S.

88. Vials, *Haunted by Hitler*, 59–87; Wall, *Inventing the "American Way,"* 112–22, 132–59.

89. Lees, *Yugoslav-Americans*, 158.

90. Ibid., 164–65.

91. Clippings from early March sent by Nick Bastasic to Adamic, October 1, 1944, box 45, folder 6, Firestone; *Hammond (IN) Times*, March 29, 1944, 22. Busby made his remarks about Adamic on March 13, 1944.

92. Clippings from early March sent by Nick Bastasic to Adamic, October 1, 1944, box 45, folder 6, Firestone; Petition to the Gary School Board, the Board of Education, and the mayor from the Gary Citizens of Serbian Descent, February 19, 1944, gradivo 6, mapa 22, Adamič M.S.

93. United South Slavs of Gary, "The Truth Must Be Heard!," part of the letter sent by Nick Bastasic to Adamic on October 1, 1944, in box 45, folder 6, Firestone.

94. Clippings from early March sent by Nick Bastasic to Adamic, October 1, 1944, box 45, folder 6, Firestone.

95. Clippings from early March sent by Bastasic to Adamic October 1, 1944, box 45, folder 6, Firestone.

96. "Adamic in Chicago and Gary," March 20, 1944, Office of Strategic Services, Foreign Nationalities Branch, microfiche collection, INT 30 YU-1308, Records of the Office of Strategic Services, Record Group 226; National Archives, College Park, MD. For more on Adamic and Poole, see Lorraine M. Lees, "DeWitt Clinton Poole, the Foreign Nationalities Branch and Political Intelligence," *Intelligence and National Security* 15, no. 4 (Winter 2000): 81–92.

97. Lees, "DeWitt Clinton Poole," 81–103; on Poole's interview with Adamic, see 92. Also see Lees, *Yugoslav-Americans*, 156.

98. Sava Kosanovich, "A Serbian Speaks Out," *Bulletin of the United Committee of South-Slavic Americans*, January 15, 1944, 2. On Adamic arguing that communism represented the best option for Yugoslavia even though it was totalitarian, see Adamic to Nick Bez, June 24, 1946, box 45, folder 6, Firestone.

99. D. Milton Ladd to J. Edgar Hoover, March 15, 1951, FOIA/FBI Adamic file 100-63760-1, FBI, Department of Justice, Washington, DC.

100. Ibid.

101. *New York Times*, March 13, 1944, 7.

102. Bridgeport, CT, Slav group to Adamic, May 19, 1944, korespondenca 4, mapa 11; Marian M. Mallery to Adamic, August 2, 1944, korespondenca 4, mapa 14; Mary E. McCoy to Adamic, March 24, 1944, korespondenca 4, mapa 14—all in Adamič M.S.

103. D. F. Fleming to Adamic, November 3, 1943, korespondenca 4, mapa 12; Kimon A. Doukas to Adamic, June 25, 1944, korespondenca 4, mapa 11—both in Adamič M.S.

104. Marion E. Hutton to Adamic, September 19, 1944, korespondenca 4, mapa 12, Adamič M.S.

105. Eugene L. R. Lanning to Adamic, June 27, 1944, korespondenca 4, mapa 13, Adamič M.S.

106. "Report to the Nation" (transcript), Columbia Broadcasting System, Sunday, July 30, 1944, box 2, folder 8, Zlatko Balokovic Papers, Immigration History Research Center, collection 274, University of Minnesota.

107. "Report to the Nation" (transcript), Columbia Broadcasting System, Sunday, July 30, 1944, box 2, folder 8, Zlatko Balokovic Papers, Immigration History Research Center, collection 274, University of Minnesota.

108. *Bulletin of the United Committee of South-Slavic Americans*, March 10, 1944, 7.

109. Lieber to Adamic June 13, 1944, korespondenca 4, mapa 13, Adamič M.S., NUK; *New York Times*, June 13, 1944, 7.

110. Larry Ceplair, *Anti-communism in Twentieth-Century America: A Critical History* (Santa Barbara, CA: Praeger, 2011), 53–57. Walter Goodman, *The Committee: The Extraordinary Career of the House Committee on Un-American Activities* (New York: Farrar, Straus and Giroux, 1964), 3–20.

111. Legal Information Institute, Cornell University Law School, *Foreign Agents Registration Act (FARA)*, https://www.law.cornell.edu/topn/foreign_agents_registration_act_of_1938, accessed July 21, 2016; Lees, *Yugoslav-Americans*, 16, 31–36. The statute was revised in 1942 to make the Justice Department responsible for enforcing registration.

112. Adamic to Bart Andress, July 3, 1944, pisma 3, mapa 7, Adamič M.S.; Lees, *Yugoslav-Americans*, 173.

113. Frank Munk to Adamic in a series of letters from May 22 through September 1, 1944, korespondenca 4, mapa 14, Adamič M.S.

114. Lees, *Yugoslav-Americans*, 175.

115. Ibid., 175–79.

116. Ibid., 180–81.

117. Baloković quoted in Lees, *Yugoslav-Americans*, 188. For the UCSSA's struggle to avoid FARA registration, see 182–93.

118. Lees, *Yugoslav-Americans*, 175.

119. Adamic to Zlatko Baloković, November 27, 1944, korespondenca 4, mapa 14, Adamič M.S.

120. Dorothy Klarich to Adamic, June 27, 1944, korespondenca 4, mapa 13; Adamic to Klarich, July 15, 1944, pisma 3, mapa 8, Adamič M.S.

121. Gregor Kranjc, "Two Solitudes Revisited: A Historiographical Survey of Collaboration in Slovenia during World War II," *Slovene Studies* 24, nos. 1–2 (2002): 4–8; Stevan K. Pavlowitch, *Hitler's New Disorder: The Second World War in Yugoslavia* (New York: Oxford University Press, 2008), 151–269; Lampe, *Yugoslavia as History*, 213–22.

122. Gerald Meyer, "Frank Sinatra: The Popular Front and an American Icon," *Science and Society* 66, no. 3 (Fall 2002): 322; David R. Roediger, *Working toward Whiteness: How America's Immigrants Became White* (New York: Basic, 2005), 239–44; John T. McGreevy, *Parish Boundaries: The Catholic Encounter with Race in the Twentieth-Century Urban North* (Chicago: University of Chicago Press, 1996), 89.

123. Adamic to Nick Bez, December 17, 1945, box 45, folder 6, Firestone.

124. Ibid.

125. Quoted in Aleksa Djilas, *The Contested Country: Yugoslav Unity and Communist Revolution 1919–1953* (Cambridge, MA: Harvard University Press, 1996), 165.

126. Stoyan Pribichevich to Adamic, February 8, 1944, korespondenca 4, mapa 15, Adamič M.S.

127. Josip Smodlaka to Adamic, February 18, 1944, and July 27, 1944, korespondenca 4, mapa 17, Adamič M.S.

128. Josip Broz Tito to Adamic, March 29, 1944, *War and Post-war* 3, September–October 1944, 2.

Chapter 4. "Peace as a World Race Problem": The Anti-imperialist in an Anticommunist World

1. The University of Chicago Round Table, "Peace as a World Race Problem," August 20, 1944, no. 355, National Broadcasting Company Transcript, 8, 11, 13, 18, and 19. For more on black leadership on anticolonialism in the 1940s, see Penny M. Von Eschen, *Race against Empire: Black Americans and Anticolonialism, 1937–1957* (Ithaca, NY: Cornell University Press, 1997), 1–6.

2. Louis Adamic, "This Crisis Is an Opportunity," *Common Ground* 1 (Autumn

1940): 62–67; Adamic to Clifton Fadiman, August 11, 1944, pisma 3, mapa 7, Louis Adamič M.S. 1858, Narodna in Univerzitetna Knjižnica Ljubljana. The American Committee for the Protection of the Foreign Born and the International Workers Order offer two examples of organizations committed to antifascism after World War II that linked fascism to colonialism. See Rachel Ida Buff, *Against the Deportation Terror: Organizing for Immigrant Rights in the Twentieth Century* (Philadelphia: Temple University Press, 2018), 169–94; Robert Zecker, *"A Road to Peace and Freedom": The International Workers' Order and the Struggle for Economic Justice and Civil Rights, 1930–1954* (Philadelphia: Temple University Press, 2018), 166–212.

3. *War and Post-war* 3, January and February 1944, 6.

4. *Chicago Defender*, June 9, 1945, 11. W. E. B. DuBois, "The Souls of White Folk," in *Darkwater: Voices from Within the Veil* (New York: Harcourt, Brace and Howe, 1920), 31–37. Also see Charles Mills, "White Right: The Idea of *Herrenvolk* Ethics," in *Blackness Visible: Essays on Philosophy and Race*, ed. Charles Mills (Ithaca, NY: Cornell University Press, 1998), 139–68; David R. Roediger, *The Wages of Whiteness: Race and the Making of the American Working Class* (New York: Verso, 1991), 3–87; Roediger, *Working toward Whiteness: How America's Immigrants Became White* (New York: Basic, 2005), 3–34 and 199–234; Matthew Frye Jacobson, *Whiteness of a Different Color: European Immigrants and the Alchemy of Race* (Cambridge, MA: Harvard University Press, 1998), 9–13; Jennifer Guglielmo and Salvatore Salerno, eds., *Are Italians White?: How Race Is Made in America* (New York: Routledge, 2003); Ian F. Haney Lopez, *White by Law: The Legal Construction of Race* (New York: New York University Press, 1996), 1–36.

5. Robin D. G. Kelley, *Race Rebels: Culture Politics and the Black Working Class* (New York: G. K. Hall, 1994), 123–60; Winston James, *Holding Aloft the Banner of Ethiopia: Caribbean Radicalism in Early Twentieth Century America* (New York: Verso, 1999); Raphael Dalleo, *American Imperialism's Undead: The Occupation of Haiti and the Rise of Caribbean Anticolonialism* (Charlottesville: University of Virginia Press, 2016), 44–69.

6. Von Eschen, *Race against Empire*, 78–85; Nikhil Pal Singh, *Black Is a Country: Race and the Unfinished Struggle for Democracy* (Cambridge, MA: Harvard University Press, 2004), 101–73.

7. Corey Robin, *Fear: The History of a Political Idea* (New York: Oxford University Press, 2004), 3 and 13.

8. Louis Adamic, *Dinner at the White House* (New York: Harper and Brothers, 1946), 159.

9. Adamic's newsletter *T&T*, midautumn 1949, 1–2.

10. D. M. Ladd to J. Edgar Hoover, March 15, 1951, FBI, Department of Justice, Washington, DC, FOIA/FBI Adamic file 100-63760-1.

11. Walter LaFeber, *America, Russia, and the Cold War, 1945–2006* (Boston: McGraw

Hill, 2008), 57–73; John Lewis Gaddis, *Russia, the Soviet Union, and the United Sates* (New York: McGraw Hill, 1990), 186–99.

12. *War and Post-war* 3, January and February 1944, 6.

13. Henry A. Wallace, "The Price of Free World Victory," in *Democracy Reborn*, ed. Russell Lord (New York: Reynal and Hitchcock, 1944), 190–91. Also see Wendy L. Wall, *Inventing the "American Way": The Politics of Consensus from the New Deal to the Civil Rights Movement* (New York: Oxford University Press, 2008), 112–13.

14. Henry Wallace, "Wallace Defines 'American Fascism,'" *New York Times Magazine*, April 9, 1944, 7.

15. *Amsterdam Star-News* (New York), December 13, 1941, 17.

16. Louis Adamic, *A Nation of Nations* (New York: Harper and Brothers, 1945), 11.

17. *Chicago Defender*, November 3, 1945, 15. See also *Amsterdam News*, November 10, 1945, 21; *Amsterdam News*, November 24, 1945, 13; *Pittsburgh Courier*, December 8, 1945, 7.

18. Louis Adamic, "There Are Whites and Whites," *Negro Digest* 4 (March 1946): 47–50. It should be noted that Adamic's thinking on the "Negro problem" was not always this militant. For just one example, see Walls, *Inventing the "American Way,"* 73.

19. Roi Ottley, *"New World a-Coming": Inside Black America* (Boston: Houghton Mifflin, 1943), 109–12; Kelley, *Race Rebels*, 123–60; Brenda Gayle Plummer, *Rising Wind: Black Americans and U.S. Foreign Affairs, 1935–1960* (Chapel Hill: University of North Carolina Press, 1995), 42–47; Von Eschen, *Race against Empire*, 1–95.

20. *Oakland (CA) Tribune*, April 5, 1946, 2; *Philadelphia Inquirer*, April 20, 1946, 1.

21. Harold L. Ickes to Louis Adamic, April 9, 1946, box 47, folder 1, Louis Adamic Papers, Rare Books and Special Collections Department, Firestone Library, Princeton University (hereafter cited as Firestone).

22. Adamic, *Dinner*, 215.

23. Ibid., 199 and 216.

24. *T&T*, March–May, 1946, 2, 13, and 14; June–July 1946, 4; January–March, 1947, 16.

25. Ibid., October–December 1946, 1–2.

26. Ibid., 2–3.

27. Ibid., 4.

28. *Washington Post*, June 2, 1946, B4, and April 3, 1946, 9. In addition to larger papers, such as the *Washington Post*, *New York Times*, and *Los Angeles Times*, articles appeared in smaller dailies. For just two examples, see *Seattle Daily Times*, April 5, 1946, 14; *Trenton (NJ) Evening Times*, July 8, 1946, 12. Also see Lorraine M. Lees, *Keeping Tito Afloat: The United States, Yugoslavia, and the Cold War* (University Park: Pennsylvania State University Press, 1997), 10–11.

29. *Socialist Call*, July 15, 1946, 4.

30. Anne Traven to Adamic, April 2, 1946, box 50, folder 1, Firestone. This letter contained the minutes from the UCSSA's October 20, 1945, meeting.

31. Adamic to Mirko Kuhel, June 22, 1946, box 47, folder 4, Firestone.

32. Louis Adamic, *The Eagle and the Roots* (New York: Doubleday, 1952), 66–72; Lees, *Keeping Tito Afloat*, 14–15.

33. John R. Lampe, *Yugoslavia as History: Twice There Was a Country* (Cambridge: Cambridge University Press, 1996), 205–6.

34. Adamic, *Eagle and the Roots*, 202–31; Jozo Tomasevich, *War and Revolution in Yugoslavia, 1941–1945: Occupation and Collaboration* (Stanford, CA: Stanford University Press, 2001), 350, 370–71.

35. Lampe, *Yugoslavia as History*, 205–6; Stevan K. Pavlowitch, *Hitler's New Disorder: The Second World War in Yugoslavia* (New York: Columbia University Press, 2008), 35–36; Sabrina P. Ramet, *Balkan Babel: The Disintegration of Yugoslavia from the Death of Tito to the Fall of Milošević* (Boulder, CO: Westview, 2002), 84–89.

36. *Cleveland Plain Dealer*, October 25, 1946, 18.

37. *Times-Picayune*, November 3, 1946, 23.

38. Common Council for American Unity, "The Stepinac Trial in Yugoslav Press," 1946. Immigration and Refugee Services of America 1918–1985, Papers, Immigration History Research Center, Collection 165, box 156, folder 6, University of Minnesota, Minneapolis.

39. Adamic, "Tolerance Is Not Enough," *T&T*, January–March 1947, 14–15. For a more recent and contextualized discussion of Slavic Americans' use of inclusive rhetoric while simultaneously rejecting actual unity, see Roediger, *Working toward Whiteness*, 235–44. For just a few examples of Adamic's attack on tolerance, see *McCall's*, August 1948; *Negro Digest*, October 1948; *T&T*, 1947–50. On the promotion of tolerance, see Robert L. Fleegler, "'Forget All Differences until the Forces of Freedom Are Triumphant': The World War II–Era Quest for Ethnic and Religious Tolerance," *Journal of American Ethnic History* 27, no. 2 (Winter 2008): 59–79.

40. Louis Adamic, "America and Yugoslavia," 1947, box 37, folder 2, Firestone.

41. Ibid. Capitalization inconsistency is Adamic's.

42. *Akron Beacon Journal*, January 14, 1947, 2.

43. *Pittsburgh Courier*, September 14, 1946, 7.

44. See *T&T* from 1947 to 1950, esp. January–March 1947, 4, 14–15, and October–December 1948, 18. Nico Slate, *Colored Cosmopolitanism: The Shared Struggle for Freedom in the United States and India* (Cambridge, MA: Harvard University Press, 2012), 2 and 161–201.

45. Louis Adamic, "America and Yugoslavia," 1947, box 37, folder 2, Firestone. For more examples, see *T&T*, 1945–49.

46. Adamic, "American Russian Relations," March 9, 1947, box 37, folder 3, Firestone.

47. Ibid.

48. Ibid.

49. Ibid.

50. Ibid.

51. Ibid.

52. *Newsweek*, May 26, 1947, 69.

53. Don Matchan to Adamic, July 24, 1947, box 48, folder 3, Firestone.

54. Adamic, "Lecture October–November 1947," box 37, folder 11, Firestone.

55. Ibid.

56. Louis Adamic lecture "Tolerance Is Not Enough," November 11, 1947, transcribed by an FBI agent at the Curran Theater in San Francisco for November 18, 1947, report on Adamic, FBI, Department of Justice, Washington, DC, FOIA/FBI Adamic file 100–63760–1.

57. Louis Adamic to Janko N. Rogelj, December 10, 1947, Janko N. Rogelj Papers, Manuscript Collection 3555, folder 2, Western Reserve Historical Society, Cleveland, OH.

58. *Philadelphia Inquirer*, September 21, 1946, 1.

59. Philip Jenkins, *The Cold War at Home: The Red Scare in Pennsylvania, 1945–1960* (Chapel Hill: University of North Carolina Press, 1999), 37–43.

60. Adamic to editor of the *Cement News*, May 9, 1948, box 51, folder 9, Firestone.

61. Ibid.

62. Lee Pressmen to Adamic, June 7, 1948, box 48, folder 6, Firestone.

63. *Peace, Freedom, and Abundance: The Platform of the Progressive Party*, July 23–25, 1948, 2–4, 7–9. Pages 7–9 focus on decolonization.

64. Thomas W. Devine, *Henry Wallace's 1948 Presidential Campaign and the Future of Postwar Liberalism* (Chapel Hill: University of North Carolina Press, 2013), xii, 2, and 131–55.

65. Thomas R. Amlie to Adamic, June 14, 1948, box 45, folder 1, Firestone.

66. On Adamic's meeting with Wallace, see Devine, *Henry Wallace's 1948 Presidential Campaign*, 125. For his overall dissatisfaction with communists in the movement, see Adamic to Lee Fryer, June 9, 1948, box 46, folder 3, Firestone. On his effort to keep a left-liberal movement going after the 1948 elections, see Fryer to Adamic, November 1, 1948, folder 3, box 46, Firestone.

67. Nina Dexter to Adamic, June 19, 1948, box 46, folder 1, Firestone.

68. Ibid.

69. Lees, *Keeping Tito Afloat*, 39–40; Silvio Pons, "Stalin and the European Communists after World War Two (1943–1948)," *Past and Present* (January 2011): 121–38; Vojin Majstorović, "The Rise and Fall of the Yugoslav-Soviet Alliance, 1945–1948," *Past Imperfect* 16 (2010): 132–64; Aleksa Djilas, *The Contested Country: Yugoslav Unity and Communist Revolution 1919–1953*. 1991 (Cambridge, MA: Harvard University Press, 1996) 174–76; Lampe, *Yugoslavia as History*, 237–50; Archie Brown, *The Rise and Fall of Communism* (New York: Harper Collins, 2009), 204–7.

70. Report by Robert C. Blount, September, 9, 1949, FBI File 65 HQ-56402/File 100-HQ-63670, FOIPA No. 1111967–000. Blount's report includes notes of meeting with confidential informants over two years. Also, Steve Nelson, James R. Barrett, and

Rob Ruck, *Steve Nelson, American Radical* (Pittsburgh, PA: University of Pittsburgh Press, 1992), 290, 382.

71. Nelson et al., *Steve Nelson*, 382.

72. Robert Szymczak, "From Popular Front to Communist Front: The American Slav Congress in War and Cold War, 1941–1951" (PhD diss., University of Lancaster [UK], 2006), 352, 386; Irving Howe and Lewis Coser, *The American Communist Party: A Critical History* (Boston: Beacon, 1957), 475–76; Devine, *Henry Wallace's 1948 Presidential Campaign*, 177–79.

73. Press clippings from various papers, including *New York Star*, August 4, 1948, 1, box 93, folder 17; August 8, 1948, box 93, folder 4; Adamic's typed response to Budenz, box 36, folder 32, Firestone.

74. US Congress, House on Un-American Activities, *Hearings Regarding Communist Espionage in the United States Government*, 80th Cong., 2nd sess. (Washington, DC: GPO, 1948), 524–25; *Philadelphia Inquirer*, August 3, 1948, 2.

75. Adamic's responses in *Kansas City Times*, August 4, 1948, and *New York Times*, August 4, 1948, box 93, folder 4, Firestone.

76. D. M. Ladd to J. Edgar Hoover, March 15, 1951, FBI, Department of Justice, Washington, DC, FOIA/FBI Adamic file 100-63760-1.

77. Adamic to John [no last name], September 1, 1948, box 51, folder 1, Firestone.

78. Ibid.

79. Thomas G. Robischon to Adamic, September 25, 1948, box 49, folder 1, Firestone.

80. Fryer to Adamic November 1, 1948, box 46, folder 3, Firestone.

81. "Constructive Criticisms of the 48 Campaign," memo 4, box 85, folder 12, Firestone.

82. Mike Miller and Burt Alpert, "Organizational Suggestions for a Permanent Progressive Party," memo 4, box 85, folder 12, Firestone.

83. *T&T*, midautumn 1949, 7.

84. Ibid., 1–2.

85. Harold L. Ickes to Adamic, September 5, 1946, box 47, folder 1, Firestone.

86. *Pittsburgh Courier*, September 17, 1949, 14. For other examples of black journalists defending Adamic, see Lucius C. Harper's obituary of Adamic, *Chicago Defender*, September 29, 1951, 7.

87. Robin, *Fear*, 3 and 13; Nelson Lichtenstein, *State of the Union: A Century of American Labor* (Princeton, NJ: Princeton University Press, 2002), 104–57; Kenneth R. Janken, "From Colonial Liberation to Cold War Liberalism: Walter White, the NAACP, and Foreign Affairs, 1941–1955," *Ethnic and Racial Studies* 21 (November 1998): 1082–91.

Chapter 5. Anticommunists and Death Narratives

1. A. H. Belmont to D. M. Ladd, September 5, 1951, in Report from New York Office to J. Edgar Hoover, May 2, 1957, and Report Newark Office to Director FBI,

May 3, 1957, FBI, Department of Justice, Washington, DC, FOIA/FBI Adamic file 100–63670–1.

2. Louis Adamic to France Adamič, n.d., Louis Adamič Collection, Mestna knjižnica Grosuplje (Public Library of Grosuplje, Slovenia).

3. Report from New York Office to J. Edgar Hoover, May 2, 1957, and Report Newark Office to Director FBI, May 3, 1957, FBI, Department of Justice, Washington, DC, FOIA/FBI Adamic file 100–63670–1; *Chicago Tribune*, September 6, 1951, 14; *Los Angeles Times*, November 4, 1951, 32.

4. *New York Times*, September 6, 1951, 64.

5. *Mt. Vernon (IL) Register-News*, September 4, 1951, 1. This is one example of many.

6. *Chicago Tribune*, September 6, 1951, 14; *Los Angeles Times*, November 4, 1951, 32.

7. Ellen Schrecker, *Many Are the Crimes: McCarthyism in America* (Princeton, NJ: Princeton University Press, 1998), 119–24, 131–36.

8. Schrecker, *Many Are the Crimes*, 134–35.

9. For informants and witnesses in the McCarthy Era, see Victor S. Navasky, *Naming Names* (New York: Hill and Wang, 2003), 1–70; Daniel J. Leab, "Anti-communism, the FBI, and Matt Cvetic: The Ups and Downs of a Professional Informer," *Pennsylvania Magazine of History and Biography* 115, no. 4 (October 1991): 535–81; Kathryn S. Olmsted, "Blond Queens, Red Spiders, and Neurotic Old Maids: Gender and Espionage in the Early Cold War," *Intelligence and National Security* 19 (Spring 2004): 78–94; Robert M. Lichtman, "Louis Budenz, the FBI, and the 'List of 400 Concealed Communists': An Extended Tale of McCarthy-Era Informing" *American Communist History* 3, no. 1 (2004): 39–52; Lichtman, "J. B. Matthews and the 'Counter-Subversives': Names as a Political and Financial Resource in the McCarthy Era," *American Communist History* 5, no. 1 (2006): 1–36.

10. Carey McWilliams, "Louis Adamic, American," *Nation*, September 22, 1951, 231.

11. For the most recent example, see Matthew M. Briones, *Jim and Jap Crow: A Cultural History of 1940s Interracial America* (Princeton, NJ: Princeton University Press, 2012), 68. Dan Shiffman is an important exception to this trend. He noted that McWilliams overstated this break, but he did not elaborate. See Dan Shiffman, *Rooting Multiculturalism: The Work of Louis Adamic* (Madison, NJ: Fairleigh Dickinson University Press, 2003), 62.

12. Odd Arne Westad, *The Global Cold War*, repr. (Cambridge: Cambridge University Press, 2017), 1–7.

13. Louis Adamic, "A Game of Chess in an Earthquake," unpublished chapter in the draft manuscript of *The Eagle and the Roots*, Library of the Slovene Academy of Sciences and Arts, Ljubljana, Slovenia. Milan Mrdenović sent me a scanned copy of this chapter, for which I am grateful.

14. Westad, *Global Cold War*, 97–109.

15. US House, Special Committee on Un-American Activities, *Investigation of*

Un-American Propaganda Activities in the United States, 78th Cong., 2nd sess., on H. 282, vol. 17 (Washington, DC: GPO, 1944), 10338.

16. Louis Adamic, "Confessions of a 33rd Degree Subversive," *Nation*, June 28, 1952, 637.

17. US House, Special Committee on Un-American Activities, *Investigation of Un-American Propaganda*, 10338–39; Larry Ceplair, *Anti-Communism in Twentieth-Century America: A Critical History* (Santa Barbara, CA: Praeger, 2011), 42–43.

18. Landon R. Y. Storrs, *The Second Red Scare and the Unmaking of the New Deal Left* (Princeton, NJ: Princeton University Press, 2013), 2–4.

19. Adamic repeats these themes in most of the articles he wrote for *T &T* vols. 2–5, 1946–49.

20. *Philadelphia Inquirer*, August 3, 1948, 2.

21. Examples of Pegler's attacks on Adamic include *Cincinnati Enquirer*, September 4, 1946, 2; *Harlington (TX) Valley Morning Star*, September 6, 1946, 4; Chester (PA) *Delaware County Daily Times*, November 19, 1947, 6; *Mansfield (OH) News-Journal*, December 24, 1947, 11; *Muncie (IN) Evening Press*, January 27, 1948, 4; *Pampa (TX) Daily News*, June 14, 1949, 8; *Jackson (TN) Sun*, July 20, 1949, 4; *Dixon (IL) Evening Telegram*, July 29, 1949, 9; *Newark (OH) Advocate*, December 17, 1949, 4; *Cincinnati Enquirer*, April 12, 1950, 3.

22. Bogdan Raditsa, "How Terror Rules Yugoslavia," *American Mercury* 63 (December 1946): 669–75; US Senate, Committee on the Judiciary, Subcommittee on Immigration and Naturalization, *Communist Activities among Aliens and National Groups*, Hearing 81st Cong., 1st sess., on S. 1832, part I (Washington, DC: GPO, 1950), 56.

23. US Senate, Committee on the Judiciary, Subcommittee on Immigration and Naturalization, *Communist Activities*, 57–62.

24. Ibid., 62–63.

25. Ibid.

26. US Congress, House on Un-American Activities, *Hearings Regarding Communist Espionage in the United States Government*, 80th Cong., 2nd sess. (Washington, DC: GPO, 1948), 524–25.

27. US Senate, Committee on the Judiciary, Subcommittee on Immigration and Naturalization, *Communist Activities*, 115, 238–39.

28. Robert Szymczak, "From Popular Front to Communist Front: The American Slav Congress in War and Cold War, 1941–1951," PhD diss., University of Lancaster [UK], 2006, 1–8, 129–70.

29. US House of Representatives, Committee on Un-American Activities, *Report on the American Slav Congress and Associated Organizations*, 39–47.

30. Ibid., 39–47.

31. Ibid., 6.

32. Mark Basic, *It Happened in Yugoslavia, It Must Not Happen Here* (Chicago: Medjrich, 1949), 66.

33. Basic, *It Happened in Yugoslavia,* 184.

34. Bentley stated that Adamic passed secrets to the Soviets when he worked for the Office of Strategic Services (OSS) during World War II, and that she learned of his treasonous act from Budenz. Budenz claimed that he never told Bentley this story. Also, FBI agents discovered that Adamic never worked for the OSS. D. M. Ladd to J. Edgar Hoover, March 15, 1951, FBI, Department of Justice, Washington, DC, FOIA/FBI Adamic file 100–63670–1.

35. Report by Robert C. Blount, September 9, 1949, Adamic FBI File 65 HQ-56402/File 100-HQ-63670 FOIPA No. 1111967–000.

36. William A. Fowler to the secretary of state, November 17, 1949, FBI, Department of Justice, Washington, DC, FOIA/FBI Adamic file 100–63670–1.

37. Ibid.

38. For just one example, see *Nashville Tennessean*, February 24, 1919, 1. Nearly 3,500 results came up on newspapers.com in 1919 alone for a search on "communist plots." Also see *New York Evening Telegram*, November 1, 1919.

39. *Los Angeles Times*, June 28, 1925, 1.

40. *Los Angeles Times*, January 4, 1926, 4.

41. David Priestland, *The Red Flag: A History of Communism* (New York: Grove, 2009), 121, 104.

42. Arthur Koestler, *Darkness at Noon*, trans. Daphne Hardy (New York: Scribner, 1968), 76.

43. Koestler, *Darkness at Noon*, 138.

44. *Washington Times-Herald* (date omitted), 1951. FBI File 65 HQ-56402/File 100-HQ-63670 FOIPA No. 1111967–000.

45. *Washington Post*, September 7, 1951, 18.

46. Ibid.

47. Ibid.

48. *Los Angeles Times*, November 4, 1951, 32.

49. *New York Times*, September 6, 1951, 64. See also *Chicago Tribune*, September 5, 1951, 6.

50. D. M. Ladd to J. Edgar Hoover, March 15, 1951, FBI, Department of Justice, Washington, DC, FOIA/FBI Adamic file 100–63670–1.

51. Schrecker, *Many Are the Crimes*, 172.

52. Larry Ceplair, *Anti-communism*, 132.

53. D. M. Ladd quoted in Schrecker, *Many Are the Crimes*, 230.

54. Ibid., 230–31.

55. Louis Adamic, press release, August 3, 1948, box 9, folder 32, Louis Adamic Papers, Rare Books and Special Collections Department, Firestone Library, Princeton University (hereafter cited as Firestone).

56. Bogdan Raditsa, "My Memories of Louis Adamic," *American Mercury* 73 (December 1951): 69.

57. Ibid., 70.

58. Ibid.

59. Ibid., 71–72.

60. Ibid., 72.

61. Ibid., 80.

62. Ibid., 72.

63. Jonathan H. L'Hommedieu, "Baltic Exiles and the U.S. Congress: Investigations and Legacies of the House Select Committee, 1953–1955," *Journal of American Ethnic History* 31 (Winter 2012): 41–67; Tony Smith, *Foreign Attachments: The Power of Ethnic Groups in the Making of American Foreign Policy* (Cambridge, MA: Harvard University Press, 2005); Gregory Mitrovich, *Undermining the Kremlin: America's Strategy to Subvert the Soviet Bloc, 1947–1956* (Ithaca, NY: Cornell University Press, 2000).

64. L'Hommedieu, "Baltic Exiles"; Tony Smith, *Foreign Attachments: The Power of Ethnic Groups in the Making of American Foreign Policy* (Cambridge, MA: Harvard University Press, 2005); Scott Lucas, *Freedom's War: The American Crusade against the Soviet Union* (New York: New York University Press, 1999), 66–67; Gregory Mitrovich, *Undermining the Kremlin: America's Strategy to Subvert the Soviet Bloc, 1947–1956* (Ithaca, NY: Cornell University Press, 2000).

65. *New York Times*, September 6, 1951, 64.

66. Stella Adamic to Louis Adamic, n.d., box 45, folder 2, Firestone.

67. Adamic to Mirko Kuhel, June 22, 1946, box 47, folder 2, Firestone.

68. F. J. Baumgardner to A. H. Belmont, September 5,1951, FBI, Department of Justice, Washington, DC, FOIA/FBI Adamic file 100–63670–1.

69. Louis Adamic to Stella Adamic, June 22, 1951, box 45, folder 2, Firestone.

70. Carey McWilliams to R. R. Wills, September 7, 1951, box 83, folder 6, Carey McWilliams Papers, 1894–1982, Collection no. 1319, Charles E. Young Research Library, Department of Special Collections, University of California–Los Angeles.

71. FBI/FOIA Adamic file 100–63670–113; Shiffman, *Rooting Multiculturalism*, 62–66.

72. *New York Times*, September 6, 1951, 64.

73. Vladimir Dedijer, *The Battle Stalin Lost: Memoirs of Yugoslavia 1948–1953* (New York: Grosset and Dunlap, 1970), 244.

74. Ibid., 244–46.

75. FBI/FOIA Adamic file 100–63670–113.

76. To director from SAC Chicago, September 13, 1951, in FBI/FOIA Adamic file 100–63670–113.

77. A. H. Belmont to D. M. Ladd, September 5, 1951, FBI, Department of Justice, Washington, DC, FOIA/FBI Adamic file 100–63760–1.

78. It should be noted that the FBI agents from New York City and Newark, New Jersey, identified journalist Stoyan Pribichevich as a possible suspect. Pribichevich accused Adamic of stealing material on Tito from him as Adamic prepared to write *The Eagle and the Roots*. Pribichevich, who fled with his family from Yugoslavia to

the United States because they opposed the autocratic Serbian monarch Alexander, returned to his homeland after Tito came to power. There he apparently had amassed a sizable debt. FBI agents surmised that Tito might have feared what Adamic was writing about him since he had refused to divulge "to anyone exactly what type of material he would include in his book." Playing on Pribichevich's anger and promising to forgive his financial problems, agents speculated, Yugoslav officials may have convinced him to commit murder. Report from New York Office to J. Edgar Hoover, May 2, 1957, and Report Newark Office to Director FBI, May 3, 1957, FBI, Department of Justice, Washington, DC, FOIA/FBI Adamic file 100-63670-1. For more on Pribichevich, see Lorraine M. Lees, *Yugoslav-Americans and National Security during World War II* (Urbana: University of Illinois Press, 2007), 82.

79. Janja Žitnik, "The Editing of Louis Adamic's Book *The Eagle and the Roots*," *Acta Neophilologica* 22 (1989): 70.

80. Louis Adamic, *The Eagle and the Roots* (Garden City, NY: Doubleday, 1952), 527.

81. Adamic, *Eagle and the Roots*, 529.

82. Ibid., 530–31.

83. Ibid., 40–42.

84. Ibid., 45–47.

85. Žitnik, "Editing of Louis Adamic's Book," 71.

86. Janja Žitnik, "The American Reception of Louis Adamic's Last Book on Yugoslavia," *Slovene Studies* 14, no. 2 (1992): 149.

87. Holograph copy of *Eagle and the Roots*, box 5, folders 1–4, Firestone; Žitnik, "Editing of Lois Adamic's Book," 80.

88. Ibid., 82–83.

89. Elaine Tyler May, *Homeward Bound: American Families in the Cold War Era* (New York: Harper Collins, 1988), 16–36; Lizabeth Cohen, *A Consumers' Republic: The Politics of Mass Consumption in Postwar America* (New York: Vintage, 2003), 111–92; Howard Brick, *Transcending Capitalism: Visions of a New Society in Modern American Thought* (Ithaca, NY: Cornell University Press, 2006), 152–85.

90. *New York Star*, August 4, 1948, 1; Alexander H. Uhl, "His Renewal of Faith," *New Republic*, June 21, 1952, 21; Shaemas O'Sheel, "Louis Adamic's Yugoslavia," *Saturday Review*, August 16, 1952, 9; Mark Gayn, "Documents for Our Times," *Nation*, September, 20, 1952, 234; Žitnik, "American Reception," 153–54.

91. *Berkshire Eagle*, May 31, 1952, 15.

92. *Saint Louis Post-Dispatch*, July 3, 1952, 2 B.

93. John Earl Haynes and Harvey Klehr, *Venona: Decoding Soviet Espionage in America* (New Haven, CT: Yale University Press, 1999), 334–36.

94. Bogdan C. Novak, "Why Adamic Shifted His Support from Mihailović to Tito," *Slovene Studies* 11, nos. 1 and 2 (1989): 185.

95. George J. Prpic, *South Slavic Immigration in America* (Boston: Twayne, 1978), 166.

96. Henry A. Christian, *Louis Adamic: A Checklist* (Kent, OH: Kent State University Press, 1971), xxviii; Rudolph J. Vecoli, "Louis Adamic, 1898–1951: A Retrospective View and Assessment Thirty Years Later," *International Labor and Working-Class History* no. 20 (Fall 1981): 62; Malcolm Sylvers, "The America of Louis Adamic: Democratic Ideals, Immigration and the Working Class Movement," in *Louis Adamic: Simpozij/ Symposium* (Ljubljana: Univerza Edvard Kardelj, 1981), 187–94; Shiffman, *Rooting Multiculturalism*, 18.

97. Haynes and Klehr, *Venona*, 334–36; Richard Gid Powers, *Not without Honor: The History of American Anticommunism* (New Haven, CT: Yale University Press, 1998), 5.

98. Haynes and Klehr, *Venona*, 371. Haynes and Klehr were among those who ignored the FBI's findings on this matter, which cleared Adamic of the charge, and offer no other proof that Adamic committed espionage.

99. Schrecker, *Many Are the Crimes*, xii, 359–65; Landon R. Y. Storrs, *The Second Red Scare and the Unmaking of the New Deal Left* (Princeton, NJ: Princeton University Press, 2013), 177–204.

100. Nick Fischer, *Spider Web: The Birth of American Anticommunism* (Urbana: University of Illinois Press, 2016), 256–82; Rachel Ida Buff, *Against the Deportation Terror: Organizing for Immigrant Rights in the Twentieth Century* (Philadelphia: Temple University Press, 2018), 30–32, 93–97; Robert Zecker, *"A Road to Peace and Freedom": The International Workers' Order and the Struggle for Economic Justice and Civil Rights, 1930–1954* (Philadelphia: Temple University Press, 2018), 211–59.

101. Greg Grandin, *Empire's Workshop: Latin America, the United States, and the Rise of the New Imperialism* (New York: Henry Holt, 2006), 96.

Epilogue

1. *New York Times*, May 12, 2017, 29 A. *The Nation*, *Harper's*, the *Atlantic*, *Salon*, and the *Huffington Post*, among others, have published numerous articles debating the fascist ethos present in the populist right. Also, *Bloomberg Businessweek* reporter Joshua Green, *Devil's Bargain: Steve Bannon, Donald Trump, and the Storming of the Presidency* (New York: Penguin, 2017), explains how President Trump's former adviser points to Julius Evola for his inspiration on how to think about nationalism. Evola was a leading profascist thinker and advised Benito Mussolini, especially in regard to the racial thinking that shaped the Nazis' views on race. Green also reports that Bannon cited René Guénon as his chief influence. Guénon believed the Enlightenment values of equality threatened Western civilization. On the dominance of the melting-pot narrative, see Paul Spickard, *Almost All Aliens: Immigration, Race, and Colonialism in American History and Identity* (New York: Verso, 2007), 1–28.

2. Rosie Gray, "Trump Defends White-Nationalist Protesters," *Atlantic*, August 15, 2017, on-line edition, https://www.theatlantic.com/politics/archive/2017/08/trump-defends-white-nationalist-protesters-some-very-fine-people-on-both-sides/537012/, accessed January 21, 2018.

3. Timothy Schneider, *On Tyranny* (New York: Penguin Random House, 2017); Steven Levitsky and Daniel Ziblatt, *How Democracies Die* (New York: Penguin Random House, 2018).

4. Louis Adamic, "A Game of Chess in an Earthquake," unpublished chapter in the draft manuscript of *The Eagle and the Roots*, Library of the Slovene Academy of Sciences and Arts, Ljubljana, Slovenia. On his critiques of Soviet imperialism, see *T&T,* midautumn 1949, 1–2.

5. Black Lives Matter website, https://blacklivesmatter.com/about/, accessed January 28, 2018.

6. Patrisse Cullors, "On Trayvon Martin's Birthday, We Remember His Life and Why We Fight for Black Lives," *THINK Newsletter*, NBC News, February 5, 2018, https://www.nbcnews.com/think/opinion/trayvon-martin-s-birthday-we-remember-his-life-why-we-ncna844711.

7. Black Lives Matter website https://blacklivesmatter.com/about/, accessed January 28, 2018; Yolanda Pierce, "Righteous Anger, Black Lives Matter, and the Legacy of King," January 16, 2018, https://berkleycenter.georgetown.edu/responses/righteous-anger-black-lives-matter-and-the-legacy-of-king.

8. Dani McClain, "Can Black Lives Matter Win in the Age of Trump?," *Nation*, October 9, 2017, https://www.thenation.com/article/can-black-lives-matter-win-in-the-age-of-trump/.

9. *Berkeley News*, October 6, 2017, on-line edition, http://news.berkeley.edu/2017/10/06/black-lives-matter-leader-in-the-fight-of-our-lives-against-fascism/.

10. Touré, "A Year inside the Black Lives Matter Movement," *Rolling Stone*, December 7, 2017, https://www.rollingstone.com/politics/news/toure-inside-black-lives-matter-w513190.

11. Mark Bray, *Antifa: The Anti-fascist Handbook* (New York: Melville House, 2017), xiv.

12. Bray, *Antifa*, 168.

13. Bray, *Antifa*, xix.

14. Louis Adamic, *My America, 1928–1938* (New York: Harper and Brothers, 1938), 94.

15. Bray, *Antifa*, xii, 207–10.

Index

Page numbers in *italics* refer to illustrations.

JOHN P. ENYEART is professor and chair of the Department of History at Bucknell University. He is the author of *The Quest for "Just and Pure Law": Rocky Mountain Workers and American Social Democracy, 1870–1924*.

THE WORKING CLASS IN AMERICAN HISTORY

Worker City, Company Town: Iron and Cotton-Worker Protest in Troy and Cohoes, New York, 1855–84 *Daniel J. Walkowitz*

Life, Work, and Rebellion in the Coal Fields: The Southern West Virginia Miners, 1880–1922 *David Alan Corbin*

Women and American Socialism, 1870–1920 *Mari Jo Buhle*

Lives of Their Own: Blacks, Italians, and Poles in Pittsburgh, 1900–1960 *John Bodnar, Roger Simon, and Michael P. Weber*

Working-Class America: Essays on Labor, Community, and American Society *Edited by Michael H. Frisch and Daniel J. Walkowitz*

Eugene V. Debs: Citizen and Socialist *Nick Salvatore*

American Labor and Immigration History, 1877–1920s: Recent European Research *Edited by Dirk Hoerder*

Workingmen's Democracy: The Knights of Labor and American Politics *Leon Fink*

The Electrical Workers: A History of Labor at General Electric and Westinghouse, 1923–60 *Ronald W. Schatz*

The Mechanics of Baltimore: Workers and Politics in the Age of Revolution, 1763–1812 *Charles G. Steffen*

The Practice of Solidarity: American Hat Finishers in the Nineteenth Century *David Bensman*

The Labor History Reader *Edited by Daniel J. Leab*

Solidarity and Fragmentation: Working People and Class Consciousness in Detroit, 1875–1900 *Richard Oestreicher*

Counter Cultures: Saleswomen, Managers, and Customers in American Department Stores, 1890–1940 *Susan Porter Benson*

The New England Working Class and the New Labor History *Edited by Herbert G. Gutman and Donald H. Bell*

Labor Leaders in America *Edited by Melvyn Dubofsky and Warren Van Tine*

Barons of Labor: The San Francisco Building Trades and Union Power in the Progressive Era *Michael Kazin*

Gender at Work: The Dynamics of Job Segregation by Sex during World War II *Ruth Milkman*

Once a Cigar Maker: Men, Women, and Work Culture in American Cigar Factories, 1900–1919 *Patricia A. Cooper*

A Generation of Boomers: The Pattern of Railroad Labor Conflict in Nineteenth-Century America *Shelton Stromquist*

Work and Community in the Jungle: Chicago's Packinghouse Workers, 1894–1922 *James R. Barrett*

Workers, Managers, and Welfare Capitalism: The Shoeworkers and Tanners of Endicott Johnson, 1890–1950 *Gerald Zahavi*

Men, Women, and Work: Class, Gender, and Protest in the New England Shoe Industry, 1780–1910 *Mary Blewett*

Workers on the Waterfront: Seamen, Longshoremen, and Unionism in the 1930s *Bruce Nelson*

German Workers in Chicago: A Documentary History of Working-Class Culture from 1850 to World War I *Edited by Hartmut Keil and John B. Jentz*

On the Line: Essays in the History of Auto Work *Edited by Nelson Lichtenstein and Stephen Meyer III*

Labor's Flaming Youth: Telephone Operators and Worker Militancy, 1878–1923 *Stephen H. Norwood*

Another Civil War: Labor, Capital, and the State in the Anthracite Regions of Pennsylvania, 1840–68 *Grace Palladino*

Coal, Class, and Color: Blacks in Southern West Virginia, 1915–32 *Joe William Trotter Jr.*

For Democracy, Workers, and God: Labor Song-Poems and Labor Protest, 1865–95 *Clark D. Halker*

Dishing It Out: Waitresses and Their Unions in the Twentieth Century *Dorothy Sue Cobble*

The Spirit of 1848: German Immigrants, Labor Conflict, and the Coming of the Civil War *Bruce Levine*

Working Women of Collar City: Gender, Class, and Community in Troy, New York, 1864–86 *Carole Turbin*

Southern Labor and Black Civil Rights: Organizing Memphis Workers *Michael K. Honey*

Radicals of the Worst Sort: Laboring Women in Lawrence, Massachusetts, 1860–1912 *Ardis Cameron*

Producers, Proletarians, and Politicians: Workers and Party Politics in Evansville and New Albany, Indiana, 1850–87 *Lawrence M. Lipin*

The New Left and Labor in the 1960s *Peter B. Levy*

The Making of Western Labor Radicalism: Denver's Organized Workers, 1878–1905 *David Brundage*

In Search of the Working Class: Essays in American Labor History and Political Culture *Leon Fink*

Lawyers against Labor: From Individual Rights to Corporate Liberalism *Daniel R. Ernst*

"We Are All Leaders": The Alternative Unionism of the Early 1930s *Edited by Staughton Lynd*

The Female Economy: The Millinery and Dressmaking Trades, 1860–1930 *Wendy Gamber*

"Negro and White, Unite and Fight!": A Social History of Industrial Unionism in Meatpacking, 1930–90 *Roger Horowitz*

Power at Odds: The 1922 National Railroad Shopmen's Strike *Colin J. Davis*

The Common Ground of Womanhood: Class, Gender, and Working Girls' Clubs, 1884–1928 *Priscilla Murolo*

Marching Together: Women of the Brotherhood of Sleeping Car Porters *Melinda Chateauvert*

Down on the Killing Floor: Black and White Workers in Chicago's Packinghouses, 1904–54 *Rick Halpern*
Labor and Urban Politics: Class Conflict and the Origins of Modern Liberalism in Chicago, 1864–97 *Richard Schneirov*
All That Glitters: Class, Conflict, and Community in Cripple Creek *Elizabeth Jameson*
Waterfront Workers: New Perspectives on Race and Class *Edited by Calvin Winslow*
Labor Histories: Class, Politics, and the Working-Class Experience *Edited by Eric Arnesen, Julie Greene, and Bruce Laurie*
The Pullman Strike and the Crisis of the 1890s: Essays on Labor and Politics *Edited by Richard Schneirov, Shelton Stromquist, and Nick Salvatore*
AlabamaNorth: African-American Migrants, Community, and Working-Class Activism in Cleveland, 1914–45 *Kimberley L. Phillips*
Imagining Internationalism in American and British Labor, 1939–49 *Victor Silverman*
William Z. Foster and the Tragedy of American Radicalism *James R. Barrett*
Colliers across the Sea: A Comparative Study of Class Formation in Scotland and the American Midwest, 1830–1924 *John H. M. Laslett*
"Rights, Not Roses": Unions and the Rise of Working-Class Feminism, 1945–80 *Dennis A. Deslippe*
Testing the New Deal: The General Textile Strike of 1934 in the American South *Janet Irons*
Hard Work: The Making of Labor History *Melvyn Dubofsky*
Southern Workers and the Search for Community: Spartanburg County, South Carolina *G. C. Waldrep III*
We Shall Be All: A History of the Industrial Workers of the World (abridged edition) *Melvyn Dubofsky, ed. Joseph A. McCartin*
Race, Class, and Power in the Alabama Coalfields, 1908–21 *Brian Kelly*
Duquesne and the Rise of Steel Unionism *James D. Rose*
Anaconda: Labor, Community, and Culture in Montana's Smelter City *Laurie Mercier*
Bridgeport's Socialist New Deal, 1915–36 *Cecelia Bucki*
Indispensable Outcasts: Hobo Workers and Community in the American Midwest, 1880–1930 *Frank Tobias Higbie*
After the Strike: A Century of Labor Struggle at Pullman *Susan Eleanor Hirsch*
Corruption and Reform in the Teamsters Union *David Witwer*
Waterfront Revolts: New York and London Dockworkers, 1946–61 *Colin J. Davis*
Black Workers' Struggle for Equality in Birmingham *Horace Huntley and David Montgomery*
The Tribe of Black Ulysses: African American Men in the Industrial South *William P. Jones*
City of Clerks: Office and Sales Workers in Philadelphia, 1870–1920 *Jerome P. Bjelopera*
Reinventing "The People": The Progressive Movement, the Class Problem, and the Origins of Modern Liberalism *Shelton Stromquist*
Radical Unionism in the Midwest, 1900–1950 *Rosemary Feurer*

Gendering Labor History *Alice Kessler-Harris*
James P. Cannon and the Origins of the American Revolutionary Left, 1890–1928 *Bryan D. Palmer*
Glass Towns: Industry, Labor, and Political Economy in Appalachia, 1890–1930s *Ken Fones-Wolf*
Workers and the Wild: Conservation, Consumerism, and Labor in Oregon, 1910–30 *Lawrence M. Lipin*
Wobblies on the Waterfront: Interracial Unionism in Progressive-Era Philadelphia *Peter Cole*
Red Chicago: American Communism at Its Grassroots, 1928–35 *Randi Storch*
Labor's Cold War: Local Politics in a Global Context *Edited by Shelton Stromquist*
Bessie Abramowitz Hillman and the Making of the Amalgamated Clothing Workers of America *Karen Pastorello*
The Great Strikes of 1877 *Edited by David O. Stowell*
Union-Free America: Workers and Antiunion Culture *Lawrence Richards*
Race against Liberalism: Black Workers and the UAW in Detroit *David M. Lewis-Colman*
Teachers and Reform: Chicago Public Education, 1929–70 *John F. Lyons*
Upheaval in the Quiet Zone: 1199/SEIU and the Politics of Healthcare Unionism *Leon Fink and Brian Greenberg*
Shadow of the Racketeer: Scandal in Organized Labor *David Witwer*
Sweet Tyranny: Migrant Labor, Industrial Agriculture, and Imperial Politics *Kathleen Mapes*
Staley: The Fight for a New American Labor Movement *Steven K. Ashby and C. J. Hawking*
On the Ground: Labor Struggles in the American Airline Industry *Liesl Miller Orenic*
NAFTA and Labor in North America *Norman Caulfield*
Making Capitalism Safe: Work Safety and Health Regulation in America, 1880–1940 *Donald W. Rogers*
Good, Reliable, White Men: Railroad Brotherhoods, 1877–1917 *Paul Michel Taillon*
Spirit of Rebellion: Labor and Religion in the New Cotton South *Jarod Roll*
The Labor Question in America: Economic Democracy in the Gilded Age *Rosanne Currarino*
Banded Together: Economic Democratization in the Brass Valley *Jeremy Brecher*
The Gospel of the Working Class: Labor's Southern Prophets in New Deal America *Erik Gellman and Jarod Roll*
Guest Workers and Resistance to U.S. Corporate Despotism *Immanuel Ness*
Gleanings of Freedom: Free and Slave Labor along the Mason-Dixon Line, 1790–1860 *Max Grivno*
Chicago in the Age of Capital: Class, Politics, and Democracy during the Civil War and Reconstruction *John B. Jentz and Richard Schneirov*
Child Care in Black and White: Working Parents and the History of Orphanages *Jessie B. Ramey*
The Haymarket Conspiracy: Transatlantic Anarchist Networks *Timothy Messer-Kruse*

Detroit's Cold War: The Origins of Postwar Conservatism *Colleen Doody*
A Renegade Union: Interracial Organizing and Labor Radicalism *Lisa Phillips*
Palomino: Clinton Jencks and Mexican-American Unionism in the American Southwest *James J. Lorence*
Latin American Migrations to the U.S. Heartland: Changing Cultural Landscapes in Middle America *Edited by Linda Allegro and Andrew Grant Wood*
Man of Fire: Selected Writings *Ernesto Galarza, ed. Armando Ibarra and Rodolfo D. Torres*
A Contest of Ideas: Capital, Politics, and Labor *Nelson Lichtenstein*
Making the World Safe for Workers: Labor, the Left, and Wilsonian Internationalism *Elizabeth McKillen*
The Rise of the Chicago Police Department: Class and Conflict, 1850–1894 *Sam Mitrani*
Workers in Hard Times: A Long View of Economic Crises *Edited by Leon Fink, Joseph A. McCartin, and Joan Sangster*
Redeeming Time: Protestantism and Chicago's Eight-Hour Movement, 1866–1912 *William A. Mirola*
Struggle for the Soul of the Postwar South: White Evangelical Protestants and Operation Dixie *Elizabeth Fones-Wolf and Ken Fones-Wolf*
Free Labor: The Civil War and the Making of an American Working Class *Mark A. Lause*
Death and Dying in the Working Class, 1865–1920 *Michael K. Rosenow*
Immigrants against the State: Yiddish and Italian Anarchism in America *Kenyon Zimmer*
Fighting for Total Person Unionism: Harold Gibbons, Ernest Calloway, and Working-Class Citizenship *Robert Bussel*
Smokestacks in the Hills: Rural-Industrial Workers in West Virginia *Louis Martin*
Disaster Citizenship: Survivors, Solidarity, and Power in the Progressive Era *Jacob A. C. Remes*
The Pew and the Picket Line: Christianity and the American Working Class *Edited by Christopher D. Cantwell, Heath W. Carter, and Janine Giordano Drake*
Conservative Counterrevolution: Challenging Liberalism in 1950s Milwaukee *Tula A. Connell*
Manhood on the Line: Working-Class Masculinities in the American Heartland *Steve Meyer*
On Gender, Labor, and Inequality *Ruth Milkman*
The Making of Working-Class Religion *Matthew Pehl*
Civic Labors: Scholar Activism and Working-Class Studies *Edited by Dennis Deslippe, Eric Fure-Slocum, and John W. McKerley*
Victor Arnautoff and the Politics of Art *Robert W. Cherny*
Against Labor: How U.S. Employers Organized to Defeat Union Activism *Edited by Rosemary Feurer and Chad Pearson*
Teacher Strike! Public Education and the Making of a New American Political Order *Jon Shelton*

Hillbilly Hellraisers: Federal Power and Populist Defiance in the Ozarks *J. Blake Perkins*

Sewing the Fabric of Statehood: Garment Unions, American Labor, and the Establishment of the State of Israel *Adam Howard*

Labor and Justice across the America *Edited by Leon Fink and Juan Manuel Palacio*

Frontiers of Labor: Comparative Histories of the United States and Australia *Edited by Greg Patmore and Shelton Stromquist*

Women Have Always Worked: A Concise History, Second Edition *Alice Kessler-Harris*

Remembering Lattimer: Labor, Migration, and Race in Pennsylvania Anthracite Country *Paul A. Shackel*

Disruption in Detroit: Autoworkers and the Elusive Postwar Boom *Daniel J. Clark*

To Live Here, You Have to Fight: How Women Led Appalachian Movements for Social Justice *Jessica Wilkerson*

Dockworker Power: Race and Activism in Durban and the San Francisco Bay Area *Peter Cole*

Labor's Mind: A History of Working-Class Intellectual Life *Tobias Higbie*

The World in a City: Multiethnic Radicalism in Early Twentieth-Century Los Angeles *David M. Struthers*

Death to Fascism: Louis Adamic's Fight for Democracy *John P. Enyeart*

The University of Illinois Press
is a founding member of the
Association of University Presses.

Composed in 10.5/13 Minion Pro
with ITC Avant Garde Gothic display
by Lisa Connery
at the University of Illinois Press
Cover designed by Jennifer S. Fisher
Cover image: Louis Adamic at work, date unknown. Courtesy Louis Adamic Papers, Manuscripts Division, Department of Rare Books and Special Collections, Princeton University Library.

University of Illinois Press
1325 South Oak Street
Champaign, IL 61820-6903
www.press.uillinois.edu